The Althouse Press
Faculty of Education, Western University
Allison, A MOST CANADIAN ODYSSEY:
EDUCATION DIPLOMACY AND FEDERALISM, 1844–1984

A MOST CANADIAN ODYSSEY: EDUCATION DIPLOMACY AND FEDERALISM, 1844–1984

by
John Allison

THE ALTHOUSE PRESS

Geoffrey Milburn, Founding Director

Paperback edition first published in Canada in 2016 by
THE ALTHOUSE PRESS - ISBN 978-0-920354-81-0
Subsequent paperback, ebook and hard cover editions published by
John Allison

Earlier versions of Chapters One and Six appeared as peer-reviewed journal
articles.

John Allison, "From Journeymen Envoys to Skilled Diplomats: Change in Can-
ada's Education-Related International Activities, 1815–1968," *Diplomacy and
Statecraft* 17, no. 2 (2006): 237–59. Reprinted by permission of Taylor & Francis,
LLC (http://www.tandfonline.com).

John Allison, "Walking the Line: Canadian Federalism, the Council of Min-
isters of Education, and the Case of International Education, 1970– 1984,"
Journal of Educational Administration and History 39, no. 2 (2007): 113–28.
Reprinted by permission of Taylor & Francis, LLC (http://www.tandfonline.com).

Editor: *Gregory M. Dickinson*
Cover Design: *The Aylmer Express Ltd., cover image supplied by iStock*

Library and Archives Canada Cataloguing in Publication

Allison, John Daniel, 1964-, author
    A most Canadian odyssey : education diplomacy and federalism,
1844-1984 / John Allison.

Includes index.
ISBN 978-0-9953406-0-2 (paperback)

    1. International education--Canada--History. 2. Education and
state--Canada--History. 3. Federal government--Canada--History.
I. Title.

LC1090.A45 2015   370.1160971   C2015-907727-3

This book is dedicated to my parents,
Jerene Louise Allison (1927–2005)
and John Aiken Allison (1925–2003).
We remember you still.
You lit the way.

Table of Contents

Acknowledgements

This book has taken the better part of fifteen years to come to fruition. Over time, my views on this subject have morphed and changed, but the core idea of the book has nonetheless remained intact. I would like to acknowledge several people and organizations for their invaluable assistance and support in the planning, preparation, and completion of this work.

Parts of Chapters One and Six of this book were previously published in a different form in the Taylor & Francis journals *Diplomacy and Statecraft* and *Journal of Educational Administration and History*, respectively (see note 1 of each chapter for full bibliographic information). I am grateful to Taylor & Francis for granting permission to republish this material.

Having begun its life as a doctoral dissertation at the Ontario Institute for Studies in Education at the University of Toronto, this book would never have seen the light of day without the support and encouragement of my doctoral supervisor, Dr. David Levine of the Department of Theory and Policy Studies. Together with Dr. Hesh Troper, Dr. Glen Jones, and Dr. Cecilia Morgan, David shaped my early views on this topic and on the deeply important task of historical writing. David remained present all along the way; his steadfast encouragement to see this project through to the end has been instrumental in the book's completion. I had no idea what an interesting but demanding journey I was embarking on when I followed his advice, with the aim of pleasing university hiring committees, to develop "two articles and a book" out of the dissertation!

Through my teaching and service at Wilfrid Laurier University and the University of Waterloo between 2000 and 2005, my thinking on this subject developed further with the support of Dr. John English at Waterloo and the members of the History and Political Science departments at both universities. During, and as a result of, my travels and work at the Academic Council on the United Nations System (ACUNS) with Dr. Alistair Edgar, my ideas on international organization and cooperation took greater form. Alistair, I am grateful for the influence you have had on my work—may you continue to travel far and wide.

My arrival at Nipissing University in 2005 marked a new phase in my career. Dr. Sharon Rich, Associate Vice-President, Academic of Nipissing University, has been very encouraging of this project. Her support, as well as that of the Schulich School of Education at Nipissing, made this work possible. Similarly, Dr. Carole Richardson, Dr. Ron Wideman, and Dr. Ron Common, Deans of the Schulich School of Education (and previously the Faculty of Education), were steadfastly helpful and encouraging. Many other faculty and staff at Schulich also pressed me to complete this work. In particular, I would like to thank Dr. Lorraine Frost for her mentorship and inextinguishably positive spirit over the past ten years. The library staff—Directors Dr. Nancy Black and Brian Nettleford and librarians Laura Sinclair, Johanna Trapper (interlibrary loans), and Jeff Sinclair—have been supportive and helpful in a variety of important ways.

Dr. Robin Gendron, Dr. David Tabachnick, Karen Strang, and the other members of the Canadian International Council (CIC), Nipissing Branch, have been helpful and reliable sounding boards over the years. In many ways, the CIC has been the backdrop to this effort. Moreover, the members of the academic societies to which I belong—the Canadian Association for Foundations in Education (CAFE), the Canadian Society for the Study of Education (CSSE), the International Studies Association (ISA), and particularly the Canadian History of Education Association (CHEA) and the International Standing Conference for the History of Education (ISCHE)—have also been sources of helpful constructive criticism and advice. Dr. Kurt Clausen, fellow historian of education and Nipissing faculty member, has played an especially effective role as devil's advocate: his rapier-like wit and humour have been constant companions during our conversations over the years. I also wish to acknowledge the contribution of four other Nipissing colleagues: Dr. John Long (Professor Emeritus), Dr. Bob Fix, Dr. Ron Phillips, and Professor Chris Hachowski. My discussions with them throughout the last several years opened up an extremely important side of Canadian education of which I had only a limited understanding—the story of residential schools, the role of the CMEC vis-a-vis First Nations education, and the current state of education of First Nations children.

At The Althouse Press, the efforts of the Director, Dr. Greg Dickinson, who took a personal hand in the editing of the text, and the Press Manager and Editorial Assistant, Katherine Butson, have been instrumental in the publication of this work. I have learned much about book publication in general—particularly about the depth of detail required in the close editing of a manuscript of this nature. I also take this opportunity to thank the anonymous reviewers for their suggestions about how the work could be improved, many of which were incorporated into a revised manuscript.

Lastly, on the press side, I would like to thank Colin Couchman, Faculty of Education at Western University, and Michelle Barrett at Aylmer Express Limited for their help in shepherding this work through the final stages of the publication process.

I reserve the most important acknowledgments and thanks for my family. The patient tolerance of my wife, Helen Fennema, and the energy of my children, Daniel, Lauren, and Ryan, have been the spurs in the completion of this work.

Lastly, all errors or omissions rest solely at my doorstep. It is my hope that the book will spark interest, discussion, debate, and ideas that may generate the kernels of further works on this subject.

Foreword

A Most Canadian Odyssey is an important, provocative, and troubling study of Canadian educational diplomacy. Beginning with Egerton Ryerson in the 1840s, John Allison defines Canadian educational diplomacy as "international or diplomatic contacts undertaken abroad in the field of education." The definition clarifies but does not fully indicate the significance of the subject, which has become more central to the economic and political agendas of all national states since the 1950s. For Canada, however, educational diplomacy has been deeply embedded in the complexities of federalism and those dense thickets obscure the management and emergence of effective policies. This book should find a place in the office of every minister and deputy minister of education in Canada. Our new prime minister should also read it.

Fortunately, reading *A Most Canadian Odyssey* brings pleasure as well as profound concern. John Allison writes clearly, has a good eye for the telling detail, and possesses a good sense of humour. But the story of Canadian education diplomacy is largely distressing because Allison reveals that Canada has never had a coherent educational diplomacy. Canadian federalism, which has been fundamental in maintaining nationhood among diverse and physically distant peoples, has failed badly in educational diplomacy. The book is a sad tale of jealousies, failures of communication, and downright stupidity. The cost, alas, is borne principally by Canadians.

Allison understands the historical context where "education" has been central to Canadian political conflict whether in Manitoba in the 1890s, Ontario during the First World War, or in Quebec in the 1950s and 1960s. Allison notes the understandable "desire on the part of the federal government not to open yet another front in the federal-provincial dialogue." He points out the challenge of Quebec nationalism in the 1960s when Quebec minister Paul Gérin-Lajoie declared that the provincial constitutional responsibility for education would be the route to an international presence for the province. The federal government was forced to respond and vigorously insisted that an independent Quebec presence was intolerable.

The provincially based Council of Ministers of Education also reacted by asserting their central role. The tensions came to a head when the OECD Country Report of 1976 gave a highly critical assessment of Canadian educational policy. Canada had insisted that the assessors be bilingual in French and English and residents of a federal state. Canadian hopes for sympathetic understanding were thoroughly dashed. A bilingual German assessor, who was also a politician, scathingly compared Canadian education policy to a Victorian prude's approach to sex: "You do it but you do not talk about it and even if you should allude to it, you never use the right words." Allison's book convincingly argues that she was right.

Although the report and other factors have compelled greater collaboration, the basic problem persists. The Harper government in pursuit of more Quebec support broke with all previous federal governments and accepted the Gérin-Lajoie and later separatist demands and granted Quebec asymmetrical privileges in international educational organizations. The federal government fumbles its responsibility for indigenous education despite horrific evidence of mistreatment of indigenous children. In the Arctic where the federal responsibility is clear, Canada alone among Arctic nations has no university. And Canada lacks a counterpart to Australia's outstanding Australian National University, which links federal interests closely with international education and educational diplomacy. In Allison's view, however, the provinces' grasp for authority domestically and a presence internationally are principally responsible for Canada's failures.

The Canadian educational system has elements of excellence and brilliance and international rankings show that Canadian students do better than most in Western democracies. Despite these achievements, John Allison convincingly demonstrates that the Canadian educational system has lacked, and continues to lack, any real "course or control." We could do so much better. A *Most Canadian Odyssey* looks to the past but points to a better path for the future.

John English,
Distinguished Professor Emeritus,
University of Waterloo,
Ontario, Canada

Abbreviations

The following abbreviations used in the book are written in full on their first usage.

AEC   Australian Education Council
ACCT   *Agence de Cooperation Culturelle et Technique*
ACDME   Advisory Committee of Deputy Ministers of Education
ASEAN   Association of Southeast Asian Nations
APEC   Asia-Pacific Economic Cooperation Organization
AUCC   Association of Universities and Colleges of Canada
AUDECAM   *Association Universitaire pour le Développement, L'Éducation et la Communication en Afrique et dans le Monde*
BNA   British North America Act, 1867
CAME   Conference of Allied Ministers of Education
CAUT   Canadian Association of University Teachers
CBIE   Canadian Bureau of International Education
CEA   Canadian Education Association
CEDEFOP   European Centre for the Development of Vocational Training
CERI   Centre for Educational Research and Innovation
CIA   Central Intelligence Agency
CIDA   Canadian International Development Agency
CMEC   Council of Ministers of Education, Canada
CMP   Conference of Maritime Premiers
CONFEMEN *Conférence des Ministres de l'Éducation des Pays ayant le Français en Partage*
CSIS   Canadian Security Intelligence Service
CTF   Canadian Teachers' Federation
DEA   Department of External Affairs
DEA   Dominion Education Association
DFAIT   Department of Foreign Affairs and International Trade
EU   European Union
FPCCERIA   Federal–Provincial Consultative Committee on Education-Related International Activities

GATT	General Agreement on Tariffs and Trade
IBE	International Bureau of Education
IGO	International Governmental Organization
ILO	International Labour Organization
IMF	International Monetary Fund
MI5	Military Intelligence, Section 5
Monbusho	Japanese Ministry of Education
MPHEC	Maritime Provinces Higher Education Council
OECD	Organization for Economic Cooperation and Development
OPEC	Organization of the Petroleum Exporting Countries
PISA	Programme for International Student Assessment
SCME	Standing Committee of the Ministers of Education
SDECE	Service de Documentation Extérieure et de Contre-Espionnage
SEAMEO	Southeast Asian Ministers of Education Organization
SSEA	Secretary of State for External Affairs
UNESCO	United Nations Educational, Scientific and Cultural Organization

Introduction

In 2009, Canadian International Council Fellow, Ryan Touhey, called for Canada to "spearhead education diplomacy in India."[1] In his book *Branding Canada*, Evan Potter argues that "Canada has no single federal organization to beat the drum on behalf of Canada's education and training sector," and "this distinguishes Canada's educational diplomacy."[2] While discussing innovation, Governor-General David Johnston advocates for the creation of a national education act, a Smart Nation Act, to address productivity.[3] Other governments, notably Australia's, are also engaged in this type of exercise, with one of their foci being education diplomacy.[4]

All of these references draw attention to "education diplomacy." Diplomacy is the field of activity of representing one's country abroad. Although I will discuss the meaning of education diplomacy in more detail as the book unfolds, the term broadly denotes international or diplomatic activities undertaken abroad in the field of education.[5] The latter definition is different from "international education," both in terms of direction—it is more focused and speaks to national interests—and in terms of linguistic precision—"international education" means many things to many people.[6] The government of Canada does not have the kind of coherent education diplomacy and education governance that Touhey, Potter, and Johnston promote. Contemporary national and international issues in education increasingly demand that the country work coherently, collaboratively, and in synchronization on an international basis, lest it lose yet more opportunities to export the "brand" internationally, to tell the "Canadian story" to the rest of the world, enhance Canadian productivity, and "bring the world in" in the form of students entering Canadian educational institutions.

The central question that this book seeks to answer is why Canada has not had, and still does not have, a coherent education diplomacy. The response to this question, and the thesis of this book, is that Canada has not had coherent education diplomacy in the past hundred years because of a series of challenges and obstacles associated with the development of and collaboration in this area of international representation. Today's reality is a tribute to the tenacity of provincial actors and the desire on the part of the federal government not to open yet another front in the ongoing federal–provincial dialogue.

The challenges of international representation have also evolved alongside the changing nature of the Canadian state and its governance. Early education diplomats had to develop a set of improvised workarounds to represent, first colonial, then provincial jurisdictions and, less so, Canada as a country. Moreover, issues of education diplomacy were sometimes intertwined with questions of religion and nationalism, as provinces highlighted their role in public education. Some provinces, notably Quebec, literally jumped ahead by leaps and bounds in this field. It can be argued that, by the middle of the twentieth century, education diplomacy came to the attention of the federal government because of Quebec's activities and then became regulated by federal policy.

Policy and evolution of governance did not guarantee consistency and coherence. Canadian education diplomacy was also buffeted by international change in the 1960s and 1970s. Just as the field of diplomacy was evolving, so too was the field of education. Consequently, what constituted education also had an impact on the nature of education diplomacy in this era. Finally, through the the 1970s and 1980s, the evolution of coherent national education diplomacy was also affected by the tug of war between the provinces and the federal government. The book will explore this history and the development of federal–provincial jurisdictional disputes over participation in education diplomacy.

Why is the question of coherent education diplomacy important and relevant? Canada's case is compelling because the development of a coherent education diplomacy is intertwined with some of the most charged moments in international and Canadian political history. Examples abound. Canada's improvised presence at the formation of the United Nations Educational Scientific and Cultural Organization (UNESCO) in London at the end of the Second World War is one such example: who should have gone, and, in the end, who went? Paul Gérin-Lajoie's breakout speech to the consular corps in Montreal in March 1965 against the backdrop of rising Quebec nationalism is another. In this instance, nationalism trumped collaboration and Quebec went it alone in education diplomacy. The 1975 Organisation for Economic Cooperation and Development (OECD) "confrontation meeting" with Canadian officials in Paris represents yet another defining illustration of education diplomacy. Changing international structures also provided a challenge to Canada's existing constitutional arrangements in education and education diplomacy was forced to respond. The emergence of international governmental organizations (IGOs) dedicated to the development and improvement of education worldwide was a welcome arrival on the international scene in the early twentieth century. The League of Nations, UNESCO, the OECD, and the International Bureau of Education (IBE) are instances of organizations that shook up the status quo for Canadian systems of education. The idea of international organizations monitoring, suggesting, and standardizing education policies was beyond the wildest imaginings of early educationalists and classroom teachers across Canada.

Coherent, collaborative, and focused education diplomacy is vital to a nation-state's broader public diplomacy, its classical diplomacy, and ultimately its foreign policy in the twenty-first century. Establishing international cultural and education organizations such as the Confucius Institute and the Cervantes Institute,[7] attracting international students to a country's universities,[8] supporting education attachés who are sensitized to the changing nature and development of a host country's education system and curricula over time (and what textbooks say about the diplomat's home country!),[9] organizing collaboration amongst domestic education-related interest organizations, and ensuring funding for education development programs represent some of the steps being taken in countries with forward-looking education diplomacy agendas.[10] Although there have been some improvements, Canada is not engaged in any of these activities in a sufficiently coherent fashion that includes overall policy leadership and direction. In the contemporary world this means many missed opportunities to position Canadian education systems amongst the best in the world, promote further education about and understanding of Canada, attract the best students to Canada, and use traditional diplomacy to further the progress of education worldwide. Understanding the past in this sense, then, becomes critical and relevant for a constructive engagement with the future.

The historical research method used in this book relies on analysis of primary- and secondary-source documents to support the argumentation.[11] The records presented come from several different archives. They are taken principally from the Archives of Ontario, now located at York University in Toronto. Documents were also consulted at the National Archives of Canada in Ottawa. Smaller archives were also important. The archives and library of the Canadian Education Association (CEA) helped fill in some of the answers to questions in the middle period. The University of Toronto Archives also provided an institutional perspective. Much of this history is generated by "official sources." Many organizations will self-edit their documentation in large part to paint their story in the best possible light. To mitigate the effects of such revisions, I have tried to triangulate the facts presented in the documents with other primary and secondary sources.[12]

Although this book covers events that take place between the colonial era and modern times, the principal period analyzed is the 1840s to 1984. It is not simply a chronology of events; rather, it examines salient decades and events from this time period in an effort to understand the variety of ways in which education diplomacy was carried out or impeded. Consequently, at times the book will jump between different eras to highlight the argument and to draw comparisons and make contrasts regarding different facets of education diplomacy. As social and education historian Cecilia Morgan notes, Canada's international contacts concerning education varied greatly from the nineteenth century onward.[13]

The nineteenth and twentieth centuries were the eras in which modern diplomacy developed. Canada's conformity to many of the diplomatic norms of these eras had implications for education and schooling. The early twentieth century was rich in terms of the spread of independent foreign ministries and the flowering of official diplomatic relations. This period is also critical because of the innovations in government that took place.

The period between 1960 and 1984 had great significance; it was characterized by expanding provincial governments, challenging federal provincial relations, and the deepening of diplomacy between many states. It was a time in which governments could have evolved very differently from the ways in which they ultimately did evolve. As of the date of this book, Canada still does not have a national ministry of education. Such an organization could have changed the nature of Canadian education diplomacy. By 1984, the end of the period covered by the book, some of the key parameters and structures of the relationship had been set. Although

1984 certainly was not the end of this story, it is nonetheless a fitting point at which to draw this particular part of the history to a close. At that time there were official (state-level) contacts among diplomats, administrators, and educators; there were also burgeoning informal contacts between teachers and their peers in Europe and around the world. In the course of these interactions, significant exchanges of educational ideas and methodologies took place. Although some would question whether these were exercises in diplomacy, this cultural component was an essential element of early international cooperation.[14] The book's primary focus on intergovernmental contacts and dialogue is but a small portion of the total picture. Moreover, the size of the time period covered in the book—approximately a century and a quarter—demanded that many of the issues were covered only in passing. Each could easily be worthy of considerable further investigation.[15]

Earlier, I briefly introduced the concept of education diplomacy, with a promise to expand on its meaning. In the context of the Canadian case, I define education diplomacy as the sum of diplomatic activities undertaken by diplomats, politicians, administrators, educators, and citizens to represent Canada abroad in the field of education. Samy Mesli employs the phrase *diplomatie éducative* to "denote the international activities of Quebec in the particular domain of education."[16] Examples of activities comprising education diplomacy include conducting personal diplomacy,[17] cultivating international networks,[18] participating in international exhibitions,[19] attending meetings with affiliated interest groups,[20] being a signatory to education-related treaties, and implementing those treaties.[21] Other related activities, which lie on a continuum from proto-diplomacy, through traditional diplomacy, to public diplomacy, include educational visits by international delegations, international exchange policies and agreements, aid programs, multilateral educational conferences that include Canadian ministers and diplomats, and the buying and selling of educational programs. Diplomatic treaties and conventions have potentially the greatest long-term impact on Canadian education. The founding treaty of the OECD was signed in 1960. More than fifty years later, the OECD continues to occupy an influential place in Canadian educational policy-making circles, whereas educational visits and exchange programs have a much more local, specific, and time-limited impact. Similarly, fundamental constitutional arrangements under the *Constitution Act, 1982*, which incorporates the *British North America Act, 1867* (renamed *the Constitution Act, 1867*),[22] play a much more powerful role than do more limited documents such as memorandums of agreement and other localized and specific policy documents. Such constitutional arrangements are critical to understanding the domestic context of diplomacy.

The term "education diplomacy" has been used in governmental circles in a variety of countries including Australia and New Zealand, and as mentioned above, in the work of Potter and Touhey.[23] In their tribute to Chinese educationalist, scholar, and centenarian, Professor Wang Cheng, Hayhoe and Arnove speak of "how China may begin to influence contemporary *educational diplomacy* through its leadership in bodies such as UNESCO, the World Bank and various NGOs."[24] In this book I will delve into the process of education diplomacy as it developed and ask several key questions: Who went where? To whom did they speak? What was their aim in doing so? What feathers did they ruffle, or not ruffle, in doing so? Did anyone care or pay attention? What impact did education diplomacy have at home?

Broadly speaking, education diplomacy cuts across classical diplomacy, public diplomacy, and the discipline of comparative and international education. The next order of business is to examine the context for education diplomacy. It is important to situate it in the field of diplomacy studies, which is in a state of contestation and change. Looking generally at the history of definitions of "diplomacy" is helpful. Recent scholarly works on diplomacy and diplomatic studies attest to the expansion of the field.[25] Several definitional distinctions can be drawn. The first is between foreign policy and diplomacy. Foreign policy is the grander, wider, strategy of a state or its "world-view." More often than not it is the realm of politicians and policy makers, although many others can influence it.[26] In contrast, diplomacy is much more about the execution of that strategy.[27] "Traditional diplomacy" often refers to any number of activities between or among states: treaty formation and beyond. Generally speaking, traditional diplomacy is performed by diplomats who have little or no contact with the public, either domestically or abroad. The activities of the French diplomat Talleyrand are characteristic of traditional diplomacy. Talleyrand was a master of negotiations, did much to foster networks of statesmen and service France's interests through successive, sometimes antagonistic regimes of government.[28]

Freeman's *Diplomat's Dictionary* includes many definitions of diplomacy. A brief sampling shows the variations in approach. Edmund Burke, the Irish statesman and philosopher, defined diplomacy as "skill or address in the conduct of international intercourse and negotiations" whereas Harold Nicholson, English diplomat and politician, defined it as "the management of the relations between independent states by the process of negotiation." Lester Pearson, Canadian diplomat and, later, Prime Minister, was more subtle: "Diplomacy is letting someone else have your way."[29] In Freeman's illustrations, there are multiple overlapping definitions of diplomacy and little agreement on the "right" one.

There is also "proto-diplomacy." Proto-diplomatic activities are those that have government sanction but not yet the support of a foreign ministry behind them. International Relations scholar James Der Derian speaks extensively about the development of proto-diplomacy in the Holy Roman Empire,[30] including reference to Carolingian caduceus-carrying *missi* or messengers in the Middle Ages.[31] Der Derian accepts the broad definition stated by Durandus: "A *legatus* is anybody sent by another."[32] The nature of the role of a proto-diplomat is also illuminated by Canadian historians Hillmer and Granatstein in their discussion of early Confederation foreign relations on the part of Canada: "[Sir John] Rose was a proto-diplomat; he acted on instructions from Ottawa, promoted trade and immigration, exerted informal influence on British politicians and officials, lobbied to achieve Canadian ends, and reported on the state of affairs and opinion in London."[33]

Another variation, "citizen diplomacy," describes the activities of members of the public who take the affairs of state into their own hands. There are numerous examples of this behaviour in contemporary times, particularly in the case of elder statesmen interceding between warring states such as Israel and Palestine.[34] Paul Sharp illustrates citizen diplomacy in his discussion of the city of Duluth, Minnesota. He characterizes citizen diplomats as "go-betweens"— citizens who simply represent one state to another in a less public role than would normally be the case with a professional diplomat. He also describes them as representative of particular sectoral, regional, or local economic interests. For example, this form of diplomacy would be characterized by cities twinning and dispatching delegations to explore economic opportunities. Sharp also speaks of citizen diplomats being autonomous agents in international relations, one example of which would be Bill Gates of Microsoft and the philanthropy associated with his wealth. Such efforts can have noticeable impacts on world affairs.[35] In contemporary times, it is also possible to speak of "cricket diplomacy"—the conversations between Indian and Pakistani statesmen while engaged in watching a cricket match,[36] although it is, of course, open to question whether these are the "off-duty" conversations of private citizens mutually enjoying a social activity on their own time or of diplomats still in governmental harness.

The recent rise to prominence of "public diplomacy" represents an exciting development in the field of Diplomatic Studies. In general terms, public diplomacy is diplomacy undertaken by a government, in the eye of the media, to engage international publics with the ultimate goal of defending and expanding the interests of the home state. Public diplomacy often includes cultural and education diplomacy, although its ambit is much wider.[37] However, education diplomacy includes elements of traditional diplomacy that would not be the focus of public diplomacy—for example, treaty signing. In *Branding Canada*, scholar Evan Potter takes an extensive look at Canadian "public diplomacy" from the standpoint of communications studies and "branding." Education examples of public diplomacy cited by Potter include Canadian studies programs and networks, scholarship programs, academic mobility agreements, and educational marketing.[38] In recent years, the public diplomacy literature has surged ahead.[39]

From this brief look, it is clear that education diplomacy is connected to most of the definitions of diplomacy. Education diplomacy incorporates traditional diplomatic practice as well as contemporary ideas of public diplomacy. Although "international education" has a bearing on this book, I try to avoid the use of this terminology. It describes a wide variety of interests, activities, and issues, as will be seen, and is much broader and more open to interpretation than "education diplomacy." There is some overlap, to be sure, but "international education" also has specific connotations in disciplines such as International Relations.[40]

Only a limited number of issues can be addressed in this book. It does not deal in a detailed fashion with issues of curriculum, exchanges, and administrative change in public, state-sponsored schooling. Although these issues all have international aspects, they are set aside in favour of examining the different tools of diplomacy and their application. In the longer run, the diplomacy sets the stage for some of these other questions to be deployed and critically analyzed.

Much of the book's attention is directed toward the evolution, role, and activities of the Canadian institutions which in one form or another, and to varying degrees, sought to fill the vacuum created by the treatment of education in the Canadian constitution. During most of the era covered by this book, the ascendant body was the Council of Ministers of Education, Canada, alternately referred to in the book as the CMEC or, simply, the Council. Despite the existence of the CMEC and other quasi-governmental and non-governmental organizations[41] that have come and gone, the authority and true power regarding K–12 schooling and higher education reside firmly with the thirteen provinces and territories, in their own right, and with the federal government in the limited sense discussed throughout the book.[42]

The analysis in the book focuses on coherence in educational diplomacy at the provincial, federal, and international levels. As a result, the dynamics of elementary, secondary, and higher education in Canada are not discussed,[43] although they are affected, in the long run, by diplomacy. Moreover, despite the acute importance of First Nations education, arguably the most challenging issue in Canadian education—because of both the history of residential schools as well as contemporary circumstances—it does not receive much attention in the book.[44] Also, the substantial literature in the fields of comparative, international, and developmental studies (i.e., aid) that deals with the international aspects of education and higher education is not examined either inasmuch as it often pertains to specific schools and institutions rather than the broader picture. Futhermore, certain domestic and international organizations such as the Association of Universities and Colleges of Canada (AUCC), the Canadian Association of University Teachers (CAUT), and the Association of Commonwealth Universities are not discussed in detail. Nor do UNESCO and the World Bank figure prominently into the book. Even though their activities speak to the question of education diplomacy and Canada, an examination of the complex interrelationship between these bodies and education diplomacy is for another work at another time.

Moreover, the federal government has a large bureaucracy and this book only begins to look at the international initiatives of the foreign ministry, as well as a variety of other federal ministries and institutions.[45] The evolving role of international governmental organizations in Canada and the influence of multinational corporations represent other areas in which this book is not exhaustive, and in which more research is critical.

Finally, a variety of other topics left uncovered, or covered only superficially in this book, are dealt with in depth in other works. For example, contemporary education diplomacy in Canada from the public diplomacy angle is well covered by Evan Potter in *Branding Canada*.[46] Other historical and general works have also more deeply probed the questions of missionaries and education abroad,[47] the role of the Canadian

International Development Agency (CIDA),[48] education diplomacy and higher education,[49] and the role of special interest organizations such as the Canadian Bureau of International Education (CBIE).[50]

Exclusions aside, what range of topics do I discuss in this book? And, in what order? I begin in Chapter One by looking at the rise of education diplomacy in the Province of Ontario. During these early days, coherency in Canadian education diplomacy was challenged by disorganization and improvisation. Through a set of different tools—networking, exhibits, conferences and policy making—provincial education diplomats had to make do. The chapter ends with an exploration of the more recent development of federal responses to provincial activities in this area.

Chapter Two considers the unique challenges presented by Quebec's involvement in education diplomacy. Because of its origins, and its ongoing pre-occupation with nationalism, Quebec remained a "special case" during much of the era covered by this book, with unique implications for Ottawa and the other provincial ministers of education. La doctrine Gérin-Lajoie, the special role that Quebec assumed for itself in international relations, is explained and analyzed for its effect on the governing bodies of Canadian education. Still controversial to some in Anglophone Canada, this doctrine nonetheless remains in play today as Mesli has detailed.[51]

The confrontational "go it alone" stance of Quebec in the late 1960s resulted in much more attention being paid to education diplomacy by the federal government, whose increasingly attuned attempts at national coherence in such diplomatic activities are the focus of Chapter Three. The genesis of the brochure Federalism and International Conferences in Education in 1968 was an important development in this period. Moreover, education was starting to mean much more than simply schooling. Most significant for government was the growth in training for the workplace through apprenticeship and post-secondary diploma programs. These two types of programs resulted in an overlap between the more traditional education portfolio and the labour portfolio.

During the 1970s and 1980s, the picture became richer and more complex, and other international influences made coherence in education diplomacy all the more difficult despite the efforts of the federal government. Chapters Four and Five turn away from looking outward to consider instead the international pressures impacting Canada and the development of education diplomacy. Significant among the international changes that had an effect on Canadian education and diplomacy were the global transformations associated with the Vietnam War and its economic aftermath. Not only did these transformations result in military clashes, but they also produced a substantial economic fallout. The inflation that accompanied the war diminished the emphasis that elites and politicians placed on education. The evolving nature of international organizations also played a role. Around the world, the policies of international education organizations became much more interventionist. This was particularly evident in the evolution of the OECD, which during the latter part of the 1960s developed a system of country reviews of education systems that took critical aim at nation-states and their education policies. The OECD Country Review of 1975 tested the ability of Canada's officials to manage the exercise and provide a consistent face to the world in education diplomacy. This historical event and its aftermath are examined in Chapter Five.

Effectively representing Canada and providing a coherent education diplomacy became very much a grinding bureaucratic exercise in the 1970s and 1980s, as Chapter Six illustrates. The growing pains of the CMEC, the most prominent national body in Canadian education during this period, resulted in unsatisfactory relations with the federal government. The CMEC took a considerable period of time to define what its role would be. Not only was the organizational question problematic, provincial education ministers were arrayed along a continuum of how much they wished to participate in the organization and what they thought its objectives should be.

The CMEC emerged during a highly combative period. The 1970s were characterized by periodic clashes between Ottawa and provincial governments over a wide range of issues. Prominent among the problems that the federal union was experiencing was a proliferation in its executive agencies. Policy questions that previously were dealt with at the administrative level became politicized. More time was spent on debate between the premiers and the prime minister—often marathon day-and-night, "the fate of the nation is at stake" sessions at first ministers' conferences.[52] Ultimately, these theatrics were not helpful. At the same time, governmental and private-sector actors (the OECD and multinational corporations) in the international system were undertaking changes that were leaving all nation states with less and less control over their territories. Moreover, the federal government had its own reasons for delaying the longer-term resolution of Canadian education diplomacy. Ottawa was fully participating in the internationalization of its resources, was still interested in "education" for economic reasons, and had diplomatic issues to resolve. In particular, Ottawa wanted to safeguard its prerogative in terms of federal jurisdiction in foreign policy concerning education. The federal government also underwent a series of internal changes that tightened the relationship between career diplomats in the field and the short-term educationalist envoys whose principal role was to attend conferences and similar functions.

The book concludes by recapping the efforts during this era to create a coherent education diplomacy for Canada and by outlining some of the ongoing contemporary obstacles to the realization of that goal.

Chapter One

A History of Innovation: Early Education Diplomacy, 1800–1967[1]

Early Efforts

The early development of national education diplomacy was halting, largely incoherent, and in many ways nonexistent in the nineteenth century because much of what constituted government was evolving at the provincial level. This chapter will look at this early era and more recent times with the aim of showing that the interest in education diplomacy by the provinces, special-interest groups, and ultimately the federal government was a prior condition of national education diplomacy in Canada. This was the era of state formation for Canadian provinces and of the construction of provincial school systems, which were developed to contribute to the transformation of independent and distant royal colonies into strong provincial states. The effort was largely a success[2] that carried forward to Confederation, under which provincial control of schooling constituted one of the key provincial prerequisites to joining the national government project in an era of enflamed nationalisms and external threats.[3]

During the Industrial Revolution states were keenly interested in the role of education in the development of a trained workforce; education, however, was not an important topic among diplomatic chanceries and foreign policy elites in the era between 1800 and 1870.[4] For example, whereas contemporary US secretaries of state periodically highlight the contributions of education and cultural diplomacy as part of America's public presentation to the world, such things were not among the interests of Charles Maurice de Talleyrand, France's foreign minister in the early part of this period. Education was nonetheless very important to empires and states both at home and in the lands subjugated through imperial expansion. Consequently, establishing and maintaining education diplomacy between countries was very much a freelance occupation and it emerged in spite of empires. As Benedict Anderson notes in *Imagined Communities: Reflections on the Origins and Spread of Nationalism*,[5] European empires encouraged a culture in which education was tied to their imperial aims and goals.

Education diplomacy remained very much a self-initiated process as educational bureaucracies did not begin to function until the mid-nineteenth century. In the provinces of Ontario and Quebec, as well as others, the initiative to collaborate with other nations lay largely with individual provincial officials, who would interact with American and European school leaders. By the end of the century, organizations began to play a role but their interests were elsewhere, as was demonstrated by the newly formed Dominion Education Association (DEA), which was formed to bring together Canadian educationalists, and anyone associated with education, with the goal of developing a national perspective on schooling.

The primary diplomatic concerns of the European international system between the end of the Napoleonic Wars in 1815 and the Franco-Prussian War of 1870 lay in war, economics, and the international pecking order—far away from education and schooling. This was also an era of relative stability, which most foreign policymakers were disinclined to disrupt.[6] The Congress of Vienna had changed the way in which European powers dealt with each other. Rather than fighting and bickering, they paid attention to empire building in Africa and Asia. Bull and Watson characterize this era as one of hegemony, but a hegemony that did not extend to the European continent. Instead, the nation-states of Europe engaged in an all-out race to control the rest of the world.[7] Mearsheimer argues that the same movement toward hegemony characterized American foreign policy in the nineteenth century.[8] In such an environment, education was seen by all the great powers as a secondary rather than principal instrument or interest in their foreign policies and diplomacy. Educators and philosophers, it was thought, would spread their ideas through the dissemination of their works rather than with the aid of diplomacy. Moreover, schooling itself was to remain the responsibility of the church during this period.

The lack of interest in education by foreign ministries and chanceries demonstrates that education diplomacy did not begin with them. What is more, the notion of going abroad in order to learn about pedagogy and methodology struck many imperialists as unconscionable. Like schooling, education was firstly the province of the established churches in some states.[9] If it was to have a life over and above that, then it was only as a means to "enlighten" conquered nations after imperial troops had pulled out.

Neither did the early colonies of the era provide the initial locus for education diplomacy. Those born of conquest differed from those occupied by early settlers from the imperial heartland: education was seen as an overtly civilizing tool in the former; whereas, in the latter, it was simply transplanted for the benefit of the colonists. For the most part, early teachers in Canada were relocated from the British Isles or France. Some were in favour of imperialism, others were against British imperialism in particular, and still others had little incentive to explore what lay beyond their classroom doors, let alone find out what other foreign educators did in their schoolhouses.[10] In the earlier period, 1660–1760, in New France in particular, the division between education and the state was very clear. Schools fell strictly under the purview of the church. As Magnuson notes, governments and citizens were not yet prepared to accept schooling as part of the public agenda, as was the case with foreign affairs.[11] By the start of the nineteenth century, it was clear that educators and practitioners from Britain and France had transplanted many of their customs into the first European schools in Canada. Audet describes some of that original cultural transference, illustrating both the "ties that bind," but also the cultural inheritance with which colonists had to come to terms. In this situation, a truly international exchange of ideas and their adaptation for colonial school systems were not even remotely considered as possibilities.[12] The first state-funded schools in Upper Canada were established in 1797 and evolved with a similar approach to pedagogy. These schools came into being after the acceptance of a petition to King George III for the endowment of a school in each administrative district and for the establishment of a university.[13]

Although it laid some of the groundwork for Canadian schooling, royal intervention did not influence the development of education diplomacy. Education remained mostly outside of public control inasmuch as schooling in Canada continued to function under the watchful eye of the Colonial Office—the overarching authority for British colonies around the world. That authority, although not principally interested in education, did have some impact on it. The Colonial Office set out the broad lines of educational policy in the colonies. Similar to the situation in New France, the Colonial Office presumed that education was to be left primarily to the established church, and the Colonial Office's role was merely to mediate disputes. Many of the early communications with the Colonial Office illustrate this point insofar as they dealt specifically with the arbitration of disputes between churches, such as claims over clergy reserves and other similar issues. Bernard Hyams suggests that the Colonial Office championed the idea that education was one with religion and critical for the youth of the colonies. He also states that the Office was very aware of the financial issues and individual needs of each colony.[14] The Colonial Office developed its influence over education through the provision of clergy reserves and the granting of university charters. Thus, colonists were on the receiving end of educational policy rather than making policies of their own. Furthermore, a rigid distinction was made between education, a church matter, and international relations, a government matter. Any examination of different pedagogical ideas would have to take place within the church itself without input from the government.

By the middle of the nineteenth century, education was becoming a secular issue and the walls between the worlds of international affairs and learning began to break down. Public school systems were being established throughout the Americas and Europe as part of the process of state formation.[15] State formation was also central to the foundation of public schooling in the Canadas. The international politics and diplomacy at which charismatic and successful foreign secretaries such as Talleyrand and Metternich excelled still meant little to administrators and teachers within the colonies, other than being of passing interest as current events. However, concurrent with the establishment of public school systems, and as part of provinces' nation building and assertion toward the outside world, there was increased interest in what educators in other counties were doing. Educational leaders in Upper and Lower Canada began to agitate for the adoption of the newest and best methods of teaching. This agitation provided the context in which the first efforts were made towards a coherent colonial education diplomacy.

Ryerson's World

Despite the fact that the Colonial Office still established official policy in the colonies, some of the emerging local colonial leaders looked outside their own jurisdictions for different ways of addressing educational problems. Amongst the first of these leaders was Egerton Ryerson, whose efforts can easily be characterized as early education diplomacy.[16] Ryerson and others were active protagonists in the development of education diplomacy for several reasons: they represented their government, participated in the rituals and culture of diplomacy, and had international objectives. While still a Methodist minister in the 1830s, Ryerson made his first contacts with the Colonial Office. In 1832, he went on his first trip to England, where he presented a petition from Methodists to the Colonial Office concerning church education and clergy reserves. He left with unformed ideas and returned with a very romantic view of Britain. On his return to Canada he did not speak about mills or comment on other social inequities in Britain. Rather he was pleased to have been received by the Colonial Secretary and impressed by the physical power and majesty of the British state.[17]

While Ryerson went about his efforts in aid of Methodism without comment on the Industrial Revolution (a political neutralism he again displayed during the rebellions of 1837 in Upper and Lower Canada), other colonial leaders and politicians also became involved in international activities. Charles Duncombe was another early education diplomat who visited other parts of the world.[18] Trained as a physician, once he entered into politics he travelled to the United States, England, France, and Prussia to observe their education systems. He reported his findings to the Assembly of Upper Canada in February 1836.[19] Although his efforts were earnest, they were destined to failure—the bill attached to his report was turned down in the Legislative Council.[20] Duncombe was also noteworthy among early Canadian educationalists for having American roots.[21] In his investigations in the United States, he studied several American cities including Lexington, Cincinnati, Baltimore, Philadelphia, Boston, New York, and Albany. Not surprising, much of the bill that sprang from his report was based on the operation of school systems in the state of New York; however, the report was forward looking and incorporated a critical examination of those systems.[22]

It was Ryerson, however, who became most prominent in Upper Canada in the mid-1830s in the role of government agent and early education diplomat. He accomplished an incredible amount in his time as the so-called father of education in Ontario, and likely Canada. It is often claimed that these accomplishments were devoid of any outside influence and that they sprang from his mind fully formed. However, Susan Houston points to the emergence of several other innovators around the same period, and documents their ongoing communication with each other. Sir James Kay-Shuttleworth in England, Victor Cousins in France, and Thomas Dick in Scotland all had a strong influence on Ryerson.[23] Each was an innovator in his own way, but they all worked in a common period of educational change. As a group, they were significant because they formed one of the first *international* networks comprised specifically of education diplomats. This web of contacts became a forerunner of subsequent twentieth-century international governmental organizations (IGOs) and contemporary diplomatic networks dedicated to education.[24]

Egerton Ryerson's participation in education diplomacy was revived in 1835 with another trip to England to solicit funding for a Methodist Academy in Cobourg. This time, the level of interaction with the Colonial Office was significant for Ryerson. He spoke with both the Colonial Secretary and the Under-Secretary about the Canadian political situation, and received the appreciation of the Secretary for his efforts.[25]

Ryerson began to assume a truly international perspective on education when he became Chief Superintendent of Education for Canada West (Upper Canada became Canada West in 1841). He now officially represented government.[26] In 1844, he travelled to Europe and remained there for thirteen months. While there, he examined European school systems in an effort to distill the best practices that could be applied to the school system at home. The transfer of the Irish curriculum to the Ontario system followed the completion of his journeys.[27] Ryerson's visit to Switzerland during his first European tour became a significant step on the road toward the development of education diplomacy for Ontario.[28] There he met the disciples of the Swiss educator, Johann Heinrich Pestalozzi, whose methods ultimately found their way to Canada West thanks to the efforts of Ryerson and others.[29] Ryerson also travelled to several other countries on that tour to learn, to absorb, and to engage in a personal diplomacy with other educationalists.

Diplomatic rituals and culture were an integral part of engaging in nineteenth-century diplomacy, and learning them was part of the apprenticeship to the diplomatic game—even for outsiders such as Ryerson.[30] One aspect of this was the presentation of letters of introduction. Scholars of the "English School" speak of an over-arching international society that establishes norms for things such as diplomacy and states. The reach of this type of society is arguable, but this was, indeed, the world into which Ryerson had become inducted.[31] At the request of Lord Stanley (the Secretary of State for the Colonies), the

Earl of Aberdeen (the Secretary of State for Foreign Affairs) furnished Ryerson with letters of introduction that were to open the doors of all the British embassies in the capitals of the countries he would visit. His 1844 trip included Holland, Belgium, France, Naples, Florence, Sardinia, Switzerland, Württemberg, Bavaria, and Prussia. Ryerson wrote about how, because he was armed with these introductions, doors were opened, bureaucracy did not impede him, and he was able to see the people most able to help him with educational questions.[32] At the same time, Ryerson was a diplomat *pas comme les autres*. In his examination of the experiences of Commander Philip Dumas, RN, a naval attaché to Berlin from 1906 to 1908, Matthew Seligmann notes the challenges of entering the world of diplomats as an outsider. Knowing the rules of golf and how to play bridge and having "worldly skills" that went beyond what Dumas had learned aboard the Royal Navy training vessel HMS *Britannia* were critical.[33] Having family members married to Germans also helped in his case.[34]

During his trips, Ryerson also widened his own learning and became more attuned to the international events and culture of the era. The 1844–45 trip, for example, spurred him to learn French. Fluency in French, he felt, would make him much better able to follow the debates in *l'Académie française* and ask his own questions rather than having to rely on others. Moreover, French was the language of diplomacy during this era and learning it continued his initiation into this new world.[35] Ryerson returned to Canada from his European tour by way of New York, stopping to inspect a normal school and thereby completing what he saw as a comprehensive picture of the educational methods and approaches of the day. Furthermore, he was developing a personal diplomatic network for the future.[36]

Back in Canada, Ryerson illustrated the value of international engagement and the development of new contacts, both diplomatic and educational. To modern sensibilities, reports of international travels by high officials sometimes take on the aspect of a travelogue, and the trips themselves, jaunts at taxpayers' expense. On the contrary, Ryerson's "take-away" and diplomatic accomplishment were breathtaking, resulting in nothing less than a transformation of the Ontario school curriculum. J. Donald Wilson argues that Ryerson stopped the Americanization of the entire Canadian education system dead in its tracks with his legislative initiatives.[37] In Walsh's view, Ryerson's travels presaged the wholesale import of the Irish curriculum throughout succeeding decades.[38] Walsh, among others, argues that this was the curriculum that dominated the

Ontario school system for the next twenty years. What exactly was it that Ryerson brought with him on his return to Canada? It was standardized Irish textbooks to be published in Toronto, an approach to curriculum, and an understanding of the Irish system of school governance. Why the Irish Curriculum? A variety of things pushed Ryerson in the direction of the Irish Curriculum and they have been discussed elsewhere.[39] Briefly, Ryerson's loyalist leanings, the invasion of American curriculum and textbooks into Canada, the presence of Roman Catholic francophones in Ontario, and Roman Catholic Quebec were all factors that influenced Ryerson's choice of this curriculum. As for its impact, the new curriculum shaped Ontario students for decades. The spread of British Imperialist ideology can be directly linked to this choice—a far-reaching outcome from something that started with a diplomatic introduction and a conversation.[40]

Ryerson continued to engage in education diplomacy in succeeding years, undertaking trips abroad in 1844, 1850, 1855, and 1867 during his tenure as Chief Superintendent of the Ontario education system.[41] The voyage of 1855 was particularly significant because it opened a new phase in education diplomacy. This time, Ryerson had both personal and professional goals for his trip. High amongst these was refreshing his personal contacts with his educationalist acquaintances abroad. On this occasion he wished to return to some of the cities he had visited in the mid-1840s, most notably Paris, Brussels, and The Hague. Prior to departure he also felt that attending the Universal Exhibition in Paris would be helpful to the Department of Education in Ontario.[42] So powerful was his role that the government declared him to be an Honorary Commissioner to the Great Exhibition in Paris of 1855.[43] His early personal diplomacy had evolved into expanded roles and opened the door to the use of new diplomatic tools such as international exhibitions.

It was in both a personal and network-building sense that Ryerson spearheaded early education diplomacy during this era. He was an official government representative embodying Upper Canada in the 1830s when ostensibly it was still under the sovereignty of the Colonial Office and diplomatic suzerainty of the Foreign Office. Also, in the best sense of diplomacy, in his travels around Europe he gained much through his participation in diplomatic culture, both personally and for the education system of Canada West in the 1840s through late 1860s. Finally, in exercising his initiative, he was able to solve problems that would later involve many layers of bureaucracy—contemporary decisions to change provincial curriculums have become massive exercises of political and bureaucratic muscle. All of what would become the Province of Ontario in 1867 benefited from the new curriculum. By the end of his tenure in 1876, his many travels in Europe had laid the foundations for engagement between subsequent generations of educationalists, thereby underpinning a coherent colonial education diplomacy and making it easier for others to follow in his footsteps. His efforts in this field also echoed the evolving nature of the provincial state, which was changing from a small colony into an increasingly robust province.

Other Canadian colonial superintendents followed similar paths towards education diplomacy in the mid-nineteenth century. Some modeled their ideas on the countries from which they had emigrated, whereas others saw the United States as the source of international innovation. Superintendent John William Dawson of Nova Scotia began his education in Scotland and felt it was natural to look to that country for inspiration.[44] Others such as Jean-Baptiste Meilleur of Quebec benefited from having been educated in the United States. This brought a more international perspective to that province's outlook on education.[45]

Exhibition Diplomacy and Associations

After the departure of Ryerson and contemporaries from the public education scene in the 1870s, education diplomacy was carried on by others and through the use of other tools. The political landscape was rapidly changing as well. The colony of Ryerson's early career had morphed into a transcontinental nation-state suitably titled the Dominion of Canada. As noted above, constitutional talks had confirmed provincial responsibility for education. Nonetheless, bureaucracies remained under-developed, providing more latitude for free-lance efforts but also leading to less coordination among departments. There was very little effort to coordinate major programs dealing with the search for excellence in curriculum design and the establishment of a Canadian education presence abroad.[46] There were, however, exhibitions, fairs, and universal exhibits that continued into the twentieth century. Indeed, representation at these types of venues continues to be one aspect of contemporary public diplomacy. Nicholas Cull argues that World Fairs were used for propaganda prior to World War II and later for public diplomacy purposes.[47] The same argument holds true in contemporary times. Whereas the earlier generation of educationists had been only to the Paris Exhibition of 1855, education diplomacy in the latter half of the nineteenth century focused on greater participation in this type of activity. Ryerson's deputy minister, George Hodgins, represented the new Province of Ontario at the 1876 World's Fair in Philadelphia.[48] Although the international exhibits were meant to showcase the best in Ontario education, in some cases the result was the opposite of what was intended. Foreign visitors who saw the admirable portraits of Ontario's education system at these fairs and who later visited the province were not impressed. In some cases they were shocked to see the lower quality of Canadian schools compared to those in Europe.[49] Thus, some forays into the diplomatic realm were not altogether successful.

Sometimes, however, educators gleaned a lot of success from the tool of exhibition diplomacy. Witness the glittering accolades bestowed on Ontario by the judges of the 1893 World's Columbian Exposition (also known as the Chicago World's Fair). Margaret Evans and Joseph Schull underline that in 1893 Ontario was the leader in education in Canada and abreast of the United States. The prizes won at the Columbian Exposition were the crown jewels. Ontario was given a unique award "for a system of public instruction almost ideal in the perfection of its details and unity which binds together in one great whole all the schools from the kindergarten to the University."[50] Not all exhibitions, however, aimed for the transfer of important pedagogical ideas. Some, such as the one at Bradford, England, in 1904, were more modest affairs.[51] An exhibition of various children's paintings and crafts, it included most of the countries of Western Europe amongst its participants, and Ontario's display simply presented the finished products of its education system.[52]

Towards the end of the nineteenth century, education came to occupy a much more significant place in Canadian governments' gaze, political consciousness, and, grudgingly, its diplomacy. In the negotiations that led to the creation of a national government through Confederation in 1867, it was agreed that education was to be entrenched as an exclusively provincial responsibility. This political compromise was indeed a critical consideration for many of the colonies in choosing to join confederation at a time of burning nationalism and uncertainty worldwide.[53] That such a compromise was necessary, and that education was the only jurisdictional matter to receive its own section (section 93) in the British North America Act, 1867 (B.N.A. Act, 1867), speaks volumes about the prominent place of education in the colonies at the time of the formation of the new state. Although many of the Fathers of Confederation, most notably John A. Macdonald, wanted a national system in which jurisdiction over education was reserved to the federal government,[54] Macdonald and George Étienne Cartier drew up section 93 at the London Conference on December 6, 1866 granting plenary power over education to the provinces. One of the biggest points of contention was the question of minorities, especially the educational rights of Catholics in Ontario and Protestants in Quebec.[55] Such rights were protected by the insertion of a provision in section 93 that gave these minority groups a right to appeal to the federal government for recourse should a provincial government abrogate their denominational education rights.[56]

Over time, by virtue of section 91(24) of the BNA Act, 1867, which granted it legislative power over "Indians," the federal government also maintained control and influence over First Nations education through the Indian Act and the use of the horrific residential school system. [57] Ottawa also operated schools for the children of members of the Canadian Armed Forces and those associated with the Department of National Defence. [58] Other areas of education that evolved under the purview of the federal government included those tied to prisons, the territories, external affairs, and economic development. [59]

With the provincial hold on education so strong, the need to establish a national vision of education for Canada continued to be debated in the 1880s. Modelled after the National Education Association in the United States, the DEA was established in 1891 to meet the definite need for such a national education presence in late nineteenth-century Canada. [60] The early efforts of Ryerson and other early colonial leaders to visit other jurisdictions, analyze their methods, and develop networks were now being taken in new directions. World fairs had begun to play an important role in encouraging international diplomacy in the field of education.[61] Education systems began to edge towards a more central position on stage. Within Canada, more efforts were undertaken to organize education across the country.

As a special interest group, the DEA did not fulfill the place of a national ministry of education. Nor was it very effective at education diplomacy. Rather, it started a more sophisticated conversation about education across Canada. In fact, it can be fairly considered to be one of the antecedents or ancestors of the CMEC. One of DEA's early and central concerns was Canada's place in the British Empire—not surprising given the ongoing relationship between Canada and London. In the early years of the DEA, the Colonial Office in London was still responsible for Canada's foreign affairs and, ostensibly, education diplomacy—of which, formally at least, there was none. Moreover, by 1895, imperialism of a much more strident form had become fashionable. "International" affairs were seen through a more focused lens as imperial adventures that children could enthuse over at home. The DEA was to be preoccupied with this imperialist mission for years to come.

Robert Stamp outlines this imperialism and its impact on Canadian education. He argues that Canadian leaders and educationalists were intent on developing Canadian nationalism but did so somewhat paradoxically by buttressing sentiment towards things imperial. The notion of two loyalties was one with which Canadian citizens were inherently comfortable. George Ross, Minister of Education in Ontario from 1883 to 1899, played a central role in fostering this colonial sentiment as can be seen clearly in his letter to George Grant, Principal of Queen's University: "We need your help for some years yet in the evolution of a higher Canadian sentiment and in strengthening that Imperialism which has practically revolutionized the attitude of the Colonies to the Empire."[62] By Joseph Schull's account, Ross—a jack-of-all-trades—was ably suited for his leading role in the campaign for imperialism. He was a teacher and part-time journalist who later rose to the position of inspector of schools. With a penchant for a good turn of phrase, Ross was an eloquent speaker and strong debater. Moreover, he was very aware of the school system and what it could and could not do.[63] It is not surprising that Ross, who was very much involved in the establishment of the DEA, would shape it into an instrument that would encourage practices extolling imperialism in the Canadian school system.

Thus, the early years of the DEA, to the limited extent that it influenced Canadian education, were characterized by a more intense focus on British-oriented education rather than the international comparisons that marked the Ryerson era. By 1890, there was little to suggest any real commitment to education diplomacy. The DEA was distinctly unsuccessful in bringing any uniformity to or creating consensus on curricular and policy matters in education. A more engaged approach to education diplomacy would await future efforts.

Education Diplomacy in the Twentieth Century

Between 1895 and the end of the First World War, new challenges and problems emerged in Canada's external affairs. Education diplomacy at the national level continued to be a low priority for a host of reasons. Provincial governments were beginning to think about international activities in a more formal sense.[64] An ongoing pedagogical focus on the British Empire inhibited Canadian educators and administrators from looking further afield for new ideas and strategies for the classroom. In Quebec, the Catholic Church's very powerful role in the education system limited the opportunities for Québécois to look to secular societies in Europe and elsewhere for ideas in education. The desire to make Canadian citizens out of the new immigrants in the west, Saskatchewan in particular, resulted in a missed opportunity to encourage those newcomers to bring their knowledge of other cultures and languages to the table and to further international links. Finally, the advent of war understandably further limited possibilities for international collaboration in education.

Nonetheless, the stage was set for these new developments at the end of the nineteenth century, albeit belatedly after Ryerson's efforts a quarter century before.[65] Soon after its founding in 1895, the DEA made contact with the National Union of Teachers in Great Britain.[66] Friendly greetings aside, this contact was important because it marked an early effort on the part of an education special interest group to engage in education diplomacy. It also illustrated clearly the continued imperial preoccupation of Canada's educators at that time. The ongoing challenge, however, was representing the non-existent entity of "Canadian education" at the national level.

Beyond relations with the British, the education diplomacy conducted by the DEA was haphazard and hampered by the lack of consensus that was characteristic of curricular and policy matters in education in Canada in this era. In the larger sphere of Canadian foreign policy at the turn of the century things were changing. As the situation in Southern Africa degenerated leading up to the Boer War, Canada faced unpleasant policy choices because of its role in the Empire. Waite notes that Sir John A. Macdonald was able to say "no" to adventures in Africa in 1884 when called upon by the Empire. It was more difficult on Laurier's watch fifteen years later. The world was a different place: more news, more transport, and more communication. In 1884, the Sudan was a far distant land; in 1899, South Africa was much closer. At the same time, empire had become an all-consuming passion for many European states.[67] When the Canadian government did not get involved in the Boer war, volunteers went anyway. Foreign policy was clearly pulled in many different directions. It was in this environment that education diplomacy began to take on a more defined shape. For the DEA, however, it was still severely limited by a very pro-imperialist agenda. At its convention in 1898, the DEA, in coordination with the various ministries of education, moved to declare May 23rd, "Empire Day."[68] George Ross, Ontario's minister of education and soon-to-be premier, sponsored this proposition. Like Ryerson, Ross was making his mark on Ontario politics and education. Unlike Ryerson, however, he did not travel extensively during either his tenure as minister of education nor his time as premier.

Prior to the First World War, the limited nature of the DEA's role coincided with the lack of a coherent pan-Canadian education diplomacy. Within the organization, too, interests were focused elsewhere; consequently, the executive of the DEA was simply unable to meet. The representatives and members of the organization were in Europe in the summer of 1911 and again in 1912, delaying a general meeting of the organization.[69]

In 1909, the Canadian government began to establish a formal bureaucracy of external relations. This initiative was prompted by the realization that the Prime Minister could no longer conduct diplomacy and foreign policy on the side as had been the practice throughout the latter part of the nineteenth century under the governments of Macdonald and Laurier.[70] There was simply too much to do. The first under-secretary of state for external affairs was Sir Joseph Pope. The activities that the new organization dealt with included the approval of passports, preparation for Imperial Conferences, and trade policy.[71] Despite the ongoing presence of the prime minister as minister of external affairs, the new bureaucracy was a definite improvement on the previous arrangement. The practice of having the prime minister play the most important role in external affairs continued for many years. The prime minister would delegate particular issues to ministerial colleagues depending on the ministers' interests and availability.[72] It was through the new External Affairs organization that nascent contacts were made between the federal government and provincial departments of education. Many of these were routine requests for information or documentation; however, as time went on and the education diplomacy of Canada developed, so, too, did the frequency and nature of the interaction between the Department of External Affairs and the Ministry of Education in Ontario, as one example.[73]

Provincial Initiatives in the Early Century
The provinces of Canada, most notably Quebec and Saskatchewan, had their own problems to contend with concerning education diplomacy in the late nineteenth and early twentieth centuries. After the trauma

of the Conquest, the shock of the 1789 Revolution in France, and the turmoil of the Napoleonic periods, Quebec turned very much toward the Catholic Church and Rome. Indeed, there was much more of the mother country–colony relationship between the Holy See and Quebec City than existed in the province's dealings with France. During the last half of the nineteenth century, the influence of the church in Quebec became more important and more entrenched. For many French, Swiss, and Belgians, the province of Quebec was the last refuge from a Europe gone mad with republicanism and godlessness. Linteau, Ricard, Durocher, and Robert note the power of the church: it was a dominant organization that did not flinch when it came to getting involved in any aspect of Quebec society, including the provision of medical and educational services.[74] The special relationship between Quebec and the Vatican was clearly evident in two educational issues—the question of Jesuit lands (which had been simmering for decades, although its origins dated back several centuries) and legislation to re-establish the ministry of education.

With the repression of the Jesuit order by the eighteenth-century pope, Clement XIV, all the Jesuit estates in Canada fell to the suzerainty of the Colonial Office. They were then given to the government of Lower Canada (subsequently the government of Quebec). When favour once again shone on the Jesuits and they were allowed to re-establish in Quebec in 1842, they laid claim to the properties that had formerly been theirs. Honoré Mercier, premier of Quebec between 1887 and 1891, finally decided the matter by compensating the Church in the sum of $400,000 and requesting that the pope distribute the money as he saw fit. In Quebec and elsewhere, this arrangement elicited a lively protest against the perceived encouragement of an external power's meddling in Canada's internal affairs.[75] Some resented the idea that the Church would decide educational policy beyond Canadian borders. Eventually, the funds were split among Laval University, Protestant school boards, and the Canadian Jesuits.

The second noteworthy occasion of Papal intervention concerned proposed legislation on the re-establishment of a ministry of education in Quebec in 1897. This initiative provoked an immediate response from Rome to the Quebec premier: "[The] Pope requests you defer action on public instruction bill. Letter follows today."[76] Although the proposed legislation was passed by the National Assembly, it was later defeated by the Legislative Council under pressure from Monseigneur Bruchési, archbishop of Quebec. In order to preserve their power over education, ecclesiastical officials in Quebec often invoked Rome's influence and intercession.

Whereas relations with the Catholic Church had a significant impact on Quebec's engagement with education diplomacy, immigration to western Canada also shaped the way in which provincial education bureaucracies viewed contact with the world outside Canada in the latter part of the nineteenth century and beyond. One of the defining phenomena of the history of the Canadian prairies, immigration had significant implications for the development of western Canadian school systems.[77] But, to what extent did prairie educational authorities attempt to understand the ideas and practices of teachers from Europe and integrate them into their educational systems by contacting European countries? Did ministers undertake to visit Europe? The record is dismal, but also reflective of the times.

Instead of following Ryerson's example and integrating the best of foreign education systems, prairie governments fired teachers who taught too much of the languages or cultures of their mother countries. As a result, many of the new teachers from normal schools on the prairies endured hard times while educating the first generation of immigrants to western Canada. Also, educational talent was lost to the system as European-trained educators were forced to work at jobs other than teaching. The nub of the issue was linguistic and cultural. Canadian teachers did not speak European tongues and government officials often viewed teachers arriving from Europe with suspicion. Issues of teacher supply and providing teachers who would "Canadianize" students won out. The challenge of enticing young teachers to small immigrant communities remained.[78]

Education, international relations, and immigration thus slammed head-on into questions of race and ethnicity. R. J. Vincent's view of the age of European ascendancy illustrates clearly the crosscurrents affecting new Canadians as they came into the education system. In contrast to the twenty-first century, when international society has outlawed, at least formally, all doctrines supporting racial superiority, the nineteenth century was one in which European ascendency was supported by acceptance of the idea of a biological hierarchy amongst human beings.[79] Hence opportunities to deploy the talents of immigrant educators were often lost because of prejudicial attitudes, racism, and fears.

The principal international and diplomatic concerns of what was later to become the province of Saskatchewan dealt with exchanges of teachers (with Britain and France), the examination of schools in Illinois, and correspondence—principally with the United Kingdom, Ireland, and departments of education in U.S. states. In Saskatchewan, in particular, as Alcorn argues, the influx of American immigrants and ideas had a very strong influence on the education system from 1905 through the late 1930s.[80] Although the system was strongly influenced by American ideas, only those foreign teachers with suitable qualifications were invited to apply for jobs.[81]

The First World War and the Interwar Period

The unsettled international environment in the era leading up to and including the First World War affected education diplomacy. The obvious agent of this refocusing was the outbreak of war, which in many ways was the last gasp of the European hegemons tired after a century of expansion in the "hinterlands" of Africa. The war resulted in an absolute decline in international educational relations between Canada and the rest of the world, because of the preoccupation with the struggle and the inability to maintain normal communications in a state of hostilities. Canada, particularly Ontario, saw the war very much in terms of the country's place and role in the Empire. Although contacts continued with the organizations within the Empire that were dedicated to education, communication with organizations based in enemy territory was out of the question. The effect of the war on pedagogy, for example, is aptly illustrated in correspondence between the Canadian Department of External Affairs and the Department of Education in Ontario. The government in Ottawa received from Britain a series of cartoons depicting the war in Belgium and the nature of German atrocities there. These Raemaeker's cartoons were to be distributed to high schools by the provincial authorities.[82] Other than to elicit patriotism, pedagogy was not a concern in the relations between nations. In the previous era, the 1880s and 1890s, Prussian and other European systems of education had garnered a great deal of interest.[83] It was not until the Germans were defeated at the end of the war that mention of Germany resurfaced at CEA conferences.

While the First World War raged, international relations were constrained pending the outcome of the conflict. Education around the world suffered as many teachers left the profession to enlist in armies. The normal mechanisms enabling education to be an effective part of international interaction were given over to other issues. In the longer term, however, the war helped to push education back onto the agenda of international relations. Globally, the political value of education increased. War also impelled Canada to pursue its own foreign policy. Although Canadian leaders, notably Mackenzie King, were generally cautious in this arena, Canada did become at least a hesitant player on the international stage. Its principal focus, however, continued to be on the domestic political agenda rather than an international one.

Armistice and the end of the First World War having occurred only days before on November 11, 1918, the Tenth Conference of the CEA was held on November 20th, 21st, and 22nd.[84] Almost immediately, references to education diplomacy began to reappear in CEA documents. The keynote address at the conference focused on educational developments in the defeated Germany, as well as in Britain and France.[85] The proceedings of the 1922 CEA conference recommended the establishment of a bureau of education in Ottawa, which, among other things, would be charged with an international mandate: "to give information regarding educational effort and results in other lands that would be informing and stimulating to all in Canada."[86] These words echo clearly the mission that Ryerson had undertaken in his trips abroad, but unfortunately they were not immediately acted upon. In the 1920s, the CEA entered into a period during which it was not active at all, let alone carrying on international activities. The legacy of the earlier DEA was again confirmed: the organization was not playing an important role in shaping national policy for public education in Canada. This situation was different from that in the United States, where the National Education Association and its offspring became much more active during this period. For the most part, international activities in Canada at this time were carried out independently through the provincial ministries of education, or they did not happen at all. On other fronts, much attention was given to returning war veterans and the training needs of Canadians. Although delegates continued to attend international conferences, they were not necessarily aligned with the CEA or any other organization.

Developments at the Department of External Affairs increased the profile of education in foreign relations in the 1920s. In particular, O. D. Skelton had recently become Under-Secretary of External Affairs. The scope of international activity undertaken by the federal government increased under Skelton's watch. During his tenure, the department started to handle more diverse issues, such as the League of Nations, relations with the Imperial government, Canadian-American relations, trade, management of foreign consulates and embassies, and issues related to defence.[87]

The rise of international agencies during this period also changed the existing environment. The International Bureau of Education (IBE), one of the foremost of these organizations, was established in the 1920s, initially as a private entity. Canadians were introduced to the IBE at the 1927 Toronto conference of the World Organization of Education Associations, an organization founded in San Francisco in 1923. The conference in Toronto was the run-up to one planned for Geneva in 1929. The hope was to interest Europeans and forge solid international links by holding the conference in a variety of cities.[88] When the IBE invited governments to become members in 1929, Canada chose not to officially join, instead maintaining observer status until 1967.[89]

By the early 1930s, the IBE had become more assertive in international affairs. It invited all the ministries of education to submit a report of their activities in 1931–1932 and to send educational envoys to the IBE Council meeting to present these reports. The provinces of British Columbia, Saskatchewan, and Nova Scotia sent reports. Twenty-four other states also participated in the meeting.[90] Canadian participation in the IBE is documented from the early 1930s onwards, with correspondence between it and Canada continuing between 1931 and 1968.[91]

The 1930s witnessed more forays by individual provinces into education diplomacy. During the mid-1930s, the government of Ontario arranged a teacher exchange agreement with Bermuda. The arrangement facilitated the professional development of Bermudan teachers in the Canadian school system and the opportunity for Canadian teachers to have some international experiences.[92] Another instance of contact of a diplomatic nature came in the form of correspondence from the New Zealand Ministry of Education, which inquired about Ontario's teacher-training program and remuneration of trainees, and sought ideas about how to deal with the Depression.[93] The Department of External Affairs fielded the initial query and the Ontario Department of Education's response found its way to Auckland through External Affairs channels.

The Second World War and Education Diplomacy
By the latter half of the 1930s, Canada's external posture became much more insular.[94] Moreover, the rhetoric of war and the disorder and mayhem of the Second World War effectively shut down the transnational operations of the IBE, which continued to function, albeit with a changed focus.[95] One of the activities that the IBE undertook was the organization and shipping of thousands of books to prisoners of war under

the Geneva Convention.[96] The IBE also sponsored the establishment of "internment universities."[97] The CEA did not participate in these IBE initiatives, because Canada was one of the belligerents in the conflict after September 1940. In the summer of 1940, the IBE decided to postpone the next conference on education until after the end of the war. Although the conference was postponed, a request was sent to member ministries of education to send reports on educational developments during the period 1939–1940 for inclusion in the *International Yearbook of Education and Teaching or Annuaire international de l'éducation et de l'enseignement*.[98] During the latter half of the war, the IBE took on the question of using foreign teaching staff to help in the redevelopment of war-torn countries.

The war ushered in other changes in education diplomacy. As in the First World War, there was a cessation of ties with enemy combatants. There was also a heightened emphasis placed on educating citizens for war.[99] Every imaginable step was taken to champion the ideals of the British Empire and Commonwealth. In the view of many people, these institutions had helped to nurture Canadian civilization. "Empire Day," which had been instituted in the heyday of the late Victorian epoch, remained a national institution.[100] The war had also prompted Canadians to increase the number of intra-Empire education contacts to demonstrate Canada's "imperial solidarity." Poster competitions were sponsored by the British Board of Trade to accelerate trade among English-speaking countries. Children were also asked to sign a statement to "Strengthen the Bonds of Empire"; the statement was sent to the King and Queen.[101]

While the end of World War II marked the establishment of a new international order and new hopes for world peace, the CEA began to broaden its international connections as a special interest group. Beginning in the mid-1940s, an array of international concerns presented themselves to the CEA. Resolutions were introduced regularly at CEA conventions regarding the formation of UNESCO. In his early work on Canadian education, Phillips discusses provincial reluctance to participate in UNESCO, attributing some of the responsibility for this reluctance to "Catholic Quebec," and "Social Credit Alberta."[102]

Although the CEA may have had its doubts about involving itself with UNESCO, an increasingly close relationship developed between UNESCO and the IBE. This relationship began in the early 1950s with an agreement between the two organizations to coordinate the use of their names and symbols and to co-sponsor the International Conferences on Public Education.[103]

The Postwar Era and Federal Engagement

During the period encompassing the final years of World War II and the beginning of the Cold War era, Canada's education diplomacy entered a new phase. Although the last part of the war saw much effort turned towards reconstruction in Europe and the evolution of the new United Nations organization, it also witnessed increased diplomatic activity in Canada.[104] The CEA became more heavily engaged again in education diplomacy. The Executive Committee of the CEA was interested in the educational reconstruction that would follow the war, particularly in countries that had been occupied by the Nazis or other Axis powers. There was pressure to have a Canadian representative on the proposed United Nations Organization for Educational and Cultural Reconstruction. The CEA offered its services to the federal government, but at the time of the exchange of correspondence Ottawa had not yet decided whether it would send a representative to the nascent UN agency.[105] The establishment of new, more permanent headquarters in Toronto coincided with a more assertive attitude on the part of the CEA. In October 1944, the CEA and the provinces were instrumental in the establishment of a bi-national panel with the United States; the Canada–US Committee on Education would continue to operate until the early 1960s.[106]

Another significant event took place in 1945. For just over a year, John Althouse had been Chief Director of Education in Ontario. It was in that capacity that he undertook a tour of England, Scotland, Northern Ireland, Denmark, and Sweden with Justice John Hope in order to examine new pedagogies that might be incorporated into Ontario schools. This tour was a preparatory exercise undertaken prior to the writing of the Hope Report, which was released in 1950. Although the sweeping recommendations of the Hope Report were not implemented,[107]Althouse and Hope had briefly revived the "Ryersonian" personal approach to education diplomacy through their voyages and meetings abroad.[108]

During this period, the federal government's views regarding UNESCO solidified as well.[109] In February of 1945, Gordon Robertson of the Department of External Affairs expressed the view that the provinces had to be consulted on UNESCO participation and wrote a draft letter to that effect to his superiors and provincial officials. The letter never made it to the provinces.[110] In November 1945, just after Canadian delegates from External Affairs participated in the final conference on the creation of UNESCO, the CEA sent a letter concerning UNESCO to the prime minister. The instructions to the delegates to the UNESCO conference had been clear: they were not to do anything that would disturb the federal nature of Canada.[111] The CEA, however, was determined not to be left on the sidelines and stated as much in its letter: "(To the Prime Minister) That the Canada and Newfoundland Education Association is the only organization representing the departments of education of the provincial governments...as such the Canada and Newfoundland Education Association is the proper body to be consulted on any educational matter affecting Canada as a whole."[112]

The pressure exerted by the organization eventually brought results, ensuring greater prominence for this special interest group. These developments are summed up in Freeman Stewart's work on the CEA. Prior to the 1950s, only junior diplomats from the embassy in Switzerland would have been sent to international education conferences in Geneva. With the establishment of UNESCO, the CEA felt strongly that it should play an important role in any Canadian participation in that international body. In November 1945, the secretary of the CEA addressed the above-mentioned letter to Prime Minister Mackenzie King. In Stewart's view these representations led to the selection of a prominent provincial educationalist, Dr. G. F. McNally, as a delegate to UNESCO sessions held in Paris in 1946.[113]

As negotiations continued between External Affairs, the CEA, and the provinces on international educational issues, tensions continued to arise. The CEA and the provinces were frozen out by the federal government from participation in certain international activities in education such as the 1947 UNESCO conference in Mexico City.[114] Despite this action by Ottawa, progress in furthering provincial representation in international activities was being made on other fronts. The CEA expressed an interest in becoming involved in representing Canada in dealings with UNESCO. On October 31, 1947, a delegation from the CEA met with the Acting Under-Secretary of State in the Department of External Affairs. The topic of the meeting was UNESCO relations with Canada. The CEA group—including the president of the organization, A. R. Lord, and its secretary, Freeman Stewart—put forth the view that the Canadian government was not doing a good job of handling the UNESCO file compared to other states.[115] The CEA, they contended, could better fulfil this role.

The 1950 conference of the CEA in Victoria was decisive, particularly with regard to the organization's relationship with the IBE. Following the war, the IBE came out of its period of stasis, and interest in education diplomacy was once again renewed. A proposal put on the table at the 1950 conference suggested that each of the biggest provinces increase their subvention to the CEA by the princely sum of one hundred and fifty dollars. Smaller provinces would increase their dues by fifty dollars. The increased subvention would clear the way for the organization to send representatives to appropriate international conferences. The provinces liked the idea and approved it. The CEA attended the 1950 UNESCO conference but was there at UNESCO's sufferance and on its tab. As of 1952, however, the CEA regularly sent a Canadian representative to the annual UNESCO–IBE conference held in Geneva, Switzerland. From this point forward, provincial governments covered the CEA's expenses.[116]

The CEA also claimed that it was not informed about the events that were taking place on the international scene, particularly those related to UNESCO. It was also critical of the frequent changes made to the Department of External Affairs staff who monitored developments at UNESCO.[117] By the early 1950s, the CEA had entered into what it hoped was a more stable arrangement with the Department of External Affairs.[118] External Affairs was to consult with the CEA on matters related to public education. All of the provinces agreed with this arrangement, reiterating many times that they expected that the CEA would continue to act in this role.[119] G. Fred McNally, secretary and later president of the CEA, reflected on these activities in his memoir of his life in the Canadian Education Association: "In 1946, on the nomination of the CEA, the Dominion government appointed me a member of the five-man delegation to the first general conference of the United Nations Educational, Scientific and Cultural Organization. I was a member of the survey committee which produced a significant report on the chief educational needs of the Dominion of Canada."[120]

By the second half of the 1950s, the nature of the CEA's relationship with UNESCO had become clearer. The head of the CEA at the time suggested to External Affairs that the CEA was a convenient organization to which the government could address particular questions. Specific provincial departments of education, in turn, would address local matters of a technical and political nature.[121] In her 1962 overview of worldwide ministries of education, Kathryn Heath discussed the CEA's evolving role. It provided "certain quasi-public functions," including liaison and facilitation, and a functional connection among the provincial ministries of education, their Canadian peers, and various international

bodies such as the IBE and UNESCO. It also drafted reports for the
Department of External Affairs based on the information available from
the provincial ministries.[122]

While these changes and debates took place at home, other
events were happening overseas. Heath noted that, for the most part,
governments were working out sharing arrangements between federal
or central ministries of education and the ministries of foreign affairs
when dealing with education diplomacy. Most of the ministries of
education were part of the federal or central government. In Australia,
the Commonwealth Office of Education was the representative of the
Department of External Affairs regarding education-related international
activities. In Japan, the Ministry of Education was the key department
once international conventions and treaties had been signed and ratified.
In Sweden, the Ministry of Foreign Affairs remained the responsible
agency, although the Minister of Education and Ecclesiastical Affairs was
to be consulted on international agreements on educational issues.[123]

The Growth of Federal Interest and Involvement

As the CEA became more prominent, so too did federal interest in the
connections between education and diplomacy in the postwar era. This
heightened interest represented another step towards national coherence
in education diplomacy. Ottawa's growing attentiveness accompanied
changes in specific government departments, most notably External
Affairs. Several competing forces influenced this department in the 1950s,
sometimes causing education to be overlooked as an area of interest.
However, as the 1960s wore on, education became more a prominent
part of External Affairs' mandate. The 1951 Massey Commission report
underscored the close link between culture and education as well as the
realization that the protection and nourishment of Canadian culture were
surely not the sole responsibility of provincial governments.[124]

In this era, the federal government was also persuaded that
French- and English-language education and training for industry were
fundamental to building the national character.[125] At the same time, it
realized that educational spending would provide national equalization of
opportunity. Thus, the federal government became more involved in the
financing of universities from the 1950s onward. Ottawa derived additional
legitimacy for its centralization initiatives from the unpredictability of
world affairs.[126] The national government was seen as the stable rock
amidst the storms of international relations.

That the nature of what was considered education had radically changed since the Second World War was also underlined in terms of its relationship to industry. The fostering of industry, a competitive economy, distinctively Canadian products, and basic research activities such as supplying statistical information added weight and importance to the role of education.[127] The federal government's expansion into education was also motivated by new ideas about economic policy.[128] Increasingly, there was a move towards recognizing the human costs and benefits of education. After 1960, the connection between a more complex society and the human capital arguments advanced by the Economic Council of Canada helped further federal projects in an already hyperactive education sector.[129] Of equal concern was the belief that education needed to be equivalent across the country. Federal incursion into provincial jurisdiction was expected to equalize opportunities and complete the goals of a previous century, albeit in a way that was previously unimaginable.[130] Societal changes also brought pressures to bear in the area of student financial aid, spurring the federal government to go over the heads of provincial authorities to put student loan programs in place.[131]

This expansion of the federal government into the traditionally provincial realm of education set the stage for an important next step by Ottawa—the assertion and extending of its place in international educational relations. The emergence of expertise specifically dedicated to diplomacy in education followed a series of changes in the Department of External Affairs during the postwar years.

The federal government began to expand its foreign affairs bureaucracy immediately after the Second World War; ultimately, the expanded offices provided a home for education diplomacy. Initially, however, this expansion and competition for recognition and resources within the "political divisions" in External Affairs resulted in a low profile for education and cultural affairs in the department. Nonetheless, it was during this period that education began to become visible in departmental thinking. The rate at which the foreign ministry expanded virtually guaranteed some presence for the field. Nossal notes the rapid growth from eight divisions at the foreign ministry in 1945 to seventy-one by 1971. By Lester Pearson's era, External Affairs had spread out of the East Block of the Parliament Buildings and was housed all over the city of Ottawa.[132]

Education came to the attention of the Canadian foreign policy establishment as the result of demands from the United Nations and the emergent UNESCO. Political problems initially directed much of Externals Affairs' energy into international security. The rapidly changing European situation, the birth of Israel, and the subsequent wars in the Middle East required new and different specializations. In addition, the rapid de-colonization and movement of displaced peoples following the end of the Second World War brought new demands for embassies and foreign-service officers.[133] Newfoundland's entry into Confederation in 1949 and growing media interest in External Affairs put pressure on the department. Moreover, External Affairs dedicated much of its resources to increasing participation in international commissions and organizations, such as the International Indochina Commission of the late 1950s.

In the backdrop behind pressing day-to-day issues, education diplomacy gained significance in External Affairs' hierarchy through departmental expansion and re-organization. Among the first critical examinations of External Affairs was the Royal Commission on Government Organization, or the Glassco Commission, of 1960.[134] Under its auspices, Maxwell Cohen of the Faculty of Law of McGill University examined the structure of the organization and its processes. The senior management of External Affairs had several suggestions for Cohen. In their view there needed to be more of a balance between the attention given to the headquarters and overseas operations. They also recommended that greater attention be paid to the number of difficult posts in developing states; the lack of generalists; and the need for more cooperation with other departments, more francophone and bilingual civil servants, and a central physical facility.[135] Cohen's findings, however, were not altogether in line with the proposals that the senior administration had put forward. Cohen saw the need for a deputy under-secretary of state. He also felt that young, probationary foreign-service officers required more training. Moreover, he argued that upper-rank positions, such as division head, be staffed by senior personnel. Finally, he suggested that support staff might also be specialized in their skills, and that staffing should be carried out accordingly.[136] Cohen's report reflected previously aired concerns about international activities in education and reiterated the complaints of non-governmental educational organizations in the 1950s, when the CEA and provincial officials had bemoaned the continual switching of the department's desk officer for UNESCO in the previous decade.[137] Stewart's work on that topic indicated that twenty-three staff changes were made in one year. Service in the Information Division, where cultural relations and education were primarily housed, was seen by foreign-service officers as a posting to be endured because, organizationally, this division was under-developed and did not have the career cachet of other international assignments.[138] Cohen's account was blunt, but it garnered results. The emergence of the Education Liaison Desk in 1964 was partly attributable to his activities.

The 1960s witnessed important international developments that enhanced the need for education diplomacy in the Department of External Affairs. One of these was the 1960 Convention that established the OECD. An economics- and finance-centred organization, the OECD came to be considered an educational organization as time went on. External Affairs tracked the organization's education diplomacy as it became more of a factor in international relations.[139] Other developments abroad in the early 1960s also raised the profile of education in the department through the addition of diplomats charged with looking after the interests of international organizations that addressed education issues. A permanent delegate to UNESCO was appointed in 1959 and dispatched to the Canadian embassy in Paris. In the following year, another official was named to represent Canada at the OECD.[140]

Grander organizational changes within the department also affected the direction of education diplomacy. Although the External Aid Office, the precursor to CIDA, had some educational responsibilities, its mandate centred on aid and development. Some of the office's activities also linked it to UNESCO and the Commonwealth education conference held in New Delhi in January 1962.[141] In the early spring of 1968, newly elected Prime Minister Pierre Trudeau immediately undertook a critical reappraisal of the organization of External Affairs. Trudeau had several specific concerns about the department. Why was diplomacy necessary? Why was so much money spent on foreign policy? Why did the advice from the department not reflect the views of the news media and the public at large?[142] Agitated by the activities of the Quebec government, Trudeau wanted to avoid any further expansion of provincial diplomacy.

A special task force had been established just prior to Trudeau's ascent to power. Alan Gottleib headed this group until he became assistant under-secretary in the summer of 1967, when he was succeed by Max Yalden. The task force met throughout 1967 and examined a variety of issues including the negotiation of cultural agreements, relations with France, a policy for French-speaking African countries, collaboration with provinces on the question of foreign aid, and the question of visits to Expo '67 in the summer of 1967.[143] Although an excellent initiative, in effect the task force was a belated recognition of issues such as provincial education diplomacy. During Trudeau's first years in office, increasing attempts were made to provide oversight for the operations of the foreign affairs apparatus. The mechanism chosen for this supervision was the Interdepartmental Committee on External Relations, which included the Clerk of Privy Council, the Secretary of the Treasury Board, deputy ministers of several departments, the president of CIDA, and was chaired by the under-secretary of External Affairs. Despite its high profile on the committee, External Affairs was given no further powers to influence international activities of other government departments.[144]

The activities of the task force and the departmental reorganizations resulted in the elevation of education into the policy structure of External Affairs. The emergence of sophisticated international organizations such as the OECD led to a higher profile for education diplomacy in the department. At the same time that new sophisticated organizations were emerging internationally, Trudeau was critical of External Affairs and the "diplomatic lifestyle" of its members and moved to create a smaller and leaner department. Despite this downsizing, the Education Liaison Desk, which Trudeau had inherited, survived because of its critical role in furthering the nation's mandate in international education.[145]

Education diplomacy eventually came to reside at the Education Liaison Desk after 1964. The development of this desk can be traced back to the early 1950s and Ottawa's need to pay attention to education in the context of UNESCO and the Conference of Allied Ministers of Education (CAME), an organization established during the Second World War to oversee the postwar re-development of European school systems.[146] Under the heading "UNESCO and International Exchanges," External Affairs' Information Division's responsibilities for 1951 are noted in the department's annual report for that year. This division was responsible for the preparation of materials and memoranda for the diplomats attending UNESCO's General Conference. It was also to be the conduit between UNESCO and Canadians interested in its activities.[147] For many years UNESCO was the only officially recognized international "educational" organization.[148] Many education diplomacy activities were handled in liaison with the CEA, as noted earlier, but they received little or no acknowledgement in official External Affairs publications, resulting in a vacuum at the foreign ministry in terms of the place of education in Canadian diplomacy and its public acknowledgment by the department.

After the election of the Diefenbaker government, education diplomacy disappeared for three years.[149] The department's annual reports for 1960, 1961, and 1962 made no mention of the Information Division that oversaw education nor did they provide any information on UNESCO and other education activities. [150] When education diplomacy emerged from the shadows in 1964 under the Pearson government, it was given a new title, "Education Liaison," and new prominence. Its coverage extended to many other educational activities, including preparation for the Third Commonwealth Education conference that was to be held in Ottawa in the summer of 1964. The planning committee established to prepare for this event included representatives of provincial education authorities, the universities and other education organizations.

Also during 1964, the Education Liaison Desk paid much attention to developing exchanges with French-speaking countries.[151] In its 1965 report, External Affairs clarified the *raison d'être* of the Education Liaison Desk:[152] it was to provide a link between Canadian organizations that dealt with educational issues and international organizations. The key domestic organizations were the AUCC and the CEA.[153] Although the report includes fulsome references to collaborative relationships, the reality, particularly in the case of Quebec, was far more combative. The message was clear: Ottawa had moved into the field and intended to stay there. By the latter half of the 1960s, not only was greater attention paid to French educational connections, but there was also a greater awareness of the widening spectrum of education diplomacy. In the 1966 annual report on External Affairs, textual information about the Education Liaison Desk received greater visibility, appearing beside a picture of Paul Martin (Secretary of State for External Affairs at the time) and Pope Paul VI at the Vatican.

In addition to the new prominence of the Education Liaison Desk, Canadian education activities within UNESCO also garnered more attention. In 1968 External Affairs was assertive in stating how education diplomacy had become an important focus in its portfolio. External Affairs was the first stop for any inquiries regarding education in Canada because there was no federal ministry of education. The department stated in its annual report that it continued to liaise with provincial departments and organizations regarding educational issues arising out of Canada's diplomacy with other states. External Affairs also signaled that CMEC, AUCC, and CEA were important advisors in such matters.[154] Throughout the late 1960s and into the 1970s, the Education Liaison Desk and all education diplomacy were ultimately overseen by the Bureau of Public Affairs.[155] It was to be one-stop shopping for liaison with the provinces regarding education diplomacy, negotiations regarding international exchanges and any incoming correspondence regarding education in Canada.[156]

Changes in federal-provincial relations and an increased focus on provincial activities were also part of the heightened awareness of and interest in education diplomacy. The late 1960s witnessed the establishment of the Coordination Division at External Affairs. This division addressed external issues that impacted federal–provincial relations. Hilliker and Barry write that the rising assertiveness of the provinces also led to the creation of a Cultural Affairs Division in January 1966. It was given broad latitude to negotiate cultural agreements, provide a link with educational and cultural agencies, and organize exchanges with other countries.[157] As a result of government centralization, several layers of bureaucracy would emerge specifically to deal with education diplomacy and the surrounding federal–provincial issues. The system, like the society it reflected, had become something vastly different from Ryerson's world a century before.

Federal Centralization
Connected to federal-provincial relations was the drive for centralization. Centralization clarified Ottawa's position regarding ultimate authority over Canadian education diplomacy and spoke to the nature of Canadian federalism during this era. The assertion of prerogative, which reflected the federal government's desire for control began during the Second World War and continued unabated into the 1960s. This centralization was directed substantially toward the fostering of a sense of Canadian identity.[158]

Gagnon underscores the protective role of government in his commentaries on the constitution. In his view a constitution is simply a document, it does not provide intellectual agility. The period after the cessation of the federal war powers exercised during World War II was a testament to his belief. Imagination was essential in the centralization of Canada through the federal use of fiscal, monetary and spending powers.[159] For a very long time prior to World War II, opinion had been widely divided over the federal government's role in relation to the provinces. In the early postwar period, the Liberal government opted for continued centralization, making its aims clear in the 1945 White Paper on Incomes and Employment, and the proposals put forward at the 1945 Federal-Provincial Conference.[160] Newly re-elected, Mackenzie King's Liberal government spelled out in detail its goal of centralizing healthcare, health insurance, pension plans, employment insurance, and public works.[161] The new centralization was underwritten by the federal spending power. Over the next two decades, Ottawa increased support for the provinces to ensure national standards in accordance with the increasingly widespread acceptance of the welfare state.[162]

As Rocher and Smith note, a centralizing federal state increasingly exercises its power at the expense of the provincial authorities, despite what the constitution or other basic laws might say about the issue. The centralizing state also relies much more explicitly on the supremacy of the ruling authority and its definition of what constitutes "the nation." Moreover, it has the financial muscle to back up its wishes.[163]

Various forces were at work in the postwar movement toward centralization. According to Finlay and Sprague, some critics accused government bureaucracies of encouraging the concentration of authority in Ottawa. Subtlety became the mark of Ottawa mandarins. "Education" became "training," and "community development" the "fight against unemployment."[164] Others have suggested that changes and innovations inspired by politicians were the prime motivators behind centralization. Regardless of the origin of the changes, the federal government became a much more activist organization in all areas. The Canada Pension Plan, the Canada Assistance Plan, Medicare, and more money for higher education and training, as well as old age security, marked the second wave of federal activism in the mid-1960s under the Pearson government.[165]

Although it is true that centralization said much about the evolving nature of Canadian federalism, it was also closely tied to the new view of education in contemporary Western states. Twentieth-century governments were at work molding education into something that was virtually unrecognizable to the architects of the British North America Act, 1867 and to nineteenth-century educationalists. The emphasis on factories, industrialization, social conformity, and an education that ended with elementary school had disappeared. Some termed this new approach "post-industrial."[166] The central difference that characterized a post-industrial society was the prominence of theory as the cornerstone of innovation and policy. The post-industrial society was also characterized by the ascendancy of the professional and technical classes and the use of "intellectual technology."[167] Education had become critically important to both efficient government and the international economy. Skilled workers and planners were now—more than ever before—necessary for the smooth operation of society. Canada, like all other western states, was caught up in these changes.[168]

If the necessary cast of skilled workers was to be created, the definition of education had to change. Both government and business came to embrace the university and secondary school systems for the creativity and innovation that they increasingly supplied. Education was equated with job training and human capital production. As Galbraith notes, the "technostructure" was highly dependent on education systems for human resources. Responsibility for innovation in science and technology comprised another significant dependency visited upon educators.[169] Business executives served on university boards of governors and in government not only for philanthropic reasons; their positions also gave them early access to new ideas and an edge in the business environment.[170]

Economic theories shed light on the history of Canada and changing federal–provincial relations in education during this era. They reveal the changing economy as a subtle cause of the increasing tension between the federal and provincial governments in the latter part of the 1960s. The arrival of large-scale economic change within the state was heralded by specific political events, which appeared as tempests on the edge of a gargantuan storm.[171] Galbraith argues that neither classical capitalism nor socialism can be seen as a framework for society. With a modern economy comes more responsibility for the state, and government intervention remains necessary. If an economy does not perform, governments will pay the ultimate political price at the polls on election day.[172]

The context of international relations and the convergence of global standards also influenced domestic politics. Business and technology became significant partners in education, and education systems—still nominally under government control—became subject to new forces. In this environment, discriminating between useful "educational" innovations and high-pressure sales became very difficult for already harried educators and officials.[173] The emergence of the post-industrial state was important, then, in terms of how education was perceived. By the late 1960s, both governmental centralization and post-industrial development had collided forcefully with education in Canada.

As the federal government became more engaged in international education, and as the CEA continued to play a role in the early postwar era as the de facto representative of Canadian education systems in international affairs, other non-governmental organizations were similarly starting to establish international profiles. A brief examination of these other organizations reveals the increasing sophistication of international relations and the centrifugal forces of greater global interaction. In particular, the Canadian Teachers Federation (CTF) was becoming more involved in global aspects of education, primarily through its membership in the World Confederation of Teacher's Organizations. In addition, the CTF was also involved in establishing the National Commission for UNESCO in Canada, entering into bilateral arrangements with teacher organizations around the world, and focusing on specific regions with which to encourage exchanges. The CTF also worked to increase educational collaboration through the Canada-US Committee on Education.[174]

The development of education diplomacy continued to be a priority for the CEA in the 1960s. The organization saw an increasing need to address questions of education diplomacy, and, in its view, there simply was no other agency that could represent the provinces abroad. Moreover, the Department of External Affairs also recognized that the responsibility for education lay pre-eminently with the provincial governments. The senior management of the CEA regularly discussed UNESCO and the International Conference on Education. Political problems and sensitivities crept onto the agenda. The organization was aware of the potential implications of these issues for teachers even though they would not normally be encountered in their day-to-day work.[175]

As Carmen Moir notes, CEA executive director Freeman Stewart travelled regularly in support of Canada's education diplomacy during this period. Moir even goes so far as to suggest that Stewart was a latter-day Ryerson—the premier educationalist-diplomat for Canada. Stewart played many roles indeed, not only as a member of many national and international committees, but also as chair and delegate, representing Canada in many locales including Geneva, Montevideo, New Delhi, Lagos, London, and Canberra.[176]

The Gilded Age
The postwar period not only marked the rise of the influence of the CEA in education diplomacy, it also saw a new importance attributed nationwide to international affairs. The true extent of this importance is arguable:

was this a "golden age" of Canadian foreign policy or simply a period of sobriety and middle-power caution as Donaghy has characterized it?[177]

Some would argue that a decline followed Lester Pearson's departure from the post of Deputy Minister of External Affairs to take on political office as Minister in 1948.[178] Under the influence of Norman Robertson, Pearson, and others, however, the department had shed its relative obscurity and become an important part of the Ottawa scene. Conflicting developments muddle the picture. The establishment of new embassies and the participation in new organizations widened the horizon greatly for political authorities. At the same time, the "middle-Atlantic" notion of the world no longer held, with the Pacific playing a much more important role in global systems. In addition, barriers to communication and transportation fell very quickly in the 1960s. With the development of jetliner travel, countries that were previously days away by ocean liner were now only hours away by plane. The establishment of an effective worldwide telephone system also narrowed the distance between continents, and for a brief time increased international relations. No longer were the ex-colonial powers and the United States completely able to call all the shots. Bull and Watson are instructive in characterizing the nature of the environment in which education diplomacy was being conducted in the 1960s. They argue that although there was enormous growth in international law, international organization, and diplomacy, states in the 1960s were less united in their interest in international structures than were their predecessors in the era between the Napoleonic wars and World War One.[179] The reasons for this relative disinterest were complex, but they included the lack of a shared background in and perspective on world affairs—unlike the situation during the era of the Concert of Europe.[180]

As the 1960s proceeded, it became obvious to the provincial ministers of education who had formed the Standing Committee of the CEA that institutional change would have to happen. The CEA was unable to carry out all the necessary tasks for the ministers and still fulfill its obligations to its other members. The organization's agenda was overloaded. This was also the reality with regard to the CEA's international activities, ultimately leading to CMEC supplanting the CEA as the home organization for education ministers and the leader in the nation's international education affairs and diplomacy.

The issue of transferring the ministers of education to a different organization arose for the first time in January 1967; the ministers finalized an agreement to establish a new council in September of that year in Regina, Saskatchewan. The main purpose of the new organization would be to differentiate the ministers of education from the CEA and to provide a venue for ministerial commentary and dialogue. However, Stewart notes that after the Council of Ministers was established, the work of the CEA on the technical side of international activities continued unabated. Its preparation of a report for the IBE and its participation at the 1968 Commonwealth Education Conference in Lagos, Nigeria, demonstrated the CEA's continuing role as a liaison with the rest of the world on educational matters.[181]

The issue of who should take ultimate responsibility for international activities naturally came to the fore. Many of the interprovincial and international activities had regularly been the responsibility of the CEA. But the CEA was now to be cut out of the loop. Instead of being channeled to the CEA's upper management, information regarding education diplomacy would henceforth be forwarded to William (Bill) Davis as chair of the CMEC. The CEA's downgraded role was further underscored when provinces began to question whether the CEA should continue to host meetings of provincial education information officers prior to their annual convention. Approval for hosting such meetings was to be sought from the Council.[182]

The chairman of the new Council of Ministers was one of the new ministers of education in the 1960s, Bill Davis of Ontario. Davis and the executive of the CEA came to an agreement. Davis felt that the CEA could continue to assume functional roles such as preparing reports for international conferences. The Council of Ministers would focus on international relations in education, in other words diplomacy, and as Davis saw it, the relationship with the federal government in a host of fields including manpower, post-secondary education, universities, and problems that departments of education could solve together across the country.[183] Although the agreement Davis crafted clarified somewhat the relationship between the CEA and the CMEC, uncertainties remained into the 1970s. By the middle of that decade, there was a clearer demarcation of the functions of the two organizations.

Education diplomacy developed in many nations in the mid-twentieth century. What remained unique about Canada, however, was the role of federal–provincial relations, and the specific case of Quebec. It is to that question that the book now turns.

Chapter Two

The Lessons of la doctrine Gérin-Lajoie: Provincial Education Diplomacy, 1960–1970

The Emergence of la doctrine Gérin-Lajoie

On April 12, 1965, in front of the consular corps in Montreal, Minister of Education for Quebec Paul Gérin-Lajoie presented the essence of what became known as *la doctrine Gérin-Lajoie*. His aim was to broadcast a new reality in education diplomacy for Quebec. The key principle was *"le prolongement international des compétences internes du Québec."*[1] In other words, Quebec reserved the right to develop international policies and represent itself in areas of provincial jurisdiction without the consent or supervision of the federal government. Gérin-Lajoie argued that his doctrine was backed up by the ruling in the Labour Conventions case of 1937.[2] According to the Judicial Committee of the Privy Council, the federal government had the ability to make treaties, but not the exclusive ability to implement them. The power to implement treaties often fell to the level of government with jurisdiction over the subject-matter of the treaties. In most cases, it was the federal government, but sometimes the provinces enjoyed sole jurisdiction over a particular field of activity. As such, they alone could implement treaties and enact laws pertaining to that subject-matter or field. A non-education example is municipal affairs (a matter of exclusive provincial jurisdiction under the *Constitution Act, 1867*) and the contemporary issue of agreements regarding waste disposal across international boundaries.[3]

This chapter will examine the evolution of this constitutional interpretation and its impact on the development of education diplomacy initiatives in Quebec as well as the other provinces. (The challenge that this constitutional interpretation posed to the presentation of a unified Canadian education diplomacy will be investigated in Chapter Three, which details the federal perspective on and response to the issue.) In a word, and after a century of priming, Quebec put its act together very quickly and has remained at the forefront of education diplomacy ever since. The chapter will also analyze the role of the Standing Committee of the Ministers of Education (SCME) and, more recently, the CMEC in the response to the evolution of Quebec's policy on education diplomacy. Other provinces paid attention to Quebec's activities and in many cases were already developing their own education diplomacies.

Ninety years prior to Gérin-Lajoie's presentation, Quebec's early education diplomacy did little to challenge the federal government's management of Canada's diplomatic relations.[4] Despite the nineteenth-century creation of the Ministry of Public Instruction by Pierre-Joseph Olivier Chauveau, the Catholic Church controlled education for more than half of the twentieth century.[5] Quebec did not have a permanently established ministry of education until the 1960s. Throughout the period from the late 1880s to the mid-twentieth century, Quebec experienced both expansions and contractions in its efforts to project its image internationally. The province's trade agencies in foreign capitals that had been opened earlier in the twentieth century were summarily closed down in 1936 by the government of Maurice Duplessis. With Duplessis's support, the influence and control over education by the Roman Catholic Church were absolute in this era. In fact, the Duplessis government dealt with international questions primarily through the Catholic Church. In particular, invitations to international conferences were routed through ecclesiastical officials. When an invitation was received, usually through the federal government, the response was worked out between the Quebec government and the Church. Duplessis would ask whether there was a priest who would be interested in going to the conference. When someone with the right qualifications stepped forward, Duplessis would award a scholarship enabling him to attend the conference in question. No report was required once the conference was over.[6] During the Duplessis era, there was ongoing ecclesiastical traffic between Quebec City and France and the Vatican, most notably the journeys of Cardinal Villeneuve. Duplessis also sent politicians to the Vatican for the start of the Holy Year in the fall of 1949.[7] However, as Neatby notes, Duplessis did not express much interest in other international sojourns, particularly those of students.[8]

The Standing Committee and Gérin-Lajoie's Treaty

The introduction of *la doctrine Gérin-Lajoie* in Quebec was a catalyst for the developing views of other provincial ministers of education on the matter of federalism and education diplomacy. Indeed, from 1960 onwards, the policies of the Lesage administration in Quebec turned government heads across Canada.[9] Many of the provincial ministers of education, although not present during the speech itself, had indeed been "present at the creation" of Gérin-Lajoie's doctrine.[10] In the period following World War Two, the CEA—although not empowered any more than its predecessor, the DEA—had been the principal locus of collegial discussion surrounding issues of education across Canada.[11] The organization brought together teachers, administrators, and ministers of education from every part of the country.[12] But by 1960, pressures for change were starting to affect the CEA. Informal discussions among ministers of education had gone on since the beginning but these now became more formalized with the establishment of a ministerial council, the Standing Committee of Ministers of Education (SCME).[13] John Robarts of Ontario was the first chair of the Committee, whose initial meeting took place at the September 1960 CEA Convention in Toronto.[14]

The rationale for this separate council was that the needs of the ministers differed significantly from those of the rank and file of members of the CEA (i.e., teachers, administrators, school principals, and superintendents). Ministers governed and so were concerned with policy, whereas educators were primarily engaged in questions of classroom management and pedagogy. At this time, the CEA was the heir to the aspirations and visions of Egerton Ryerson and other nineteenth-century promoters of education in Canada.[15] The progressive notion of educational improvement was deeply ingrained in the organization's vision at a grassroots level. Concurrently, ambitions to play on an international stage continued to bubble up. For the ministers of education, their separation from the rank and file was both beneficial and questionable.[16] Some ministers felt that the CEA and the standing committee were still too close.[17] As a Liberal member of the Quebec National Assembly and a cabinet minister, Paul Gérin-Lajoie was active in the establishment of the SCME. Initially, he did not share his vision of an autonomous Quebec with the organization,[18] in large part because Jean Lesage's Liberals were still working through the implications of their policy transformations.[19]

However, the CEA taught Gérin-Lajoie much about English Canada's role in education diplomacy. What he saw in his Committee activities confirmed the prevailing view amongst members of Quebec City's political elite: Canadian anglophone international affairs involved primarily anglophone countries.[20] At the same time, Gérin-Lajoie's participation in the SCME gave anglophone ministers a much better appreciation of the changing situation in Quebec. In 1963, Gérin-Lajoie became chairman of the SCME. It was in this role that he addressed the CEA Convention in Quebec City in September of that year.[21] In his speech on the future of education he discussed ongoing developments in Quebec and dealt with educational finance concerns. Notably, although he did not speak about international competence in the field, he did observe that Canada's role in international education was dependent on creating centres of learning of the highest standards.[22] By this point, as Gendron notes, Gérin-Lajoie and the Quebec government were busily furthering plans for education diplomacy, whether through taking control of aid or other measures.[23] Throughout 1964, the government of Quebec became increasingly active in its attempts to gain control of education assistance being sent to Africa.[24] May 1964 also marked the re-establishment of the Ministry of Education in Quebec: Gérin-Lajoie became its first minister.

During the mid-1960s, the SCME became more receptive to the highly charged ideas that were taking form in Quebec. As a very small part of the CEA, the SCME had a meagre budget and, by 1965, many ministers felt that the support staff and budget of the CEA should be increased so that the SCME could become a more effective agency.[25] However, despite the establishment of the SCME, Canadian education diplomacy remained much as it had prior to this era. The direction of the CEA remained overwhelmingly English Canadian and the international educational organizations to which Canada belonged were predominately anglophone. With the exception of the IBE,[26] and eventually UNESCO, Commonwealth organizations were at the centre of the international agenda.[27] Commonwealth Conferences on Education were common throughout the 1960s. During his term as chair of the CEA, Gérin-Lajoie co-hosted the Third Commonwealth Education Conference in Ottawa in September 1963.

The development of *la doctrine Gérin-Lajoie* was catalytic for anglophone ministers because of the energy with which the Quebec government re-interpreted the Canadian constitution concerning the international application of provincial powers. The membership of the SCME watched with interest as Quebec politicians surged forward in their re-imagining and re-balancing of the constitutional distribution of powers. By 1963, the winds of change had been blowing within Quebec for some time. Inside Lesage's government it seemed that transition to something different was inevitable.[28] The government's initial international activities in education seemed innocuous enough. In the tradition of Ryerson and Meilleur, and as part of the effort to restructure the system, the president of a Quebec commission of inquiry into education, Alphonse-Marie Parent, traveled to Europe to examine new developments in curriculum and educational administration in other jurisdictions.[29] In 1964, however, the government's aims became clearer. Under the title *The External Co-operation Service*, the Ministry of Education's 1963–1964 Annual Report stated flatly that provincial jurisdiction in education extended beyond Quebec's borders.[30]

Stating an intent to do something different is one thing, carrying it out is quite another. Catalytic or transformative change in education diplomacy was dependent on action.[31] On February 27, 1965, Canadians, foreign diplomats, and ministers of education witnessed such action when Quebec signed an entente with France and publicly declared its new independence in this field.[32] This accord addressed various aspects of education including a series of exchanges among scientific researchers and university professors, notably, from faculties of education.[33] French specialists in curriculum, particularly those who could set up pilot-programs in Quebec, were to be brought in from France. The accord also focused on secondary school technical education in Quebec, student exchanges, equivalency of diplomas, and the establishment of a permanent commission on cooperation between France and Quebec.[34]

The Ministry of Education had continued to develop the relationship with its counterpart in Paris following the initial contacts between France and Quebec in the early 1960s. The accord signed by Gérin-Lajoie came about as a result of meetings between government officials on both sides that took place at the Ministry of Foreign Affairs in Paris and the Department of Education in Quebec City during the summer and fall of 1964.[35] Under Canadian constitutional law, Quebec did not have the power to sign diplomatic treaties, but Gérin-Lajoie had alerted the federal government to Quebec's intentions during a meeting with the Secretary of State for External Affairs, Paul Martin, early in the summer of 1964. According to Gérin-Lajoie, Martin "raised no serious objections" but maintained that treaty-signing power remained a matter of federal jurisdiction.[36] This laissez-faire approach resulted in the creative use of words to determine the best title of the proposed deal. Eventually, the term "entente" was settled on.[37]

Ottawa was technically able to claim that jurisdictional niceties had been observed through an exchange of *accords-cadres* with the French government in late autumn 1965.[38] A second exchange of understandings between the governments of Canada and France was inked on the same day that the accord between France and Quebec was signed. These federal actions had the effect of sanctioning the entente, notwithstanding that they took place after the fact.[39] Had there been no federal response, the possibility of other provincial education authorities also striking out on their own would have become much more real. Not surprisingly, both educational and governmental authorities in Quebec City felt they had made a significant diplomatic breakthrough. Memoirs of the senior participants reflect this feeling: for example, Claude Morin, Deputy Minister of Intergovernmental Affairs, described it as the first "international treaty" signed by Quebec.[40] For many, signing an international agreement was a surreal and euphoric experience. In a meeting with Charles de Gaulle, President of France, Gérin-Lajoie hinted that this would be the first of many agreements with other French-speaking countries.[41]

Anglophone ministers of education within the SCME saw their ties to international organizations and groups such as the British Commonwealth reflected in Gérin-Lajoie's ongoing efforts to establish an international francophone organization—an initiative favoured by de Gaulle, although he expressed reservations about its feasibility.[42] The proposed francophone organization was to be in many ways structurally identical to the Commonwealth, and, in Gérin-Lajoie's estimation, the obstacles were not insurmountable.[43]

The articulation of *la doctrine Gérin-Lajoie* in Gérin-Lajoie's April 1965 speech to the consular corps in Montreal provided further grist for the members of the SCME.[44] In the group's 1965 meetings the Quebec minister made the special situation of Quebec clear, not only in education diplomacy, but also across several other areas including higher education and university and college admissions.[45] Many felt that, because it had received the support of Jean Lesage, Gérin-Lajoie's position was the basis for future policy. Had Lesage opposed his minister's plans, the diplomatic initiative of accords and voyages that followed would never have taken place.[46] Canadian Prime Minister Lester Pearson, Secretary of State for External Affairs Paul Martin, Sr., and, later, Deputy Minister of External Affairs Marcel Cadieux all gave strong responses to the April 1965 speech.[47] Martin's was the most pointed: "Canada has only one international personality in the community of sovereign states," and "only the Government of Canada has the power and authority to enter into treaties with other countries....A federal state... whose members actively possess [such powers] would consist of an association of partially sovereign states."[48] Gérin-Lajoie's main message to the diplomatic corps had been that the extension of Quebec's jurisdiction in areas of its competence beyond its borders was a natural development in an ever-smaller world[49]—a viewpoint rejected out of hand by Martin and all other federalists.

By the mid-1960s, provincial governments were already much more interested in and aware of the possibilities that international engagement offered across many policy fields. In Ontario, the government sustained five international trade offices abroad, and the Education ministry was becoming involved in its own diplomacy project with the Bahamas: Operation School Supplies.[50] Ontario was also engaged in other international diplomatic activities. In particular, new attention was being paid to interaction with US state governments in the Great Lakes area.[51] Other provinces were also becoming more active internationally, particularly with their own US neighbours.

Provincial Engagement and Cooperation: The Rise of the CMEC

Increased momentum for change in the SCME was evident as the gap between the nature of the organization and the rising expectations of political office continued to grow in the mid-1960s. Some ministers of education disliked the connection between the Standing Committee and the CEA.[52] Moreover, the role of ministers was becoming increasingly political, seemingly distancing them from the educational concerns of the communities they represented and their schools, and rendering them more the representatives of the cabinet and governmental policy in their electoral communities. Education diplomacy was only one of the broad policy issues framing the evolution of this political office. Pressure on the office of education minister was also added by the growing media coverage of schools and education issues.[53]

Practical demonstrations of interprovincial congeniality in the course of education diplomacy began to emerge during this period. In July 1967, a Canadian delegation went to the thirtieth international conference on public education sponsored by the IBE,[54] which was attended by approximately 250 delegates from ninety-eight countries. Present from Canada were Jean-Marie Beauchemin (Assistant Deputy Minister of Education for Quebec), J. Corbeil (Vice Consul, Canadian Mission in Geneva), and L. H. Bergstrom (Head of Delegation from the Saskatchewan Department of Education). The congeniality of the Canadian delegation was notable in a period of increased federal–provincial tension. Bergstrom, the author of the delegation's report, wrote that he believed the delegation had worked well together. Role delineation had posed no problems. He was also quick to point out that there was support from the Canadian mission when needed. His only criticism of the process was a call for an earlier briefing session in which members could prepare to work as a group in advance of the opening of the conference.[55] Composing this delegation, however, had led to friction with the federal government over the future composition of diplomatic contingents.[56] This issue eventually came to the attention of the newly minted Council of Ministers of Education (CMEC) in the autumn of 1967.

After much consultation, the Council of Ministers of Education, Canada was established on September 26, 1967 at a meeting of the CEA in Regina, Saskatchewan.[57] In his capacity as the first chairperson of the new organization, Ontario's Minister of Education, Bill Davis, communicated the news of its birth to the Secretary of State for External Affairs, Paul Martin, Sr.[58] His correspondence began a dialogue on the precise nature of the CMEC and its responsibilities in the realm of foreign affairs. Martin quickly wrote back in support.[59] From the beginning of the discussions on the CMEC, Davis made it clear that he wanted to do his utmost to cooperate with the federal government. In his letter to Martin, Davis went out of his way to assure the federal minister that the objective of the CMEC was to offer "full cooperation with the federal government on the part of the Council in matters of mutual interest."[60] Davis was simply being realistic about the nature of the Council: at this point, it was very small and creating enemies was not a sensible survival strategy.

Subsequent correspondence between the acting secretary of the CMEC, E. J. Quick, and Marcel Cadieux, Under-Secretary of State for External Affairs, began to define a role for the Council of Ministers in education diplomacy.[61] Cadieux brought to the table a position paper entitled "Working Paper on Selection of Delegates for International Education Conferences during the Period 1965–1978," which outlined the federal government's position on CMEC activities. In this document, Cadieux and the Department of External Affairs were careful to underline the pre-eminent federal role in this area. The federal officials also highlighted their need to assess the nature of the educational conferences in order to determine their level of participation.[62] Cadieux's working paper went on to detail the participation of agents of the provincial governments in the primary bodies sponsoring international education conferences— the Commonwealth, UNESCO, and the OECD—while also addressing the question of how delegates should be selected and appointed.[63]

Unlike the Government of Quebec, the anglophone premiers, and by extension the SCME and the CMEC, did not enter into bilateral diplomatic relations with other sovereign states concerning educational matters. This was a real and distinct restriction on the activities of these organizations. There were several reasons for this limitation. Anglophone ministers continued to adhere to a tradition of working through the federal government in their international dealings. Apart perhaps from some of Ryerson's early initiatives, the anglophone provinces had never really established high-level ties with sovereign states. Moreover, some provinces feared federal retaliation if they went too far in developing international personas. The concern over encroaching on federal jurisdiction was particularly expressed by British Columbia's Minister of Education, Donald Brothers, who stated at an Executive Committee meeting of the CMEC in 1968 that the mere action of setting up a special committee to examine the question of education outside Canada might be "construed as *a challenge to Ottawa* and his Province's government might have reservations about such policies."[64]

Bill Davis, Minister of Education for Ontario from 1962 through 1971, stands out as a provincial politician with considerable national influence during this time. Like the majority of anglophone ministers of education, Davis was federalist in his orientation. At the same time, however, he advocated provincial visibility around education diplomacy, a position he made clear in the September 1968 discussions of the Executive Committee of the CMEC. In his view, "Canada had a role to play in international education and nobody would be more qualified for this than the Provincial Departments of Education. The Provinces as the constitutional authorities responsible for education should make their influence felt, and this whole area should be explored by the full Council."[65] In the same discussions, Jean-Guy Cardinal, Quebec's Minister of Education, proposed that a group be set up to address this question. He recognized that there might be areas of agreement among the provinces, even taking into consideration the special perspective that Quebec brought to the question. He also pointed out that there were different levels of international meetings; some might appeal specifically to Quebec whereas the rest of the provinces would be more interested in others. Although he advocated for a common policy, he argued there should be a separate policy for Quebec with regard to French-speaking states. In Cardinal's view, the federal government should interact with the CMEC, who in turn would determine the composition of Canadian delegations to international conferences. In the case of Quebec, and specifically concerning francophone conferences, the Council would then turn to Quebec to decide who the representatives would be.[66]

Quebec, de Gaulle, Francophone Africa, and the CMEC

As mentioned, none of the anglophone provinces had experienced a tie with a sovereign state like that forged between Quebec and France. To get a true sense of the nature and importance of the interaction between Quebec and France, one must appeal to counterfactuals.[67] The significance of the interaction that characterized Franco-Quebec relations in education in the 1960s would be similar to that of British Columbia signing a bilateral accord today with the People's Republic of China addressing curricular exchanges or other educational issues.[68] It would be implausible without some federal government participation. If the Quebec Government was original in the formation of its bilateral relations, it also had the advantage of a unique moment in the history of Franco-Quebec relations. Similar confluences of advantageous factors did not come to pass in the histories of the anglophone provinces. Quebec was able to re-fashion the traditional norms of diplomacy in education because it found common cause with France. In a metaphorical sense, it found a willing dance partner who could and would lead. French diplomatic and educational authorities during this period were being buffeted by strong historical and political tides, not the least of which was embodied by French President Charles de Gaulle. Encouragement in the diplomatic dance came also from francophone African states, which, beyond their ties to France, saw gains in having links to Quebec. Had France and the nations of francophone Africa not seen things this way, Quebec's more assertive approach to education diplomacy might not have occurred.

The new propinquity between Quebec and France established in the early 1960s was also an alliance born out of geopolitical necessity. The shared history of Quebec and France went back centuries: it was at the same time a history of "family ties" and estrangement. In many ways, Quebec owed its soul as a society to the French colonization and settlement of the territory in the era of the "Sun-King," Louis XIV.[69] Organized education, although severely limited and highly regulated by the Catholic Church, grew out of that colonial period. On the other hand, French-Canadians became estranged from France after the Conquest, the hand-off of their colony by Louis XV, the subsequent revolutions in France, and the secularization of the nineteenth century. For some, the end of French rule was lamented; for others, it meant a less restrictive national agenda and more freedom of trade. With the exception of the early comings and goings of agents-general, the twentieth century was remarkable only in the lack of engagement, except for occasional hostility and disagreement, that characterized the relations between these two French-speaking societies.[70]

France ultimately became a willing patron of Quebec's 1960s education diplomacy initiatives because Quebec offered a key to the North American citadel. Postwar geopolitics had dealt President de Gaulle some poor cards. Not only was de Gaulle dealing with the breakup of the French empire, he was also searching for a strategy to confront and limit the development of US power in Europe. At the same time, he wished to ensure that the Americans remained favourably disposed toward the Europeans in the event of conflict with the Soviet bloc.[71] For the French, Canadian constitutional minutiae and education diplomacy were sideshows and small walk-on parts in the global grand strategy it wished to stage. By annoying the Americans in their own backyard, de Gaulle thought he could effectively refocus attention away from France and carry forward his own foreign policy agenda.[72] Quebec, moreover, was *not* the target of *la mission civilisatrice* of the traditional cultural diplomacy and education programs of the *Alliance Française*.[73] The province had evolved in a very sophisticated manner since de Gaulle's wartime visits to Canada. During the Second World War, his Free-French assistant, Father d'Argenlieu, was sent to Canada to convince the Québécois that they and the Free French shared similar views and to recruit them in their fight against the Nazis. He returned empty-handed.[74] Following the war, de Gaulle became more deeply involved in French politics, and after becoming President, visited Canada again in early 1960. At this point, he was not convinced that anything new was happening in Quebec. The stagnant legacy of Duplessis was still everywhere to be seen.

With the election of Jean Lesage and the Liberal Party of Quebec in 1960, the geopolitical puzzle pieces fell into place for the French. The opening of La Maison du Québec in Paris in October of 1961 cemented the new relationship and marked a significant departure from traditional province-to-state relationships in Canada through the bypassing of the Canadian embassy in Paris and Canadian government scrutiny.[75] On the French side, de Gaulle, although not one of the directly involved principals, oversaw the whole series of events from the top. The movement toward proto-embassies in Paris began when Georges-Émile Lapalme, former leader of the Quebec Liberals, went to Paris to present the idea of a French-Canadian trade office to the French government. By incredible luck, he was able to talk to one of the leading French ministers, André Malraux, within a day of arriving in France. Malraux was encouraging and waxed poetic in his appreciation of the proposed initiative.[76] De Gaulle was rapidly reassessing the possibilities for Quebec, and the favourable response by Malraux was an indication of his new views toward the province.

Equally important in solidifying the ties between France and Quebec was the move by the French president and government to give the consulate in Quebec City additional powers. Again, this move represented a marked departure from state-to-province relations in other parts of Canada. De Gaulle altered standard diplomatic practice by having the consulate report directly to the French foreign ministry at the Quai d'Orsay in Paris, rather than go through the embassy in Ottawa. This manoeuvre not only changed perceptions of the role of Ottawa, but it also raised the eyebrows of a great number of French bureaucrats in Paris.[77] The 1967 annual report of the Quebec Ministry of Education, however, portrays this event as purely procedural. There would be direct links between the consulate in Quebec City and the French government in Paris.[78] Education diplomacy also became an easy tool for the French to use during the 1960s because a pro-Quebec faction that had developed within the French civil service was highly supportive of Quebec's post-1960 goals. Within the French Foreign Office, Jean-Daniel Jurgensen, Director of North American Affairs, was substantially responsible for creating the network of pro-Quebec bureaucrats. Interestingly, the Service de Documentation Extérieure et de Contre-Espionnage (SDECE), the French equivalent of Canada's CSIS, Britain's MI5, and the American CIA, was one of the organizations that de Gaulle used to keep informed about the Quebec situation. It has been hypothesized that the SDECE had a unit working in Quebec during this period.[79]

Quebec also went beyond the bounds of anglophone education diplomacy in its unique diplomatic link with the African state of Gabon. Although the particulars of what is colloquially termed the "Battle of the Flags" will be addressed below as they relate to the CMEC, for the purposes of the present discussion the Government of Quebec had diplomatic contacts in the winter of 1968 with the sovereign state of Gabon without the acquiescence of Ottawa.[80] The participation of France was essential to the realization of Quebec's ambitious education diplomatic agenda during the 1960s and the French connection played an important role in its relations with Africa.

Canada's interests had been developing in French Africa since the late 1940s.[81] Some scholars attribute Gabon's participation in the diplomatic imbroglio with Canada and Quebec to pressure from the French government. Although France undoubtedly had a great deal of influence in many African states, particularly those emerging from the French Empire such as Gabon, the reality was again more complex. It is important not to underestimate the significance of multi-state contacts for post-colonial states. During this era, these states were in a period of profound upheaval. Empires collapsed and newly independent nations emerging from the wreckage had to learn how to do everything at once. Some succeeded, but others did not, leading to a diplomacy that sought safe havens, encouragement, and support. It was also a diplomacy that valued speed rather than reflection on the longer-term consequences of actions. The history of Quebec missionary proselytization and education in Africa also had some influence on the favourable disposition of the new French African states towards Quebec. Attempts at aid programs and established aid during the Quiet Revolution also predisposed these states to actively participate in Quebec's diplomatic agenda.[82]

The ongoing necessity of participating in international conferences in education and the application of Gérin-Lajoie's doctrine to Quebec–Gabon relations sparked a search by CMEC for a niche in education diplomacy. Quebec's foray into Gabon was particularly problematic for the CMEC. It attracted concerted federal attention and intensified federal–provincial strife around the issue of foreign policy and education.

This backlash did not help the fledgling CMEC. It was also problematic in that it prompted the search for a more secure policy framework and structure by which federal–provincial relations and education diplomacy would be conducted. This search began in the early 1960s under the SCME, continued through the era of Gérin-Lajoie, and did not end with the signing of memorandums of understanding in the 1970s and 1980s.

The 1960s was very much a period of growth in multilateral and international education organizations that dealt primarily with the social and functional aspects of education in the international sphere.[83] Although the CEA continued to send delegates to UNESCO and IBE conferences throughout the latter part of the decade, Quebec City had begun to participate in these organizations in a different and much more public way, engendering complex power struggles. Did sub-national governments with jurisdiction over education have the legal authority to join new international organizations and sit at the table with sovereign states? Who would represent Canada and Quebec at international conferences on education put on by these organizations? Finally, how did these developments fit with the existing arrangements and the newly established CMEC? These were new questions, none of which was straightforward or easy given the labyrinthine nature of Canadian federalism.

Things came to a head when Quebec became a member of an international francophone education organization established in 1960.[84] The primary mission of the *Conférence des Ministres de l'Éducation des Pays ayant le Français en Partage* (CONFEMEN), which was essentially an early French homologue of the Commonwealth, was to hold annual meetings to discuss common educational issues. Francophone African ministers of education were invited to these meetings as a matter of course, and the secretariat of the organization had its headquarters in Dakar, Senegal, after 1966. Jacques Foccart, a French official at the Élysée Palace, who was also the Secretary-General for Francophone Community, African and Malagasy Affairs, was instrumental in ensuring Quebec's participation in CONFEMEN.[85] In joining the organization, Quebec—with France's support—was taking provocative steps to which the federal government had to respond. Indeed, it would be several years before the vexing issues of "member country," "participating government," "delegation," and "representative" would be ironed out between Quebec and Ottawa. Final and lasting agreements on the issue were never reached in this early period; rather, as each francophone conference approached, there was a series of ad hoc accords.

Particularly bitter federal–provincial strife surrounded the CONFEMEN conference held in February, 1968, in Libreville, Gabon. The rationale for this conference was to convene francophone countries to determine how they could help each other with their pedagogical needs. Conference topics included educational economics, pedagogy, administrative structures, and teaching programs.[86] An early unofficial invitation to the conference was sent to Quebec City, but not to Ottawa.

Disputes over participation in the conference began soon after the federal government learned that Quebec was going to take part in it.[87] Believing that the federal prerogative in foreign affairs was threatened, Ottawa began to take a much more active interest in education diplomacy. Its response, although slow in the beginning, quickly became more focused once the implications of Quebec's actions became clearer. The need for a decisive and active stance became urgent following de Gaulle's splashy and provocative pronouncement *"vive le Québec libre"* on the balcony of the City Hall in Quebec City on July 24, 1967.[88] Senior bureaucrats in Quebec felt that the province should not try to obtain an invitation for Ottawa to this conference because the presence of a federal delegation in Libreville would reduce the impact of Quebec's participation. In a cabinet memorandum, Quebec Premier Daniel Johnson made clear his feelings that jurisdiction over education ensured the province's inclusion in the conference, and if Ottawa could obtain an invitation in another fashion, it was up to the federal government to do so. Quebec would not participate in a federal delegation.[89]

Ottawa went on the diplomatic offensive and tried to secure an invitation to the meeting, but to no avail. One of the options presented by Marcel Cadieux, the federal Deputy Minister for External Affairs, was the combination of a Quebec "presidency" with a Canadian delegation. Ottawa also suggested that the establishment of a Canadian delegation would ensure the inclusion of francophone representatives from other provinces with large French-speaking populations, notably New Brunswick and Ontario. A letter that Lester Pearson wrote to Daniel Johnson at the beginning of December 1967 had this idea as its central theme. Johnson received the letter but did not respond, preferring instead to stay his course and let the federal government figure out its own solution.[90]

The matter became more critical for the two levels of government as the conference, scheduled for early 1968, approached. By the end of December 1967, Quebec had not yet received an official invitation to the conference and was becoming increasingly worried about whether it would arrive. As time pressed on, contact was made with Quebec's Delegate-General in Paris, Jean Chapdelaine, who was enlisted to argue Quebec's case. Chapdelaine was a useful contact because prior to his current posting he had been Canadian ambassador to several South American and African countries.[91]

The Gabonese, for their part, insisted on the presence of Quebec and the exclusion of Ottawa, thus deepening the federal government's exasperation.[92] In early January 1968, the Canadian government issued diplomatic notes to other francophone African countries to enlist their support: the central message was that any move to send invitations to education conferences to the individual provinces would be regarded as interference in Canadian affairs, and that all such invitations should go to the national government in Ottawa.[93]

In the end, Quebec Minister of Education Jean-Guy Cardinal received a formal invitation to the conference.[94] The same day that the letter was received, Cardinal responded, saying that he would bring two colleagues to the conference.[95] Gabon acknowledged the acceptance within a day. Cardinal, an advocate of *la doctrine Gérin-Lajoie*, felt that Quebec should proceed with this venture, underlining the importance of the province's jurisdictional primacy in education.[96] Cardinal's tenure as minister of education and deputy premier often put him at odds with Premier Jean-Jacques Bertrand. He was much more active in his desire to extend Quebec's jurisdiction than both Union Nationale premiers, Daniel Johnson and Bertrand. He was therefore closely watched as he signed three additional accords with France just prior to the resignation of de Gaulle. Cardinal's approach exemplified the divisions between the nationalists and federalists in the Union Nationale Party: as a nationalist, Cardinal was inclined to press for further diplomatic initiatives, whereas Bertrand, a federalist, was less disposed toward doing so.

In the final run-up to the conference, the federal government made several last-ditch efforts to secure its participation. The Canadian Ambassador to Cameroon attempted to obtain an audience with the Gabonese president. He was refused, having no standing in Gabon. A Canadian trade-mission that "just by chance" was scheduled to come to the region—and to Gabon at the very time when the conference was about to end—was also refused.[97] In the end, Ottawa was unsuccessful in its attempts to attend the Gabon conference.

However, the conference was a complete success for Quebec. In a note sent to the Gabonese embassy in Washington, the Canadian government protested its exclusion from the conference and emphasized its prerogative in setting Canadian foreign policy and governing Canadian diplomatic activities. Although Quebec had a recognizable legal competence in the field of education, it was applicable only within Canada. Paul Gérin-Lajoie's assertion of an extension of provincial competencies was not acceptable to Ottawa. Foreign policy and diplomacy were, in Ottawa's view, exclusively within federal jurisdiction. The Canadian government retaliated against Gabon. On March 4, 1968 the Canadian ambassador did not present his credentials to the Gabonese president; consequently diplomatic relations with Gabon were not normalized and, in fact, were suspended.[98] The government's actions against Gabon foreshadowed Pierre Trudeau's clash with de Gaulle, in the course of which he seriously considered breaking diplomatic relations with France.

The confrontational period in education diplomacy between Quebec and Ottawa came to an end following another series of conferences in Zaire in 1969. With the election of the Bourassa government in Quebec, there was a desire to "normalize" the relationship with Ottawa regarding international activities in education.[99] Until the election of the Parti Québécois government and the 1977 CONFEMEN conference, political attention turned elsewhere.[100]

In late February 1968—close to the time of the Gabon conference—Prime Minister Lester Pearson had written to Premier Daniel Johnson to promote the CMEC as the appropriate vehicle for education diplomacy.[101] In L'Art de l'Impossible, Claude Morin, former Quebec civil servant and Parti Québécois cabinet minister, reflects on this period of wrangling between Ottawa and Quebec and the place of CMEC in it. He observes that because the CMEC was composed of all ten provincial education ministers, it played a useful role in the coordination of matters of national (referred to in provincial circles as "interprovincial") educational importance. Morin points out that the fact that the organization did not have any formal links to the federal government was significant to Quebec. This lack of official connection prevented Ottawa from having any influence on the field, which it might otherwise have been tempted to enter with all its jurisdictional force.

What differentiated Quebec from the rest of the CMEC members, in Morin's view, was the propensity of English-speaking provinces to reach compromises with the federal government. Provided that Ottawa continued to finance programs and continued the flow of grants, anglophone ministers did not have the same fundamental desire to be independent in these issues.[102] For leading Quebec nationalist politicians such as Morin, the CMEC was thus seen as a shield from federal meddling, but an ineffectual avenue in the broader quest for sovereignty. Working within the confines of the CMEC was seen as tantamount to reaffirming provincial status. Quebec had aspirations of a wider role on the world stage. Effective implementation of *la doctrine Gérin-Lajoie* could not support participation in the CMEC as the only course of action. Elsewhere, the federal government was crafting its own responses to CMEC and provincial actions in the 1960s.

Chapter Three

Ottawa's Evolving Role,
1960–1970

Mitchell Sharp and Refining the Federal Role

In 1968, Mitchell Sharp, Secretary of State for External Affairs, published a pamphlet entitled *Federalism and International Conferences on Education*,[1] which was as much a response to contemporary efforts by Quebec governments, as it was the portent of a broader, more sophisticated approach to the issue of education diplomacy. Sharp's publication was significant because it marked a step in the direction of federal leadership over, and the imposition of coherence on, education diplomacy. The booklet's emergence also neatly coincided with an accelerating federal interest in education. Changes in the Department of External Affairs and the establishment of a section specifically dedicated to education diplomacy also occurred during this period. Moreover, it came during a time when the federal government, using a revised definition of education, made important inroads into the field of technical training, which also had implications for education diplomacy.

Pierre Trudeau was actively expanding the federal government's reach during an era of sustained economic growth[2] and there were many areas other than technical training—including official language policy and education, citizenship education, and multicultural education—in which the federal government was active, but they are not covered here. Although some of these have emerged as enduring policy-rich areas of federal activity (e.g., bilingualism), the area of technical training remains particularly challenging to this day.[3]

Sharp, Trudeau's first Secretary of State for External Affairs, held the post during the most turbulent period in education diplomacy: 1968–1974. Like Trudeau, he assumed his position in a period of frequent crises in this area.[4] A career civil servant, Sharp had also served as a cabinet minister in other departments. His credentials in government were strong, but he had little direct experience with education diplomacy. This deficit was quickly erased by Quebec's stance in federal–provincial relations, which was directly linked to the province's international initiatives. Sharp's legacy during this period was his codification, for the first time, of federal governing principles in this field, which represented a stab at a coherent policy for the country.[5]

Federalism and International Conferences on Education was clearly aimed at a Quebec audience.[6] A secondary and subtler purpose was to convey to the other provincial governments that Ottawa was committed to taking on an enhanced role and control in matters it deemed to be under federal jurisdiction. As the federal state grew, so too had Ottawa's propensity to undertake activities in fields that were previously the sole responsibility of the provinces or non-governmental organizations. Sharp's document addressed several key questions and spelled out a federal policy and direction in education diplomacy. Concerns regarding the nature of foreign policy, general international conferences on education, francophone issues, international aid, and future proposals were each dealt with in separate chapters.[7] The booklet was thus a sophisticated articulation of the federal position after several years of increasingly heated disagreements.

Its central message was that the federal government took precedence in international relations; provincial interests came second. Foreign policy was not divisible, regardless of whether the policy issue fell under provincial jurisdiction. Sharp supported this assertion with a decision from a 1937 court case that distinguished between internal legislation and external obligations. Of particular import was the distinction between being able to legislate on some issues and being able to sign treaties on all matters:

> The case decided that the Parliament of Canada could not legislate in areas of provincial jurisdiction simply as a result of the Canadian Government's entering into international agreements. However, the judges of the Supreme Court...explicitly recognized that the Canadian Government could enter into treaties on all subjects....

> Thus, in no respect did the judges question the external
> affairs power of the Canadian Government as such or
> support the view that provincial competence extended
> abroad.[8]

Sharp further declared that federal and provincial governments had to
work cooperatively toward the implementation of international education
treaties.[9] Moreover, he argued that a condition of partial sovereignty—
each province acting with its own international persona—would render
it very difficult for the federal government to coordinate policy. The
result would be increased conflict between the federal and provincial
governments, particularly if there were a difference of opinion on a specific
policy. Partial jurisdiction would also confuse the issue of who would take
on the lead role in education diplomacy. Thus, the concept of divided
sovereignty was completely unacceptable to the federal government.

Spurred on by Quebec's actions with respect to the Gabon
conference in 1968, the federal government needed to clarify the issue
of participation in international conferences. Making reference to past
international events, Sharp's pamphlet asserted that although diplomatic
delegations were to be composed of a variety of officials, the federal
government would scrutinize all nominations. Naturally, there would be
consultation with the provinces. He singled out the CMEC as part of this
process. He saw that the Council, and before it the SCME and the CEA,
worked well as a liaison office for the provinces. They had also carried out
the work of setting up international delegations sent to Commonwealth
meetings on education. Sharp also pointed out that, in all of these cases,
the delegation had represented Canada as a whole.[10] A similar system was
proposed for relations with UNESCO and its specialized agencies. Within
his series of federally oriented guidelines, the federal minister encouraged
the participation of provincial ministers at UNESCO conferences.[11] In
1967, the Canadian government had finally made arrangements to attend
IBE conferences in an official capacity, rather than just as an observer
or in a private capacity. Referring to the newly developed relationship
with the IBE, Sharp emphasized the growing federal role, rather than the
reasons for Ottawa's past refusal to participate.

In addressing la francophonie, Sharp applied the same principles
and maintained an emphasis on the federal role. The government took
the high ground in educational relations with the French, focusing on the
harmonious relationship the two governments had enjoyed in the past,
rather than on the recent acrimony.[12] On the specific issue of education

diplomacy, Sharp set up a framework for forthcoming conferences with francophone states and reiterated Lester Pearson's comments on sovereignty: "A sovereign state—and Canada is one—must maintain responsibility for foreign policy, and for representation abroad, or it ceases to be sovereign."[13] Much of this rhetoric was directed at the governments of Quebec and France, but it effectively set the ground rules for other provinces with regard to international conferences.

Sharp's final goal was to restate the federal view in the clearest possible and most hands-on terms. Any delegations sent to international conferences on education should speak for Canada. Delegations could, and should, include a substantial provincial component and be headed by a provincial minister of education, if possible. The CMEC should have a primary role in choosing delegations. This proposal was not meant to increase provincial power, but rather to identify Quebec's interests with those of the greater community of ministers of education. International educational questions were to be decided by the provincial governments or the CMEC. The federal government would be present at all international meetings, but would involve itself only insofar as broader issues of foreign policy and budgetary matters were concerned.[14] It was expected that provinces would not, in future, take on freelance education commitments, as Quebec had done in the case of Gabon. That type of activity would conflict too openly with the established constitutional order and be rewarded with censure by the federal government.

The Debate over Technical Training

Mitchell Sharp's booklet came out during a time when the federal government, using a new definition of education, made significant inroads into the field of technical training, broadening the parameters of education diplomacy and opportunities for federal leadership. By 1968, a lively debate was being conducted over the meaning of training and its relationship to education, and hence the federal government's role in the area. It is worth exploring this debate in order to understand how training came to be mixed up with education diplomacy.

By the end of the 1960s, economic theorists and governments had come to view education as being in the service of the state. According to this position, education should be designed to train an increasingly capable workforce that would enhance national productivity.[15] Others, notably philosophers (but also educationalists), who were particularly provincially oriented adopted a different, more humanist stance, in which education was not seen simply as an economic tool. For them, the distinction between an educated person and a trained person was facile. Simply training someone was shortsighted and linked only with economic policy.[16]

Federal officials, on the other hand, expressed concern that human resources would not be available to exploit emergent economic opportunities. Skills had to be there when they were needed.[17] Similarly, educational institutions had to be able to change quickly to respond to the latest economic developments.

The 1960s was not the first decade in which the federal government became involved in various schemes to encourage training in Canada. Throughout the twentieth century, particularly in times of national emergencies and need, Ottawa intervened in this field. In the 1920s, the Department of Labour formed a bureau of technical education to support the increasing industrialization of the country. The Department, however, did not undertake any new initiatives; rather, it concentrated on supporting existing programs.[18] The 1942 *Vocational Training Co-ordination Act*,[19] developed during World War II, advocated a primary role for the central government. Following the war, the federal government spent $25 million on training in order to re-introduce veterans into peacetime society.[20]

This original training act remained in effect until 1960 when the Diefenbaker government replaced it with a new *Technical and Vocational Training Assistance Act (TVTA)*.[21] The new act differed from the original act in that it addressed the question of jobs that were becoming obsolete and allocated much more money to training.[22] For the six-year period after April 1, 1961, the *TVTA* authorized the federal government to enter into agreements with provinces and contribute toward vocational education. Federal money would be used to build and equip vocational training facilities and to train more vocational teachers and encourage their hiring.[23] Once the *Act* became law, a steady stream of requests for financial assistance came in from technical and vocational organizations. By 1965, the number of new projects that were exclusively financed by the federal government had risen substantially and by March of that year there were over 251,000 new places for students in vocational programs.[24] These projects were worth more than $80 million annually. The federal government had contributed $350 million to technical training in the space of five years.[25]

Ottawa's penetration into provincial jurisdiction was particularly significant in terms of the additional support it provided for high school vocational programs. The regulations made under the TVTA ensured that the letter of the Constitution was being followed: the federal government would assume only fifty percent of the cost of TVTA programs and the federal funds could not be spent on capital projects.[26] The monies allocated under this project were to be used specifically to support courses in which at least fifty percent of school time was devoted to subjects of a vocational nature. The regulations also stipulated that courses must be set up to prepare students for the job market or for further training in a particular vocation.[27] The influx of federal monies promoting extensive vocational training changed the nature of secondary education and schools in this era.[28]

Two other developments illustrate how the federal government's involvement in vocational training furthered its centralization project. Not only was money going directly into secondary school programs, there was also an increasing effort to establish interprovincial standards in the area of training. In particular, apprenticeship exams were to be developed to a national standard. As the 1960s continued, each trade was developing a national Canadian component in the form of inter-provincial certification.

The second change associated with the TVTA was the establishment of an Advisory Council. Although this organization met very infrequently, it was nonetheless important. Through its operations and committees, it brought together a broad spectrum of Canadians interested in the education of tradespeople. Educators were significantly represented among them. Two of the main committees were the National Advisory Committee on Technological Education and the Inter-Provincial Technical and Vocational Correspondence Courses Committee. The former was made up of a wide cross-section of experts from industry and government, whereas the latter was composed primarily of correspondence course experts.[29] Given the distribution of educational representation on the committees, these bodies could easily have been converted into components of a federal ministry of education.[30] Particularly in light of what has been characterized as "Father Knows Best" federalism (the predominance of the senior level of government), this could have been a natural progression had the political winds blown in a different direction.[31]

The TVTA also had an impact on community college development.[32] Much of the funding from the Act went to technician training programs in colleges across Canada, the aim of which was to standardize, on a national basis, the certification of technicians as separate from tradespeople.[33]

In 1967, the *TVTA* ended and a new scheme—adult occupational training—emerged to deal with technical instruction. In establishing this scheme, the federal government attempted to distance itself from vocational education and concentrate specifically on adult instruction.[34] A complete change from the orientation of the *TVTA*, the new program was more in keeping with the economists' view of education and training: it focused on training for national productivity and human-capital development. The older system, which had targeted secondary schools, gave way. Adult occupational training led to the collapse of the provincially oriented system. Federal training and placement were to be overseen by a different group of federal officials.[35] Because of the competing views regarding education and training and different responses to the questions of who was to be trained and how, an increasingly bitter confrontation developed between the two levels of government. Throughout 1966 and 1967, federal and provincial officials hammered out an agreement on the new legislation—the *Adult Occupational Training Act* (AOTA) of 1967.[36] The outcome was an entirely new system. The two levels of government did not emerge from these scuffles agreeing on a philosophy of training. Rather, both retained their own orientations regarding training as the end of the 1960s approached. Their constituents and bureaucracies bore the brunt of the changing approach. Adolescents and single mothers, in particular, were turned away from the system.[37]

It was evident by this time that the centralist and federal government approach had made much headway: economists, rather than educationalists, were playing the determining role in developing training programs for adults. The situation in Ontario was typical of the new federal domination in this sector of the education system. Planning for future training had to take into account the federal labour market. Additionally, the machinery of intergovernmental liaison changed, upending the traditions of the previous twenty-five years.[38]

Although the federal government had the economists and greater economic clout, the provinces continued to be the primary suppliers of institutions and to oversee the specific curricula under which revitalization of the workforce was to occur. The federal government now planned to purchase training from various organizations. These could be provincial institutions such as schools and school boards or industrial plants and corporate agencies. The federal government emphasized the purchase of institutional training. Through negotiations, Ottawa was forced to guarantee institutional referrals at 90 percent of what they had been in the previous year.[39]

A serious difficulty for Ottawa in the purchase of training from private industry was that Canadian industry was generally unprepared to offer training programs.[40] In this environment, provincial institutions continued to garner federal dollars. Resistance to federal centralization under the AOTA centred on these provincial organizations. The provinces established the basic entry requirements for training programs. At the lower end, they expected a minimum of Grade Eight or Grade Six education for persons entering the various training streams. During the late 1960s, over 40 percent of Canadian males had not gone beyond an elementary education.[41] Thus, the provinces substantially influenced who got into federal training programs and who did not. As a result, there was an increased demand for basic education to fill in the gaps that existed in candidates' backgrounds.[42]

While the federal government continued down the path of centralization, the provinces were also re-examining training. By the time of the appearance of the AOTA and Sharp's booklet, they had left internal squabbles behind and were turning to face the reality of the new federal presence. During the early part of the 1960s, no branch within the Ontario Ministry of Education was responsible for training. When a training branch was eventually created, its role and philosophy were both derived substantially from the views of educationalists within the ministry and the school system rather than economists.[43] At the same time, the provincial Department of Labour experienced a period of revitalization, part of which involved the broadening of what constituted an apprenticeship. Industrial training beyond the apprenticeship was now within the ambit of the Department.[44] This sparked an early interdepartmental turf struggle at the provincial level. The provincial labour minister was now able to enter into multiple agreements with his federal counterpart with regard to manpower and apprenticeship.[45] The pitched battles and sniping between the province's education and labour departments absorbed a great deal of energy, and, by the mid-1960s, the premier had to intervene.[46] The issue was still raging by the time the TVTA ended in 1966, but the new world of adult occupational training forced the two provincial departments to drop their differences in order to come to terms with the new federal program.[47]

Ottawa's drive to centralize and the ongoing conflicts over jurisdiction with the provinces spilled over into Canada's foreign policy and education diplomacy. The rapidly changing global environment that promised economic advantage in exchange for a skilled workforce did not make allowances for ongoing feuds over jurisdiction. Opportunities provided by multilateral organizations and by transnational corporations had to be seized or lost. Ottawa was forced to take a hard look at its internal arrangements concerning international representation and training, which were shown to be lacking and confused. There was little coherence between the international activities of External Affairs and those of other ministries involved in this field. Historic collaboration between the provinces and the federal government on some international training and labour issues eventually gave way to an era in which the federal government acted unilaterally for speedier ratification of international regulations.

Throughout the twentieth century, the issue of training on the international front was tied closely to the International Labour Organization (ILO). Established in 1919, it set standards and conventions for labour and fixed thresholds for particular skill-sets. Traditionally, External Affairs had overriding authority in Canada's relationship with the ILO, but the issues addressed by that organization were quite clearly understood to be within the purview of the Department of Labour.[48] Any "educational" aspects were continually downplayed.

In the early 1960s, Ottawa expanded the scope of the branch in charge of international labour activities to better reflect Canada's continued interest in the ILO. The branch became involved in a wider range of activities that included attending international conferences, evaluating ILO conventions on training and labour conditions, and importantly, coordinating international labour responsibilities within the broader federal jurisdiction.[49] The 1966 Department of Labour report provided an overview of its expanded activities. Forty-four percent of the Canadian ILO budget was used for "manpower" organization, including vocational training. Canadian specialists were sent on missions abroad in states undergoing development. There was also an effort to compare Canadian law with ILO standards, with the aim of ratifying ILO Conventions as soon as possible.[50]

During this period "the number of [ILO] member States doubled" and, in 1960, the organization "created the International Institute for Labour Studies at its Geneva headquarters and the International Training

Centre in Turin in 1965."[51] These changes broadened the reach and awareness of the ILO and made it a more sophisticated international actor and evaluator of Canadian training schemes.

The emergence of the OECD also emphasized how education, training, and their associated international activities were defined. Training had a considerable history with the OECD. Despite ongoing efforts to accommodate all educational viewpoints, the economic priorities of the organization had a significant guiding effect on what it did. As suggested by Papadopoulos, the specific sub-text was to connect education to training and consequentially to economics. This is not to say that only educationalists' interests were being served. Instead, educationalists were pushed to broaden their horizons by relating to other sectors and exploring how the links established between these sectors could better serve the state and society together.[52]

The economic priorities of the OECD were also evident in the wide-ranging review of science training undertaken in the late 1950s. In several instances, discussions by the organization did not centre on educating the whole person. Rather, "higher education training systems" were to be studied, and training for the longer-term "manpower" needs of the economy pursued.[53] Little thought was given to examining the micro-level of implementation. Efforts were made to widen the scope of views within the organization, but industry's increasing technological sophistication also influenced this mindset and reinforced a training rather than general education focus. As a result of the OECD's priorities and the connection between economics and technical education, the Canadian civil service and public paid increasing attention to industrial training.[54]

Ministerial Turf Wars in Ottawa

Domestic training disputes and the evolution of multilateral organizations influenced the direction of education diplomacy in the international sphere. At home, the federal government also had to contend with jurisdictional sniping over the issue among its own ministries. As government institutions expanded their international competencies, and as the definition of education became more economically focused, bureaucracies began to overlap, causing increased friction within the federal government. A variety of agencies and departments was involved in different facets of Canada's external relations. In addition to External Affairs, the Department of Trade and Commerce and the Department of Manpower and Immigration maintained foreign branches. Many departments that were represented abroad and implementing federal programs resisted the coordinating efforts of the Department of External Affairs in this area.[55]

In 1966, when implementation of the *TVTA* was transferred to the newly created Department of Manpower and Immigration from the Department of Labour, training was connected to immigration—another internationally oriented policy area. Federal jurisdiction over immigration has always been an important issue in education: educated immigrants make an enormous difference to the country.[56] Despite the increasingly international orientation of the training portfolio, closer collaboration with External Affairs was not forthcoming until the Trudeau government's ascension to power in 1968. Hilliker and Barry note that no blueprint for interagency cooperation came out of this era. There was no centre of power in External Affairs to manage relationships with other departments. Eventually an approach was developed for dealing with the Department of Labour, but a comprehensive strategy to address the large number of officials from other departments working abroad never emerged.[57]

Even after Trudeau took power, ongoing debates over jurisdiction and departmental infighting at the federal level continued. Despite these turf wars, the new economically focused definition of training had redefined how the federal government viewed both Canadian and international training and education. The new definition continued to affect how international activities in education were seen during the early years of the first Trudeau government.

Perhaps not surprisingly, training had not historically registered on the Canadian foreign policy agenda. Although Mitchell Sharp mentions the ILO and training obliquely in his Department of External Affairs booklet, the advocates of training were still struggling for recognition at that time. The booklet noted that educational matters involved foreign policy. It also suggested that it was not easy to divide up matters into those that were purely provincial or "technical" matters and those whose purview fell under the umbrella of the federal government. UN agencies were cited as proof of co-operation in technical fields.[58] Collaboration with the provinces on training had proceeded in a functional way in the past. International relations had been channeled through the federal Department of Labour. April 1950 saw the Federal Deputy Minister of Labour, Dr. MacNamara, receive a letter and report from his Ontario counterparts in labour and education, F. S. Rutherford and J. B. Metzler, respectively, in which preparation for an ILO conference was discussed.

This type of discussion of procedural details was at the core of the functional relationship between provincial authorities and the federal labour department in this era.[59]

The movement of trainees through the Ontario education system and industrial sites, under the auspices of the Columbo Plan (a human resources development umbrella group) and the UN technical assistance administration, was another area in which the two levels of government collaborated.[60] International development schemes often brought with them a necessary level of collaboration—a victory of sorts for pragmatism.

By the late 1960s, the federal government began to press the provinces to change other aspects of their involvement in international training. In particular, Ottawa wanted quick ratification of ILO conventions that addressed several different aspects of labour and training. Federal leadership in this area was such that, by 1970, Canada had signed a total of twenty-four of these conventions.[61] In the past, Ottawa had experienced difficulties in getting provincial ratification of those conventions that fell under their jurisdiction.[62] As part of this new drive toward centralization, the federal government wanted more control over the signing of such international agreements.

In 1962, Ernest Gill submitted the *Report of the Committee of Inquiry into the Unemployment Insurance Act*[63] to the federal government. Created during the period of the *TVTA*, Gill's commission focused on the *Unemployment Insurance Act* of 1940[64] and ended by making a long list of forty-five recommended changes to it. Of particular note was Gill's charge that Ottawa was inadequately fulfilling its role in post-training placement of workers. Adult training and instruction often came from provincial sources and the provinces also had responsibility for national placement and the overall functioning of the labour force in the early postwar period. Referring to federally ratified ILO *Convention* 88, which set out what constituted an effective manpower system, Gill pointed out that the federal government had failed to comply with the international regulations set out in the *Convention*. The result was to effectively shame the federal government into compliance. In so doing, however, Gill also unwittingly gave Pearson and the Liberals a tool that furthered Ottawa's centralization initiative.

The federal government moved toward establishing better-funded Canadian Manpower Centres in the 1960s and a vertically integrated human resources plan.[65] Hence, the ratification and implementation of ILO *Convention* 88 became part of the ongoing federal–provincial disputes over training and manpower policy. The interconnectedness of federalism, international relations, and educational training activities was becoming unavoidable. In the sophisticated worldwide environment of multilateral organizations, however, such connectivity was also increasingly important.[66]

Chapter Four

Economic Crisis and Education: The Impact of World Economic Change on the Canadian Education System, 1970–1978

Astride the International Stage: War, Oil, and Economics

The end of the 1960s witnessed important milestones in both Canadian education and the diplomacy associated with it. The publication of *Federalism and International Conferences on Education* in 1968 marked the federal government's heightened attention to institutional conflicts between Ottawa and the provinces, even as debates over what constituted training further fueled jurisdictional disputes among federal ministries and provincial governments. Familiar forces on a grand scale—the international economy, federalism, and changing educational theories—were at work, but in new ways.

This chapter focuses on broad international considerations in the 1970s, linking them to education diplomacy. The shift in orientation, and the rationale for it, are simple. The 1970s was a period when the old ways of doing things no longer worked and new responses were not fully formed.[1] The implications were worldwide. An increasingly interventionist international system (through country assessments, UN resolutions, and Chapter 6 and 7 interventions under the UN Charter in some parts of the world) contributed greatly to a major shift in Canada's approach to the world. International politics and wars continued to play havoc with nations' economies and societies, even those not directly involved in the conflicts. The Vietnam War and the economic changes that arose out of it had unavoidable impacts in the form of the downsizing of education systems. Moreover, newly ascendant actors strode onto the international stage. Active transnational enterprises and the increasing mobility of human capital had a telling impact on the international environment. There was even talk of the rise of a "transnational class." In addition, more efficient international educational organizations affected Canadian education diplomacy. These outside organizations attempted to influence countries, encouraging broader adherence to their goals and compliance with their economically focused policies. These changes combined to help set the stage for a different type of education diplomacy in the 1980s—one that was less focused on traditional diplomatic interests and activities and more attuned to indicators, economic numbers, and outcomes.

The Vietnam War

The Vietnam War changed the environment of Canadian education diplomacy by undermining the economic stability that had buttressed education systems throughout the 1950s and 1960s.[2] The international climate that accompanied the war was generally inhospitable to many education diplomacy initiatives. The changes and associated crises that the war caused in the economies of the United States and other countries transformed governments' approaches to schooling.[3]

At the broadest level, the war can be linked to global economic adjustments initiated by the United States. By the late 1960s, the conflict had caused the US government to engage in self-serving policies that had a significant effect on the world economy. As Gilpin explains, "beginning with the escalation of the war in Vietnam and continuing in the Reagan Administration, with its massive budget deficit, the United States exploited its hegemonic position in ways that released inflationary forces and contributed to global economic instability."[4]

Inflation was one of the first adverse economic consequences of the Vietnam War after 1965. Ever-higher prices became a serious issue as increasing amounts of money were spent on the war, a trend that accelerated when decisions were taken in July 1965 to broaden the conflict.[5] Prices climbed as the demands of a wartime economy became felt. The contradiction between these demands and the domestic programs of Lyndon Johnson's "Great Society"—a spending package designed to deal with pressing social problems such as poverty and educational reform—became unavoidable. The Great Society became a target for successive Congressional budgetary cuts.[6] The monies clawed back from anti-poverty programs to fund military operations fueled the inflationary cycle as military costs spiraled out of control. Campagna notes that military expenditures had a direct impact on price instability: "While this concurrence [of price instability and increased defence costs] seems extraordinary, there is widespread agreement that the inflation of the next decade began here and was a direct result of increased military spending."[7]

The choice between fighting the Vietnam War and funding other programs was faced daily by the president and Congress. The war was directly responsible for American diplomacy's having taken a back seat to military expenditure. The world of Senator William Fulbright, a champion of international education and of congressional opposition to the war, was crumbling. As Theodore Vestal exhaustively documents in his seminal book *International Education*, a legislative initiative known as the *International Education Act* was proposed, enacted, and then ultimately starved of funds by a restive Congress.[8] Others, notably Seymour Melman, argue that the American military expenditures were a permanent holdover from the Cold War, with monies spent on defence and military equipment outstripping all other budgetary priorities and the value of American industrial assets at the time.[9] While the definitive characterization of America's choices during this era remains subject to interpretation, large increases in military spending unquestionably changed the economic face of the nation and the prospects for US-directed international education in the 1960s.

In Canada, the consequences of the Vietnam conflict, including America's experience with the *International Education Act* and funding cuts, helped to set the stage for future education diplomacy. In particular, what type of education system would emerge for diplomats to discuss? By the end of the Vietnam War era the education system had become impoverished and radically different from that of the 1950s. Initially, the overheated American military economy had acted as a stimulus for Canada's education system. As the United States experienced an increased demand for goods and services, the demand for Canadian imports also shot upwards. By stimulating the Canadian economy, the war had an impact on government spending, but also on inflation. As Gonik notes, the increased spending included educational projects: universities, road works, and healthcare all received dramatic infusions of funding. As prices spiked in 1965, inflation increased.[10] Although the added demand produced benefits on both sides of the border, it quickly became apparent that the inflationary surge that accompanied it was not going to slow down any time soon.[11] Once this realization sank in, governments started to look for solutions.

In the United States, inflation brought with it a massive trade deficit.[12] Soon after the inauguration of Richard Nixon in January 1969, economic policies pursued by the new administration resulted in a planned economic downturn, just as the country began its long, slow military withdrawal from Southeast Asia. Economists and government officials thought that the end of the war and the slowing down of the economy would put a brake on inflation. However, to their surprise, this was not the case.[13] As the inflationary bubble continued to expand, the United States considered it necessary to change its relationship with the international economic system.[14] In August 1971, the Nixon administration decided to abandon the fixed conversion exchange system based on the dollar and implemented a 10 percent tariff on all goods entering the United States.[15] Prior to this policy change, the US economic system had dominated the international scene and financed its endeavors exclusively in American dollars. While the United States played havoc with the international economic system, the news for educationalists became more alarming.[16] The economic consequences of the war had become more ominous for education on both sides of the Canada–US border than for many other sectors[17] and concern mounted amongst those charged with governing and financing education in Canada.[18]

In addition to these economic consequences of the Vietnam War, other outcomes deriving in part, and likely indirectly, from that conflict changed the environment for education diplomacy in industrialized nations. As a result of the oil crisis of 1973, Western states' economic arrangements became even more exposed and vulnerable.[19] The rise in oil prices was, at least for OPEC states, a peculiar sort of payback. Campagna argues that, in many ways, oil price increases had a purely practical economic function—to regain some of the purchasing power that oil-producing countries had lost after the Vietnam War because of the rising price of imported goods from the United States and other countries with inflated economies.[20] The oil crisis contributed strongly to the end of the Western economic optimism that had prevailed in the previous two decades. For the first time since the Second World War, the idea of scarcity began to return to economic thinking. In Canada, provincial governments (notably that of oil-rich Alberta) and Ottawa hotly debated the new state of affairs, complicating the already-fraught state of federalism.[21] Papadopoulos discusses the oil crisis and its impact on education systems in OECD member states. He considers the turning point to be the start of the 1973–1975 recession that resulted from the first oil shock. In his view, the expansion of education systems worldwide had been slowing down for some time. The collision of resource constraints, extraordinary levels of unemployment, and demographic change directly affected education systems and how society viewed schooling, politicizing and souring the debate over education generally.[22]

The effects of the Vietnam War and subsequent events shifted Canadian foreign policy priorities. The interest in education diplomacy that had peaked with the publication of Mitchell Sharp's 1968 booklet waned. Instead, the Department of External Affairs became intensely focused on continental integration,[23] global economic trends,[24] and interdepartmental power struggles over energy policy.[25] The top priority of provincial education administrators was the upkeep of the vast educational state that they had just laboured to expand in the face of massive economic change. At the same time, as Dibski and Lawton note, new interprovincial disparities were also causing inequities among domestic education systems.[26]

The Impact of the General Agreement on Tariffs and Trade (GATT)[27]

One significant but under-appreciated economic consequence that altered the environment for Canadian education diplomacy was the start of the Tokyo Round of GATT negotiations in 1973.[28] On the surface, these discussions were designed to regularize international trade regulations, deal with the problem of national governments' intervention in the workings of their own economies, and address the increasing interdependence of all nations in a new globalizing international system.[29] Although the Tokyo Round focused mainly on technical issues, including subsidies, trade barriers, licencing procedures, and customs valuations, it laid the groundwork for how service industries and questions of "training" (read education) would be dealt with in the future.

The key paradigm shift that affected education came with the discussion of non-tariff issues and common codes of conduct. Non-tariff- and code-related questions considered at the Tokyo meeting included government procurement, health care subsidies, and pricing policies of government-run liquor control boards.[30] This list would grow to include education issues. Moreover, as the GATT talks began to deal with non-tariff issues, there was increasing room for federal–provincial discord and for provincial governments to fall out of line with national policies. Indeed, much of what was discussed in the non-tariff category fell under provincial jurisdiction.[31]

The changing orientation of the global trade regime reflected economists' continued efforts to champion good education as a factor in international competitiveness. Gilpin's analysis of Japanese macro-economic policy reflects these views. He argues that the Japanese and some of the newly industrialized countries were exceptions in their use of macro-economic policy. The pursuit of growth-oriented fiscal and monetary policy, as well as large investments in education, was aimed at increasing the efficiency of their economies. Gilpin concludes that this form of state intervention was successful in these cases.[32] From this economic perspective, education was no longer aimed at the whole person. Rather, it conceived of students as a factor of production that would produce favourable economic results. In the increasingly cutthroat environment of the 1970s, economists urged educators to focus on the purely economic benefits of education and training. The Western governments participating in the GATT process generally accepted these views. It was in the Tokyo Round that participants were given an indication that government "factors of production" would be the subject of future discussions.

The conjunction of these external consequences—America's catastrophic war in Vietnam, the economic fallout of the war, the oil crisis that came quickly on its heels, the changing perception of education as a factor in international economic policy, and demographic change as baby boomers left the K–12 school system—helped induce the shift in governmental attitudes toward education in the early 1970s.[33] These developments clearly altered the direction in which Canadian education was headed.[34] In the emerging world, federal-provincial relations became even more fractious, and the goals of education diplomacy began to reflect the move toward economic imperatives.[35]

The Rising Prominence of Multinational Corporations

The environment in which education diplomacy played out was also buffeted by the appearance of new, powerful actors on the international stage. The growing prominence of multinational corporations was being felt everywhere. By the 1970s, transnational enterprises in Canada had been around for a few centuries and, despite the recent crises, many were flourishing.[36] They, particularly the Hudson's Bay Company, had also been historically influential in education.[37] Although no longer directly involved in running schools, transnational corporations were much more numerous, financially persuasive, and global in their reach by the 1970s.[38] They were also becoming more important in the operation of Canada's regional economies and local education systems. Moreover, they influenced the movement of human capital.[39]

Despite the economic turbulence of the times, the enhanced reach of transnational corporations increased their influence in Canada in the early 1970s. Indeed, author Raymond Vernon saw them as becoming coequal with governments. The advantage of large enterprises, in his view, portended well for their long-term popularity.[40] Although Vernon's prediction was not borne out, transnational organizations' penetration of markets resulted in an increasing homogenization of goods and, to a lesser extent, worldwide culture during this period.[41] Their expansion was also greatly affected in the latter part of the 1970s by governments that nationalized the holdings of foreign companies inside their borders.[42]

Eden theorizes that three factors characterized the development of multinationals in this period: convergence, synchronization, and interpenetration.[43] Convergence was the increasing trend within the most economically advanced states to bring production, financial, and technological structures to a common standard.[44] Eden sees education as one of the factors of production, although "bringing it to an equal standard" in the countries of the West, let alone worldwide, was a much trickier proposition.[45] Of similar importance was synchronization. In the past, cycles of business fluctuated in different parts of the world and did not have substantial impacts on other economies. By the 1970s, however, business cycles of the industrialized West moved beyond their national foundations.[46] Finally, Eden uses the term "interpenetration" to refer to "the growing importance of trade, investment, and technology flows" both in and out of national economies.[47] All of these factors were significant in the development of transnational corporations' policies on labour and education in individual states because they pushed the companies to a more global level of operations and increased the pressure on individual governments to conform to their expectations.

Not only did American, European, and Japanese corporations develop a truly global reach during this era, they also became more involved in the development of regional and sub-national economies. In

Canada's case, the presence of so many provincial governments made this a challenging undertaking. As Rugman notes, when corporations focus on Canadian provinces it is with some frustration. Costs increase as eleven governments, their different regulations, bureaucratic cultures, and tensions with the federal government have to be understood and taken into account.[48] Nevertheless, multinational corporations still became a visible part of provincial economies by the 1970s. For the most part, the establishment of a local head office and plant, or in more remote locations, resource extraction facilities, characterized their appearance. In practical terms, these activities had some impact on local education structures. They drew people to work in plants and changed the composition of local schools, sometimes resulting in the construction of new facilities. Transnational corporations were also attracted to Canadian provinces where there were highly skilled and innovative labour forces that were usually supported by sophisticated education systems.[49]

The persuasive presence of these organizations in Canada soon began to influence the direction of education and schooling.[50] Books, computers, and the physical plants of schools started to fall under the sway of the international marketplace in the 1970s. Multinational corporations, although influential through their market presence, were unlikely to support the education sector, particularly universities, with direct funding. When such funding did occur, its aims usually were to enhance public opinion about the corporation and to finance building projects. As well, decisions made in transnational head offices abroad had an extensive provincial and regional impact.[51] They affected the choices Canadian school systems made at the local level about the physical necessities for the school year. Simply put, energy prices, the cost of materials, and fluctuating markets impacted the very ability of school districts and school organizations to operate. They also influenced boards' capacity to borrow money and finance the building of new infrastructure.

Although the role of teachers and consultants was not only to teach, but also to create curriculum, the practical reality of education made it much easier to purchase off-the-shelf resources from specialist international enterprises, especially during times of economic change. Educators were less likely to highlight local literature in the curriculum. Local authors, regardless of their quality, did not get the same exposure as authors in commercial flyers or other promotional material sent to school libraries by big international publishing houses. Although supplies were often purchased from commercial organizations that were considered local, the broader transnational origins of these companies did not figure into schoolboards' thinking.[52] Indeed, by the 1980s and 1990s local boards of education negotiated agreements with multinational computer corporations for exclusive access to sales and maintenance of computer systems in their jurisdictions. Throughout the decades, international corporations were increasingly successful in influencing attitudes, policies, and behaviours in local education systems concerning the purchase of athletic equipment, school clothing, food services, textbooks, and classroom technology, among other things.[53]

The increasing mobility of human capital in the 1970s also had a pronounced environmental effect on Canadian education and education diplomacy during that period. Changes in transportation made borders more porous for all, but two groups in particular comprised what was normally understood to be human capital: transnational citizens and university students. Multinational corporations, Sklair argues, encouraged one segment of the newly footloose through their fostering of a transnational class. The transnational capitalist class sees things from a global rather than a more limited point of view; they come from many nations and see themselves as global citizens as well as citizens of particular countries.[54] Hobsbawm also points to the increased international transience of university students in the late 1960s and early 1970s. He characterizes them as transnational, moving across borders, and communicating globally with an effortless ebullience that left their home governments bewildered and breathless.[55]

Thus, business professionals were more on the move while national education systems were suddenly greeting new and bigger international constituencies for their programs. Students from other countries, as well as international corporations that wished to obtain the best-educated managers, could shop globally for education systems that fit their needs. There were several implications for Canadian education systems and federalism. Human capital, or "stock" as Young terms it, was being educated in Canada—nationally and in individual provinces—for the benefit of the country itself.[56] Some of this Canadian-bred human capital, however, was destined to work and live abroad. Moreover, undergraduates who came to Canada from all over the world returned to their countries of origin after completing their university educations.[57] Education in Canada—primarily at the tertiary level, but also to an extent at the elementary and secondary levels—became a question with international implications. Competition among provinces and universities for the best faculty was no longer just internal or completely national; in some cases, it developed a continental and international character as well.[58]

The growing ease with which people could cross borders as students, the "business class," and immigrants provided formidable challenges that pressured national foreign policy officials, immigration officials, and provincial education authorities to work in unison throughout the decade.[59] In an economic crisis, however, the direct correlation between education and economic development as expounded by the originator of the human capital theory, Gary Becker,[60] did not always apply. Olssen, Codd, and O'Neill note that this link does not necessarily hold in recessionary conditions. Indeed, the prognostications of economic theorists regarding education seemed to be wildly inaccurate in this economic environment.[61] The economic opportunity for education heralded by human capital theory and the rise of the transnational corporations proved to be much more elusive than governments had hoped. It took another player— the international educational organizations—to organize the Canadian educational system such that it could begin to make sense of the massive transformations of the 1960s and 1970s.

The Influence of International Organizations

The more efficient strategies pursued by international educational organizations also affected the environment in which education diplomacy was conducted. In the 1970s, these outside organizations attempted to encourage countries to adhere to their broad goals and comply with their economically focused policies. They also contributed to the new reality in education in significant and sophisticated ways. Green argues that their contribution coincided with the economic changes of the early 1970s. The extraordinary exchange of educational ideas was accelerated through the activities of the OECD, the European Centre for the Development of Vocational Training (CEDEFOP), and the World Bank, and through numerous personal exchanges among policy makers. The acceleration was also aided by economic competition and the growing importance of education for personal advancement. Unemployment and recession in the 1970s focused minds in this regard. Although acknowledging and defending the role of the nation state in the evolution of international relations, Green identifies international organizations as being among the key players in the expansion of the international discourse in education. [62]

The changes that international education agencies worked hard to achieve were not imposed through an enforced system of compliance;

rather, these organizations counted on their newfound role as dispensers of legitimacy. Most nation states wanted to be seen as countries that worked within the frameworks of international conventions and standards. Hence, most member countries within international organizations were relatively quick to apply new regulations to their own jurisdictions. International education organizations, however, were not always successful and did not always meet with the approval of sovereign states, as evidenced by the spectacular breaks that the United States and the United Kingdom made with UNESCO in the mid-1980s.[63] "Legitimacy granting" was thus a new tool used by these agencies to influence states. Its mechanisms included requirements for legal ratification of international regulations under state constitutions, scrutiny and review of local national conditions, reporting on those conditions to increasingly sophisticated and critical publics, and the establishment of regional centres of expertise and technological demonstration projects.

Finnemore describes another way in which international organizations influenced states' education systems through what she calls "technical experts" and "the teaching function."[64] As McNeely notes, these experts "taught" states why it was significant to adhere to procedures and practices in certain ways.[65] Although Finnemore—whose examples derive primarily from the developing world—acknowledges a bias towards international organizations, her work demonstrates persuasively the new assertiveness of worldwide education agencies during the 1970s.[66]

In concert with international education organizations, regional economic and educational organizations were also providing educational systems with an impetus to change. In Southeast Asia, organizations such as the Association of Southeast Asian Nations (ASEAN) and the Southeast Asian Ministers of Education Organization (SEAMEO), established in 1967 and 1965, respectively, encouraged development and became more interventionist in education.[67] SEAMEO immediately became deeply involved in educational policy, whereas ASEAN's involvement did not become pronounced until the 1970s. Newly emerging nations had to establish survival strategies in a world that had been indifferent and hostile at the time of their birth. Ashton and Sung note that the late-industrializing Pacific Rim economies faced significant challenges in dealing with the international economy, in which competition from established economies such as Britain and the United States was fierce and there was also rivalry from Germany and Japan. Consequently, tight ties between education and industry were crucial.[68] The incentive for

Southeast Asian nations to find "like nations" in similar circumstances was overpowering and the advantage in sharing educational resources amongst themselves was keenly felt. State formation in the Pacific Rim, or "Tiger" countries, was thus very closely tied to the development of education systems.[69]

SEAMEO and ASEAN responded collaboratively to the educational standard set by Singapore and Japan, which they were determined to emulate.[70] The tiny city-state and the re-born constitutional monarchy were examples *par excellence* of state formation in overdrive.[71] With the most advanced education and training system among the newly industrialized countries of the region, Singapore quickly became a hub of ASEAN and SEAMEO efforts. Ashton and Green point out that Singaporean education had two main goals in the 1960s: to establish a sense of committed national identity and to sustain economic development. Human capital was a key piece in the nation's strategy. Once industries came online, human capital was to maximize the use of physical capital; the link between an educated workforce and production was to be extremely tight.[72] This linkage of the Singaporean education system and economy was multiphasic. In the first phase, elementary education and low-wage jobs were crucial to the city-state's success. This was followed by a period in which the country moved away from basic industrial production to more value-added products—a transition that affected the country's education system. The system was upgraded, new training programs were put in place, and its focus became fixed on the technical. The Singaporean government also sought to augment the skills of the existing labour force through programs aimed at these workers.[73] Pacific regional education organizations adopted this model and used it to help governments expand their educational expertise in a variety of areas.[74] SEAMEO and ASEAN established Singapore as a hub for training through several regional ASEAN award schemes and other incentives.[75]

The Asian developments did not happen without implications for Canada. Even though Canada did not enter into a relationship with these organizations until much later, and multinational centres of excellence were not a feature of the North American educational landscape, the intensity of the Asian effort, the noticeable results in the Tiger-country economies, and the praise that continued to be heaped on the economic and educational achievements of the region by economic theorists and international business attracted the attention of Canadian policy makers in the 1970s.[76] The view that there was a link between education and economic profitability was reinforced yet again, and the consensus that education must be further integrated into a country's economic cycle in order for it to be competitive globally gained ground.

The Rise of the OECD

As Asian international organizations became more effective in their dealings with nation-states and employed more sophisticated tools to shape education systems, progress was also being made in the North American and European contexts. One of the most important examples of this progress was the development and implementation of the OECD National Reviews of Education process. This level of scrutiny changed the dynamic of education diplomacy.

The OECD's interest in molding education systems was essentially a derivative of its focus on economic productivity.[77] Papadopoulos points out that education was not even mentioned in the original 1960 OECD Convention. It is referred to only obliquely in Article 2(b) of the organization's Charter, in which countries are encouraged to develop their resources in science and technology, and notably, "vocational training."[78] From this inauspicious start, education gradually became more important in the agency's work.[79] As the OECD became an economic powerhouse, whose members "produced more than two-thirds of the world's goods and accounted for more than four-fifths of this trade," it began to recognize its "universal responsibility." [80] Ultimately, this sense of responsibility led to a formalized policy on education. Effective education systems were seen as essential to maintaining the economic gains that member countries had made in the 1960s. Education's inclusion in the agency's mandate was also derived from the OECD's tendency to be independent and critical of government policy.[81]

Throughout the 1960s, the OECD, like UNESCO, developed distinct educational research programs. Papadopoulos notes that these programs fell into four distinct areas, each of which encouraged an understanding of ways in which education systems could be tied more tightly to the productivity of developed states. Of particular importance were the Education Committee and the Centre for Educational Research and Innovation (CERI). These two agencies, which dealt with the full gamut of educational issues, were controlled by intergovernmental bodies in which all the member states could participate.[82] Essential to these programs was the development of surveys of national education systems to evaluate their progress and promote change. The development of these surveys built on the organization's initial commitment to examine scientific institutions in its member countries. The early 1960s saw a great deal of interest in the scientific and technical side of state formation.[83] As a result, the OECD wished to scrutinize national training structures for science in order to encourage their orderly development. Scientific training, however, turned out to be the tip of the iceberg. The reviews evolved and became entrenched instruments of international evaluation, the scope of which became much broader with time. The tipping point for OECD analysis of state policies was the widespread distribution of countries' national educational planning arrangements.[84]

As country-specific scientific and technical reviews evolved into education "Reviews," the Task Force on Education provided administrative leadership for the process. This body selected Examiners who conducted country studies and presented final reports—both to the country in question and to the OECD—at the Château de la Muette in Paris, the organization's headquarters.[85] A summary of the Examiners' findings was provided at a final "Confrontation Meeting" between the Examiners and a delegation from the country in question. During this presentation, aspects of the education system under review were brought forward and discussed. Critical commentary would often follow. After this session, the final report of the Examiners would be published together with a summary of the meeting. As Henry, Lingard, Rizvi, and Taylor note, the Confrontation Meeting was often a test of countries' resolve to put more money into education in order to further economic growth.[86]

When the OECD conducted its first series of broader surveys in Europe, it demonstrated the power of the Country Review as an instrument to examine distinct components of education systems. The Reviews highlighted not only the differences among member countries' approaches to education but also the commonalities. One of the themes that continually recurred was the key role played by education in a competitive economy.[87] It was with the goal of strengthening the ties between education and economic health that the OECD attempted to reshape the environment for national education systems. A clear example of the OECD's interest in strengthening the international acceptance of this linkage is the Irish Review of 1966 (published in 1969). The report emanating from this Review lauded Ireland's systematic steps in its economic development and their connection to education: "Educational progress, as the cornerstone of this effort, is meant to ensure that Ireland will benefit fully from the fruits of economic and technical progress."[88]

The legitimacy-granting subtext of the OECD Reviews was simple: states either had to get on side with the economics–education connection or risk being deemed "less effective," thus having less legitimacy in world affairs.[89]

The Reviews also examined the educational planning process. In so doing, the OECD encouraged broader visions and longer time frames for planning. Initially, the planning model emphasized the one-to-one relationship between economics and education. Holland's experience was illustrative. The main concern of the Dutch, as presented in their 1969 Review, was to make society more productive. By 1976, however, they had broadened their goals for education, feeling it necessary to see education as a whole.[90] In later iterations of the OECD planning model, goals became more socially oriented, but the emphasis on productivity continued to provide an underlying focus.[91] Expenditure also remained an important indicator that needed to be tracked.

The OECD's interest in its members' political arrangements became evident in the Reviews' new focus on governance.[92] This emphasis on politics and leadership—something that educational organizations had not concerned themselves with before—may have sprung from the original economic mission of the OECD. In the Reviews, examiners often focused on the structural nature of educational governance and the level of participation of government. Governance questions arose not only with respect to Canada but also the German federal and state governments. The Examiners felt that issues of federalism were not "wholly independent from new demands for participation."[93] In Holland's Review, the Examiners were concerned that the distribution of rights and authority to confessional groups and others would unduly empower these groups. Should they—rather than elected state authorities—control schooling, a new authoritarianism might emerge.[94]

Given the importance placed on the relationship between education and economic productivity, the role of good governance was paramount, particularly in times of economic crisis and change. Heyneman notes that developing countries paradoxically may have more experience with economic change than developed countries because of their relatively late introduction to the vagaries of the market.[95] Mundy contends that "disciplinary" and "defensive" policies characterized multilateral organizations' approach to the economic instability of the 1970s. She also argues that there was, in effect, little consensus among OECD countries on the issue of economic change and that it would be another decade before new approaches, such as monetarism, would become ascendant.[96]

By the end of the 1970s, education diplomacy was in a new world. Education was now to be harnessed in the service of capital. The shocks of the Vietnam War, the rapidly changing economic system, and the evolution of human-capital economics set the new world stage. The new titans on this stage, the multinational corporations, led the way in the assertion of this new regime, which had as its concomitant the rise of a transnational class of global citizens. International governmental organizations also moved decisively in a more interventionist fashion to shape education systems worldwide. The OECD Country Education Review process, in retrospect, was only the beginning. The discussion turns next to its evolution and application to Canada.

Chapter Five

Evaluating Canadian Education: The 1976 OECD Country Review and the Realities of National Educational Governance, 1970–1979

The International Comes Home

From the 1950s through the early 1970s, Canadians were regularly told how wonderful their education system was and how it was inevitably linked to their own wellbeing and happiness as well as that of generations to come. In the Preface to *The Development of Education in Canada*, C. E. Phillips declared that "one purpose now of education under public control is to strengthen the ability of successive generations to decide—in education as in other affairs of life and government—the means and ends of their own lives."[1] Education's promise in the mid-twentieth century was put even more grandly by G. Fred McNally, the author of the book's Foreword, who told readers that forward-looking education would reveal the eternal vision of "the spires of the city of God...wherein Truth and Beauty and Justice hold sway," a city toward which pupils will set out with "higher hopes and braver hearts because of their Teacher's help."[2] These heady promises would likely have been embraced readily by Canadians who, in Phillips's words, needed "no convincing that life in Canada today is the best kind of life we know, who see better people than themselves in the younger generation, and who look to the future for a golden age."[3] One would have been hard pressed not to believe that the sun rose and set on education and that, through the great progressive strides that had been and would be taken, the nation was, indeed, about to enter a proverbial "golden age."[4]

However, the changing international and economic environment of the 1970s forever altered this view and, more importantly, the policy choices of Canadian governments. Cracks in the structure began to appear, and quickly. Under the pressure of uncertain economic times, the progressive education spending bubble burst in 1973.[5] By the mid-1970s, when the OECD was invited to evaluate Canada's education system, a grittier reality had taken hold as the impact of the energy crisis and subsequent economic downturn frustrated any longer-term vision of Canadian education. Political exigencies became the order of the day.[6] This chapter examines the incursion of the OECD into Canadian domestic education governance and policy. It also analyzes the OECD Country Education Review that took place between 1973 and 1976 and explains its implications—simply put, Canadian education diplomacy became reactive rather than outward looking. The chapter discusses the nature of the OECD Review, the positions of the Examiners, the storm of controversy that the process provoked in terms of Canadian constitutional structures, and the Canadian response to the OECD Country Review process. Also considered are the jurisdictional tensions between the federal government and the provinces around participation in education diplomacy and international activities in general. Once again, the focus is on process, politics, and policy. Did the system work? How did Canada respond to the international review of its systems of education? This is the story to be told.

New International Scrutiny: The OECD and Canada

The National Landscape
The Canadian OECD Review process probed and questioned the essential character of Canada's educational "system"—a group of ten distinct entities that nonetheless had many things in common. It encouraged Canadian educationists, but provided few new or creative governance solutions to their problems. The outside evaluators were clearly puzzled by Canada's approach and "divine guidance" ultimately was not forthcoming from an international organization abroad. Rather, Canada's dispersed system of educational government muddled through the Review process as it had muddled through generally throughout its history. Each aspect of the

OECD process—from the Examiners' visit, through the Confrontation Meeting with Canadian officials, to the publication of the final report—revealed a firmly entrenched, provincially centred system.[7] Canada lacked a national education policy.[8]

The lack of a national policy is not surprising given Canada's unique constitutional and educational history. As discussed in previous chapters, Canada did not have a national ministry of education; rather, education was assigned to the provinces by the Constitution. Prior to 1867, the colonies of Upper and Lower Canada had developed their own distinctive education systems,[9] and the constitutional distribution of powers at Confederation guaranteed that all provinces would follow suit. State formation and the construction of a system of government in Ontario that supported social integration and citizen-building resulted in a well-entrenched common school system in the nineteenth century; whereas, in Quebec, religiously based confessional schools, mostly Roman Catholic, became the main feature of that provincial system until the 1960s.[10] In some other provinces, funding was originally provided solely for non-denominational schools. In British Columbia, the 1977 enactment of Bill 33, the *School Support (Independent) Act* extended funding to private and religious educational institutions.[11] From 1871 onward, elementary schooling was compulsory in Ontario, whereas compulsory attendance did not become law in Quebec until 1942.[12] Public secondary education also differed across provinces: in Quebec, it came very late, finally being established in 1968; in Ontario, it had existed prior to Confederation.[13]

Over the years, a constitutional and policy patchwork became the defining feature of the Canadian educational landscape as provincial governments conceded little to the federal government in terms of jurisdiction over education. With the nationalist governments in Quebec City in the 1960s, and a declared separatist government by 1976, the difficulties of coordinating interprovincial activities in Canadian education persisted.[14] Until recently, publicly funded schools, with the exception of second-language programs, did not receive direct funding from the federal government. Moreover, the maintenance of separate and federally funded schools for the children of armed forces personnel and distinctive federal schooling in the northern territories, predominantly attended by First Nations peoples, compounded the idiosyncrasies of the Canadian system.[15] In 1946, with the striking of the Special Joint Committee of the Senate and the House of Commons on the *Indian Act*, it was clear that federally sponsored residential schooling for First Nations children was unacceptable and that these schools needed to be closed.[16]

The National Review Process

The development of the OECD from the 1960s to the late 1970s illustrates a changing approach to education diplomacy and the analysis of national education systems. During this era, the approach became intrusive, critical, and pointed. OECD Examiners held "Confrontation Meetings" with national officials.[17] For all parties concerned, these were difficult affairs. The organization's twenty-first century focus, however, is more on educational outcomes.[18] Canada has posted stellar results under the contemporary system. Concurrent with the OECD's outcome-based emphasis, there has been a shift away from the analysis of educational policy processes and governance. The new system involves large-scale scrutiny of the work of the classroom.[19] States are able to find out exactly what their education systems are accomplishing. However, the system fails to address the deep structural questions associated with educational governance, such as implementing new international research in pedagogy on a global scale, national curricula, and common teaching credentials.[20] The evolution of the OECD process is helpful to bear in mind when considering Canada's inaugural Country Education Review of 1975.

The progression of Canada's OECD Review process, from its early beginnings to its latter stages, revealed the lack of both Canadian federal and provincial authorities' interest in a "national" education policy and longer-term coordination and coherence regarding education diplomacy. The twin goals of completing the Review process as quickly as possible and showing the world the progressive nature of Canadian education dominated the agenda of the Canadian participants. For all of the ministers and groups concerned, the term "Canadian education" was a polite veil hiding the control that the provinces had held since before Confederation. Indeed, the question of governance in education was part of a much longer and larger debate on federalism and interprovincial relations in Canada. Both the provincial governments and the federal government were very good at some aspects of educational governance. There was a depth of knowledge, understanding, and institutional memory among the provincial ministries of education, for example, which was not replicated by the federal government. Provincial departments were seen as having the greatest degree of expertise in matters involving the appropriateness of curricula and the administration of school systems.

They were highly conscious of local needs and the sometimes parochial questions that intersected the daily running of schools. With regard to education diplomacy and any broader engagement with the world, however, provincial governments lacked a ministry and the federal government assumed the lead role.

Because of its significant overlap into both provincial and federal spheres, education represented a unique challenge—namely, to provide not only an educated workforce but also to equip young people with appropriate citizenship values.[21] Doing so was, in a word, critical to Canada's economic and democratic well-being, if not outright survival. Educating for good citizenship was complicated by the fact that although provincial governments provided sound governance in many matters of education, education policy varied across the country.[22] Moreover, Quebec placed an elevated value on active citizenship and economic mastery over its own house— being, in the words of one campaign slogan, *maîtres chez nous*. The province's Quiet Revolution of 1960 emphasized the development of institutions that were native to Quebec, whether governmental or in the arts.[23] At the same time, education and schooling were used as a vehicle to promote Quebec's nationhood, irrespective of Canada's direction.

The decision to move forward with the OECD Review elicited many compromises as the political stakes became obvious to all parties. The first compromise came shortly after the OECD proposed a Country Education Review to the CMEC in late summer of 1972.[24] The issue was whether to accept the OECD's invitation. The OECD Review process was nothing less than a written and oral test of Canada's education systems by outsiders. In contrast to the non-intrusive tone set by other international organizations in earlier decades, this was the first real occasion on which the governance of Canadian education would be critically examined from the outside.[25] When the OECD approached Canada about the possibility of a national evaluation, Ottawa quickly signaled its willingness to submit to the process. The reputation of the OECD Review was spreading and the organization was becoming increasingly popular with states outside the initial membership group. Pressure from peer nations, as well as from younger states that were becoming interested in the OECD, made the invitation to participate in the Review difficult to resist; either accepting or declining it would have repercussions.

Despite the government's willingness to participate, the Review encountered some significant organizational hurdles. The careful crafting

of the response of the Council of Ministers to the OECD invitation was
a case in point. All members of the Council thought that, generally
speaking, Canada's participation in an OECD Review was a good idea
and agreed to set up a taskforce that would address all questions related
to it. It was also suggested that a final decision on "the points of focus" of
the OECD Review be deferred until after a similar German Review was
completed and comparisons could be made with that study.[26]

When the invitation to participate was finally accepted,
discussions continued between the Department of External Affairs and
provincial education authorities. The first of a series of challenging issues
regarding Canada's participation in the Review was the question of who
would pay the bills for the process. This question was eventually resolved
with decisive intervention from Ottawa. A decisive key letter from the
Department of External Affairs' Secretary of State, Mitchell Sharp, to
François Cloutier, Chair of the Council of Ministers, outlined the funding
that the provinces were to receive: in summary, Sharp agreed to provide
a maximum of $500,000 toward the completion of the OECD Review.[27]
Despite this financial commitment from the federal government, provincial
doubts persisted, as reflected in marginalia in a CMEC document:

> Nat. Council Committee...called for more than Sec
> of State will agree to. Can recover, however, so long as
> we agree that Feds are involved when 'federal concerns
> are clearly involved.' However earlier correspondence
> (Miller-Sharp) should have cleared this. Q is, why this
> backtracking? But we will go along, if things get rough,
> we can pull out.[28]

Accepting the invitation and sorting out the funding of the
OECD process broke new ground for Canadian educationalists, and the
international process would initiate renewed discussions between the
two levels of government on the question of their relative roles in the
governance of education. The federal government, in particular, wanted
clarification on what role it would play in the international process.
In a letter dated November 28, 1973, to the Council of Ministers,
L. Amyot, Director of Federal–Provincial Coordination, proposed that
federal representatives work with the coordinating committee and have a
decision-making role because of the federal government's responsibilities
in international affairs and other areas of its jurisdiction.[29]

The lack of a national and economically driven agenda became apparent as Canadian educationalists wrote an internal profile of the system for the OECD. This background report forced authorities to address questions of jurisdiction and overlapping authority and to look closely at what they had developed, but it did not cause them to look deeply at economic questions. Rather than providing "interregional" reports that would come out of one central office (i.e., the CMEC Secretariat), particular provinces and regions (Atlantic Canada, Western Canada, Ontario, and Quebec) wished to prepare their own reports on the state of education in their jurisdictions.[30] The federal government did not participate in the writing of these reports, with the exception of those that discussed areas in which it had sole jurisdiction (i.e., the Northwest Territories, Defence, etc.). The coordinating committee also recommended that there be no inter-regional study, rather a common introductory section.[31] Unlike an examination of education in a unitary state such as Greece, the volumes comprising the OECD report addressed five discrete, regional education realities. When put under international scrutiny, the Canadian federation came across as multi-faced, rather than cooperative and flexible. Nonetheless, the voluminous report that emerged in April 1975 from Canada's internal survey drew favourable reviews.[32]

The volume of the report entitled *Review of Educational Policies in Canada: Ontario*, gave little indication of the rapidly changing financial environment. Information on how economic change was affecting Canadian education was scarce, particularly with regard to Ontario's K–13 system. A closer tie was drawn to the new economic realities, however, in the report's discussion of post-secondary education. Nevertheless, its most specific section, "Financing Post-secondary Education," still failed to address the broader macroeconomic changes impacting the system.[33] The Western Region volume provided a better analysis of the economic issues facing Canadian education systems.[34] Not surprisingly, the various volumes of the internal report strove to draw a favourable picture of the education systems in the five regions.[35]

The political nature of the exercise became apparent when options for the membership of the team of Examiners were presented by the OECD. To ensure that the best possible Examiners would be chosen, the CMEC/Government of Canada Committee[36] recommended several membership criteria including holding citizenship in a federal state, being bilingual, having experience and expertise as educationists, and having international recognition.[37] These requirements narrowed considerably the pool of eligible Examiners.[38]

With the internal report in hand, the education and foreign-policy communities welcomed the OECD Examiners into the country to conduct a specific appraisal of the Canadian system in June of 1975.[39] Despite their qualifications, those chosen as Examiners were still hard pressed to understand the context into which they had been dropped. Federal–provincial relations in Canada were not something to which they were accustomed as they congregated for the first time to look at Canadian education in operation. Hildegard Hamm-Brücher, a member of the German Bundestag and an experienced politician and civil servant, pulled no punches in expressing her views about the Canadian federal system as it pertained to education: "[Policy relations were like] sex as it used to be in times of prudery. You do it but you do not talk about it and even if you should allude to it, you never use the right words."[40]

Both levels of government in Canada had decided to collaborate despite their various misgivings. In numerous meetings of the CMEC preparatory committee, the visit was meticulously planned and the nature of the Review and destinations were mapped out. The basic issue of who would meet the Examiners, and for what length of time, dominated committee discussions. Although the visit was to include all regions of the country, there was much debate over exactly where the Examiners should spend their time.[41] Discussions with the Examiners finally led to a compromise that undermined the effectiveness of the trip. Too many people from both levels of Canadian government wanted too much time with the foreign dignitaries.

The inspection tour was ultimately an exercise in scheduling, as Hamm-Brücher described in her reflections. It seemed as if almost everyone in government received an audience with the Examiners, who were run ragged by the pace. Hamm-Brücher also complained about the tempo of meetings and the inability to reflect and undertake "quiet work." She noted, moreover, that there was a sea of documentation that was mostly unread and underappreciated.[42] The inspection tour concluded, but federal and provincial collaboration continued in preparation for the Confrontation Meeting in Paris.

The Paris Confrontation Meeting
OECD Review Confrontation Meetings were designed to give governments and Examiners a second opportunity to look at issues facing

education systems at the national level. Governments in Canada, both provincial and federal, worried about the degree of risk the Review process posed to their public image. Consequently, the preparation of a high-level diplomatic team to attend the meeting at the OECD headquarters in Paris was of the utmost importance. The concerns of both levels of Canadian government are evident in a status report on the OECD Review provided by the CMEC/Government of Canada Coordinating Committee in early January 1975. It proposed that the delegation be led by the Chair of the CMEC and that it include at least two ministers of education, the Secretary of State for Canada, Regional Directors of the OECD Review, and one representative from each province.[43] The issue was also aired in an exchange of letters between Allan MacEachen, Secretary of State for External Affairs, and Thomas Wells, Chairman of the CMEC and Ontario's Minister of Education.[44] In order to pick the most diplomatically prepared team, both federal and provincial authorities wanted a commitment to strong regional representation on the confrontation committee.

Concerns that arose as the educational envoys prepared to go to Paris in the autumn of 1975 reflected the weakness of Canada's educational governance structures. In a detailed submission to a meeting of the CMEC on November 13 and 14, 1975, Dr. James Hrabi, Chair of the Coordinating Committee for the OECD Review and Deputy Minister of Education for Alberta, set out points of information, recommendations, and opinions on the preliminary report received from the Examiners. Hrabi noted, somewhat presciently, the contradiction between regionally prepared Canadian reports and the Examiners' pan-Canadian approach to the issues.[45] (This issue would reappear at the confrontation meeting in Paris.) This turn of events was alarming for the Committee—there had been an expectation that the Examiners would respond to the regional reports with regional rather than national critiques.[46] The Committee also had several other worries. Some dealt with factual errors, whereas others were more specifically geared toward the issue of federal–provincial relations, which all agreed was to be avoided and sidetracked if at all possible in the interests of a common front and the minimization of any diplomatic repercussions from the Review. From the outset, the federal members of the Coordinating Committee had been wary in agreeing to the pre-eminence of the CMEC in educational matters.[47] However, it was agreed that if federal government officials were pressed on educational questions, then provincial viewpoints would take precedence. This *modus operandi* took advantage of the OECD as a forum but also demonstrated

Canada's unwillingness to air the toughest questions in that public an arena. Bluntly put, the Canadian Constitution was off limits in the discussion. A written list of questions and responses was seen as a way of addressing the federal–provincial reality and minimizing the discussion of relevant, but taboo, subjects.[48] The agreement achieved during federal–provincial preparations for the Country Review came at the high cost of deferring any discussion of national educational governance in Canada, thus serving to prolong the status quo. How the OECD Examiners would respond, however, was not under the delegation's control.

Once the Canadian delegation arrived in Paris, collaboration for limited ends was the group's motto. There was heavy representation from the provincial ministries of education and the federal Department of the Secretary of State among the nineteen people from both levels of government. There were also representatives from the federal Ministry of Indian and Northern Affairs and the federal Ministry of Manpower and Immigration. The federal Department of External Affairs was also represented in the delegation in order to ensure diplomatic protocol was followed and to handle any questions on foreign-policy issues. This heavy oversight on the part of numerous federal government departments, albeit tolerable in the short term, was deliberate overkill that irritated the provincial delegates.[49]

The OECD Confrontation Meeting focused a strong beam of light on the nature of educational governance in Canada. The meeting that took place at the Château de la Muette headquarters of the OECD in Paris on December 9 and 10, 1975, was without precedent in Canadian history and marked the culmination of a period of federal and provincial collaboration in education. The probing questions of the OECD Examiners exposed provincial educationists' agendas and interests, especially because there was insufficient opportunity for the Canadian delegation to coordinate their replies.[50]

It quickly became evident that more than the Canadian curriculum was under scrutiny. The Examiners opened the Confrontation Meeting by presenting their report. They outlined effective aspects of the Canadian education system before moving on to what they considered to be general problem areas.[51] Among the latter was the sensitive question of intergovernmental relations, particularly with respect to development and change.[52] The Examiners bluntly commented on the activities of the more senior government ministers and officials involved in education, directing particular criticism at the frequent turnover among ministers of education.

In their view, the administrative background and knowledge of ministers of education were insufficient to overcome the shortness of their tenure in office. The revolving door of ministers might make political sense, but there were few other reasons to commend it. Because the short tenure of Canadian ministers of education seemed to preclude their developing and taking a longer view of education, the OECD Examiners were willing to offer advice and constructive criticism on matters of educational planning at the national level.[53]

Despite Canadian objections, the Examiners took aim at the forbidden question: the place of education in the Canadian Constitution. In the Examiners' view, the absence of a federal ministry led various federal officials to carve up the field of education into portions over which they seized jurisdiction for their own flourishing departments.[54] The Examiners were quick to question this feature of Canadian educational governance and place it in the proverbial laps of the diplomatic delegation sitting in front of them. Short-lived, ad hoc cooperation between the two levels of government in education matters was seen as a fundamental flaw in achieving momentum in the Canadian educational endeavour. They encouraged a greater emphasis on a pan-Canadian education system rather than bilateral agreements between provinces.[55] For the Examiners, a better approach would be to assign a central role to the CMEC or to create a robust federal office or national ministry of education.[56] A high-profile CMEC would be influential in Canadian educational policy formation, more representative of all groups (the federal government included), and less of a gathering place simply for ministers of education.[57] Although not explicitly mentioned in this discussion, one of the subtexts of this critique was the ability of other federal states in which constitutional authority for education resided with the state rather than federal governments to successfully work together. The United States and Australia were foremost amongst these.[58]

The Canadian envoys' response to the critiques attributed the conflicts and problems of educational governance to the country's still being young and not yet fully mature in its internal arrangements. In keeping with the spirit of their temporary accord on the OECD process—and possibly as a measure of the immaturity they had raised in their own defence—the delegation, in the full glare of the international spotlight, adopted the joint position of refusing to respond when issues strayed into the constitutional and political realm. The delegation stated unequivocally that it was not the OECD's role to discuss the

constitutional politics of education.[59] Federal and provincial officials at
the meeting further stressed that CMEC sub-committees and committees
composed of provincial as well as federal officials obviated the need for a
federal ministry of education, a national policy, or any reconsideration of
Canadian educational governance.[60]

The nature of Canadian educational governance became
clearer in the exchanges between the Examiners and the delegates from
Quebec. Examiner Hamm-Brücher, an experienced politician within
a federal state, opened the discussion with a series of questions dealing
with intergovernmental relations. Two of the questions explored possible
avenues of cooperation between Ottawa and the provinces in the area
of education and the degree to which finances were crucial to opening
up such avenues.[61] Following commentaries by Ben Hanuschak (Chair
of the CMEC) and Peter Roberts (an official from the federal Secretary
of State) which failed to address directly the Examiners' questions,
Maurice Mercier, Quebec's Assistant Deputy Minister of Education, took
the floor.[62] Mercier was realistic about the limits of federal–provincial
cooperation in education and his role as an educational envoy for Canada.
He explained that Canadians show interprovincial and federal–provincial
solidarity by agreeing not to talk about certain issues (in this case, the
Constitution).[63] Mercier did not explicitly reject "official" exclusion
of the federal government from educational policy formation, insisting
instead on provincial primacy in the governance of public education.[64]
He also felt that the provinces were to be commended on their "national"
achievements.[65] The Quebec delegate's emphasis was clearly on minimal
collaboration and the enhancement of provincial accomplishments.
Mercier's attempt to defend the interprovincial vision of the education
system ultimately failed: the other envoys stuck to their own provincial
positions, reinforcing the Examiners' critiques.

It fell to Canadians to evaluate the OECD's examination of the
country's education system. Once the Confrontation Meeting concluded,
the OECD Secretariat moved quickly to publish the Examiners' external
report. Their role in examining the Canadian system was finished. Back
home, however, the collaboration among provincial and federal officials
quickly ended as the delegates returned to their respective capitals, and
as the media and academic commentators began to digest the OECD
exercise. The end of the Review also marked the end of the involvement
of the Department of External Affairs in the OECD process—at least
for the moment. However, it released an explanatory communiqué,

engineered in discussion with the CMEC, announcing the issuance of the Examiners' external report in August 1976 and summarizing the OECD process.[66] Toward the end of the communiqué, the Department struck a measured tone, stating that the OECD Examiners had found much to admire in Canada's education system and that Canadian authorities would carefully review their report.[67] The Department of External Affairs, however, returned to its other responsibilities and devoted little further energy to education diplomacy during 1976.

Although having consulted with External Affairs concerning the response to the issuance of the final report of the OECD Examiners, the CMEC released its own version of events in its 1976 Annual Report. Mostly a simple factual recounting of the significant events of the previous three years, it did little to foster a deeper understanding of the problems the two levels of government faced in undertaking the Review process.[68] Broader response came when the OECD report was opened up for analysis by other groups within the Canadian education community, such as the CEA. Open discussion of the report was a delicate matter, not only because of the critical nature of the Review, but also because it risked a reconsideration of the CMEC's role in the Canadian education system and whether there should be national as opposed to interprovincial cooperation in the field. The CMEC gave brief consideration to inviting all associated special-interest groups (e.g., the Canadian Teachers' Federation) to a national conference on the subject. This idea was dropped, however, in favour of soliciting written submissions from the organizations.[69]

The domestic response to the Review quickly made it apparent that changes advocated by an international organization would not occur in the face of a tried-and-true constitutional structure and an existing pan-Canadian policy process. The politesse the envoys had summoned in the name of interprovincialism did not change the underlying ambiguities and bottlenecks created by the existing federal structure and the lack of well-defined paths for national educational governance. As one would expect, different segments of Canadian society responded with comments about those aspects of education that reflected their specific concerns. Those preoccupied with the education diplomacy represented in the Review and the related questions of governance divided into two groups. Some wished to expand the dialogue on educational structures at the national level, whereas others continued to defend the status quo. Among the reformist-minded replies, the dominant and cynical view was that the deeper questions of political power and the Constitution would remain unaddressed. Bringing about "improved mechanisms of federal–provincial co-operation," let alone the goal of constitutional change, was not attainable in 1976.[70]

The Canadian news media were the first to comment on the OECD Review. In *The Globe and Mail* of August 18, 1976, following the release of the report, journalist Jeff Sallot echoed the provincial education ministers' view that the report was flawed by its national rather than interprovincial or purely provincial perspective on education. Rather than offering a critical examination of the issues of governance and curriculum, Sallot merely explained the governmental position behind the carefully crafted Canadian presentation in Paris.[71]

Canadian Press and *Toronto Star* journalists had little to say about the OECD Review, but what coverage there was implied that the federal–provincial collaboration in Paris was little more than a temporary exercise. In effect, they reiterated the OECD Examiners' position that the governments in Canada must work harder to collaborate and plan policy.[72] However, the *Toronto Star* did not quote any of the provincial ministers of education nor did it convey provincial premiers' responses to the Review.

The journalistic tone in the Quebec press was much more critical. There continued to be intense skepticism about national collaboration and a single international face for Canadian education. Memories of earlier and ongoing encounters with the federal government ran deep.[73] *Le Devoir* summarized the Examiners' report, drawing particular attention to both the positive and negative critiques of the Canadian education system. The absence of a national vision for the future of Canadian education was central to the *Le Devoir* article, which prompted an editorial in the paper focusing on the question of bilingualism and the distinctiveness of Quebec's education system in Canada.[74]

The OECD process was accorded little attention by most of the Canadian business community, mostly because of government action with respect to the Review. In the course of guarding access to the OECD process, the governments had failed to elicit corporate interest or participation. Although not explicitly excluded from the process, business briefs were not solicited; therefore, business organizations did not make any presentations during the Examiners' Canadian tour.[75] After the publication of the results of the Review in 1976, school finance leaders were vocal about their dislike of the waste and conflict in educational affairs.[76] They called for renewed cooperation to ensure that Canada did not fall behind in its "industrial competitiveness."[77] Dealing with the standards of one ministry of education may have been a far simpler proposition for business than dealing with twelve different sets of school standards, but the idea of nationalizing educational policies was not popular in all quarters of the Canadian business community.

Some parts of the community also maintained their scepticism and highly contextualized view of Canadian federalism and education. For many in this constituency, anything that complicated productivity and slowed growth was to be deplored. The OECD Review confirmed some of their convictions, especially their belief that Canadian governments did much to inhibit the smooth flow of policy and limit the creation of conditions that were suitable for business to flourish.[78]

In contrast, the non-governmental groups involved in education quite uniformly supported the temporary nature of federal–provincial collaboration and dismissed the notion that there should be a national educational authority. After the CMEC, the CEA was the most representative of this position. Even after the CMEC had split away from it in the latter part of the 1960s, the CEA continued to present itself as broadly representative of all the constituencies of Canadian education. Provincially funded, it included in its ranks a number of upper-echelon provincial bureaucrats. One of its major tasks in the 1970s was the promotion of bilingualism, both internally and externally.[79]

In his discussion of the OECD Review, Freeman Stewart, the long-serving Executive Director of the CEA, endorsed the continuation of the interprovincial approach. He was convinced that it was the best way to resolve issues between the federal government and the provinces.[80] Defending the provincial standpoint, he argued that the existing state of affairs was necessary to hold Confederation together and ensure federal–provincial peace—high stakes, indeed!

CEA President Carmen Moir also dismissed the notion of thinking beyond the temporary arrangements exhibited in Paris and emphatically supported the interprovincial status quo. He mounted a vigorous defence of provincial prerogatives in education and argued that provincial collaboration already constituted a national plan and system.[81] Moir reiterated the provincial response to the OECD exercise and did not see the utility of exploring other forms of constitutional organization. As noted above, other federated states were also busy at this time trying to work out the dynamics of cooperating on educational issues. Notable amongst these was Australia.[82] In an interesting contrast, during the same period in the United States, President Carter elevated education to its own cabinet-level position with the creation of the U.S. Department of Education.[83] No similar move was to occur in Canada.

Analysis and critique of the OECD Review continued for the next three years as organizations addressed the final report and its implications. One organization to respond was the AUCC,[84] which agreed that the CMEC should be strengthened and become the principal federal–provincial body in education and that there should be federal representation on the Council, possibly the Secretary of State. The AUCC did not consider the ad hoc accords that governed education diplomacy, in general, and diplomacy with the OECD, in particular, to be constructive models for future activities.

Following the end of the Review process, the OECD Examiners reiterated, in a peer-reviewed article in the *Canadian Journal of Higher Education*, their view that the fragile nature of Canadian educational governance distracted the governors of the education system from discharging their principal responsibilities towards their end-users, the students. They pointed out that the general changes they had advocated were not being implemented and that the specific structural changes to the educational governance system that they had recommended were not occurring as quickly as they had hoped. They expressly highlighted the national as opposed to interprovincial role that the CMEC could assume.[85] In reflecting on the outcomes of the process, the Examiners also noted that there continued to be a lack of long-term national planning and research in education. It was feared that any possible momentum that might have been generated by the OECD Review had long since evaporated.[86]

Examiner Harold Noah stated that there was "an absolute vacuum of officially-sponsored consideration of a Canadian policy for educational development."[87] In his opinion, the Review was intended to be a catalyst for change. Noah believed that the impetus built into the Review process could propel a country to do many things with its education system, if that energy were sustained. He optimistically disagreed with his colleague, Hildegard Hamm-Brücher, who believed that any potential for progress in Canada had lost momentum after the completion of the Review.

While outside parties discussed the outcomes of the OECD Review, the provincial insiders returned to business as usual, continuing to defend their views on Canadian education and its system of governance. For them, the process had done much to reinforce these views, and they were resolved that change in the governance of education and in the evolution of educational diplomacy would come only if and when the provinces considered it in their best interest. Many of the provincial participants, once freed from the strictures of membership in the delegation, turned any feelings of discontent outward—toward the process, and toward OECD itself. Interacting with the outside world had left a bad taste. Prior to the Review, only Quebec had expressed international education interests; increasingly, however, other provinces had joined in. As international agencies became bolder, so, too, did individual governments.

The temporizing that occurred concerning Canadian educational governance left an unpleasant aftertaste for all concerned. The ambivalence extended to the members of the delegation. The chair of the Canadian Coordinating Committee, Dr. James Hrabi, gave the OECD Review his qualified approval. At the annual convention of the CEA, Hrabi stated that the Canadian delegation to the Paris meeting had not been happy with the draft of the OECD Review. [88] In reflecting on the question of establishing a federal presence in education, he saw obstacles as well as opportunities for change in this area.[89] Despite his apparent openness to change, Hrabi did not elaborate on the nature of the tactics that might be required to encourage this transformation while still indulging the eccentricities of Canadian federalism. In the end, he attributed the failings of federalism listed in the OECD report to the Examiners' inability to understand the nature of Canadian fiscal transfers and the peculiarities of the Canadian federal system.[90]

Not surprisingly, bureaucrats in Quebec also upheld the status quo in federal–provincial relations in education. Jean-Marie Beauchemin of the Ministry of Education asserted Quebec's unique status in Canada, particularly in the field of education. As the only francophone province, Quebec was a province unlike the others.[91] In Beauchemin's view, the OECD Examiners were very much directed by their "Canadian interlocutors," and the formulations of Anglophone interprovincialism looked suspiciously like cloaked federalism. Not wishing to associate himself with this process, Beauchemin highlighted Quebec's distinctive position.[92] He did not view the OECD as an international organization that was performing a "teaching function" in the way that political theorist Martha Finnemore has posited.[93] Rather, the OECD process had a limited impact on provinces and their relationships among themselves.[94] Beauchemin also took aim at the idea of a federal ministry of education, arguing that, in their haste to avoid discussing "political-party" differences over education, the Examiners had seized on the idea of a strengthened CMEC or a federal ministry of education to solve their dilemma.[95] Instead of seeing a need for change, Quebec bureaucrats were more than willing to retain the existing system and use it to their greatest political advantage.

Whereas provincial officials were of the general view that the status quo in educational governance would continue, local government officials clamoured because they had been left out of the Review process altogether.[96] They charged that the authorities responsible for setting up the Confrontation Meeting delegation had made no effort to include representatives from the local level, including school board trustees.[97] The CMEC and the Coordinating Committee had been blunt about their exclusion of local officials from the international process prior to the Confrontation Meeting. However, they had tried to temper their restriction on local representation by providing for a broad regional spread among delegates.[98] Local officials took the view that a federal ministry of education would allow them more representation than they enjoyed within the organizations that existed at that time.

Provincial politicians also aired their views following the publication of the final external report. In addition to generally defending the extant system of education and educational governance in Canada, provincial governments took issue with particular conclusions within the Examiners' report. The government of Ontario, particularly the Minister of Colleges and Universities, held the view that the OECD report did not fairly represent the reality of education in Canada. Dr. Harry Parrott, minister at this time, rejected the contention that colleges were "holding areas" for students not wanted in universities.[99] He argued that this sort of relationship was not characteristic of the Ontario system.[100] From the perspective of many provincial politicians, international reviews such as the OECD's were useful only so long as they portrayed provincial policies and actions in a positive light.

More OECD Diplomacy:
The Second Engagement and the Statement

Federal government attention was centred on the Review only fleetingly in the wake of the 1976 Examiners' report.[101] However, with the echoes of the confrontation meeting and the entire Review process still reverberating, another round of Review-related education diplomacy was launched in 1978.[102] Despite the time lapse and the learning that had ostensibly taken place during the Review, the two levels of government acquitted themselves no better the second time around. The temporary accords that had marked the earlier exercise continued.

In part, the second diplomatic engagement with the OECD sought to soothe the wounds from the earlier Review and address the critiques of Canadian educational governance. Upon receipt of the OECD's invitation to participate in a retrospective analysis of country education reviews in general, the federal government issued a *Statement by Canadian Authorities for the OECD Appraisal of Country Educational Policy Reviews*. Emanating from the Government of Canada and the CMEC,[103] the *Statement* was significant because it offered an opportunity for Canadian politicians to have a final word on OECD's Canada Review. They were able to revisit recent history and rebut some of the harshest criticisms of the Canadian education system. Moreover, several points brought forth in the earlier Confrontation Meeting were reiterated.[104] The two levels of government once more collaborated to take their views about education and education review processes to the international stage. Making fellow-OECD states aware of the Canadian position on the Country Review process became a diplomatic objective of both the Canadian government and the CMEC, despite the curious fact that little attention was paid to the *Statement* in the publications of External Affairs.[105]

Many of the comments in the new document dealt with areas in which the Examiners were critical of Canada or in which Canadian officials felt that the process was too intrusive into domestic concerns. The lines dividing the provinces and the federal government remained quite clear in the *Statement*. Where the two levels of government agreed was in their criticism of the Examiners and the Confrontation Meeting process. They suggested several remedies, including more precise guidelines, earlier appointment of Examiners, and better communications.[106] The *Statement* also criticized the way in which the international organization had handled the planning phase.[107] The Canadian team recommended that the OECD set up a series of guidelines governing future reviews and the scope of the organization's involvement in education.[108]

The federal and provincial governments made it abundantly clear in the *Statement*'s introduction that Canada's constitutional arrangements were fixed and not open to discussion in a forum such as the OECD.[109] In explaining and justifying the divergence among different levels of government and the reasons why national programs were not favoured, the *Statement* cited the predisposition of the provinces.[110] Put simply, the ten provincial governments expected the status quo to continue. The status quo demonstrated the temporary nature of collaborative arrangements in the field of education.[111] The CMEC had learned from experience to tread cautiously in federal–provincial relations so as to maximize the possible returns on any actions that they might wish to take. Thus, it was underlying concern about political costs and the ramifications of structural change that lay beneath the continuation of the united front.

Authorities from both levels of government also distinguished between their own internal reports (authored early in the process) and the external report authored by the Examiners.[112] Floating the possibility that another volume offering a national perspective on education might add a "new dimension" was an adroit way of handling questions of education on a Canada-wide basis. It also brushed under the carpet the notion that there was a history of "education as a national concern" and a history of various leaders' thoughts on structural change in education going back to Sir John A. Macdonald, Canada's first prime minster.[113] The possibility of change was an issue that both levels of government, to varying degrees, wanted to keep nebulous and undeveloped.

Ottawa and the provinces further argued that the views of grassroots educational organizations had been considered in the initial response to the Review. However, despite the post-Review participation of these groups, the emphasis in Canada had remained on these groups "submitting views" and developing "a forum for discussion" rather than sharing ideas for revolutionary institutional and structural change within government.[114]

The short-term collaboration in educational governance also led the governments to object to OECD's charge that the Canadian education system lacked any particular course or control.[115] A temporary response to the divided views that emerged in Canada following the conclusion of the 1975 Confrontation Meeting, the *Statement* ultimately reaffirmed the status quo and defended provincial jurisdiction over education.[116] Moreover, it rejected the reforms that the OECD had advocated. The net result was a commitment to an educational system driven mostly by provincial priorities and expectations.[117]

The nature of these criticisms implied a concern about future reviews. It is improbable, however, that the Canadian reproaches had any substantial impact in other world capitals. The impact at the OECD headquarters was also muted—probably because the organization itself had initiated the process leading up the *Statement*. Although the OECD would eventually make changes, they came as the result of the pressure of global economic events rather than countries' critical responses to educational reviews.[118] Moreover, the types of criticisms voiced in the *Statement* were not anything new for the OECD. The emphasis of the organization's Education Committee and Examiners was on the critical evaluation of *all* aspects of a country's education system, pointing out both the good and the bad. Critical responses were often directed to the Education Committee.[119] Critical feedback from a large number of countries, all of which complained to some degree about the process, did not overwhelm the Committee. Nor did these countries quit the OECD. Rather, despite their complaints, most countries—Canada included—would not jeopardize their standing in and connection with the OECD over these issues. Hence, although the *Statement* was part of Canadian education diplomacy, it was done *sotto voce*, without threat to other ongoing economic initiatives with the OECD.[120]

Whether Canada's OECD Country Review would have long-term effects remained to be seen. It undoubtedly had given various Canadian organizations the incentive to consider how they approached education. Over time, however, the outcomes of the Review became less important and its suggestions more muted as other items moved onto the educational agenda. In this sense, intrusive international education diplomacy as later practised by other international organizations (e.g., the IMF and the World Bank) had yet to have a substantial impact on Canada. Instead, the economic change that had begun in the early part of the 1970s continued apace, with the result that all possible reforms to education or any other part of the human-services sector had to be considered in light of increasingly tight government purse strings.[121]

Chapter Six

The CMEC, *Federalism, and "the Ottawa Way" in Education, 1970–1984*[1]

The 1970s—Finding Ways to Communicate

While the shifting international scene profoundly altered the environment for Canadian education diplomacy, at the level of implementation the 1970s and early 1980s were marked by communications challenges, accords, and compromises. This chapter returns to the examination of post-1968 education diplomacy as an evolving and convoluted part of Canadian foreign policy. In part, the challenges were institutional. The emergence of the CMEC and its evolution from a committee of the CEA to a larger separate organization with its own secretariat contributed to the contingent nature of the relationship between federal and provincial authorities in the field of education diplomacy. Accommodating the growing pains of this new agency led to circumstantial agreements on a wide range of educational issues, including education diplomacy. Self-definition remained an important matter for the CMEC during most of this period.

Moreover, the integration of the Council of Ministers into the wider context of Canadian federalism retarded the regularization of education diplomacy. Throughout the 1970s, and more recently, the emergence of numerous new agencies had a profound effect on the day-to-day operation of federalism in Canada.[2] Examples include the CMEC, of course, but also the Canadian Council of Ministers of the Environment, the Health Council of Canada, and the Provincial–Territorial Council of Ministers of Securities Regulation. High-level politicians and administrators, despite their resistance to change, benefited from the ongoing revolution in air travel and telecommunications, which made it possible to bring previously isolated provincial and federal elites closer together, thus invigorating and altering the dynamics of the federal-provincial relationship.[3]

Continued federal involvement in education at the international level, however, did not ease the conflict between the two levels of government. Federal attention became more intense as internationalization affected economic systems and governments around the world.[4] Nationalism and Canadian unity were the forces behind the federal government's interest in education diplomacy, both in matters of strategic importance and in the minutiae of policy.[5] In an era of increasingly close alignment among events, news, and response time, the federal government saw that it was in its best interest to ensure that its transitory envoys (i.e., ministers and bureaucrats) briefed its traditional envoys—the ambassadors and consuls who served in "line" positions in Canadian embassies in foreign countries.

During the CMEC's first fifteen years, the evolution of its organization and mission contributed greatly to the provisional character of its relationship with the federal government in educational diplomacy. The organization's search for a role at both the national and international levels during this period permeated the ad hoc collaboration between the provincial and federal governments. Repeated attempts to establish a place for itself in Canadian international relations were concurrent with the organization's evolving view of its capacities in this domain. The possibilities were myriad. Full control and monitoring of international education activities— effectively taking on the role of a national ministry of education—would potentially involve the responsibilities of sixty federal agencies[6] and include international educational activities in everything from CIDA to the Ministry of Labour. The small size of the CMEC secretariat, however, made such an expansive role unfeasible. Simply working with the Department of External Affairs, by contrast, was a much easier but weaker option. External Affairs had begun to deal with a much narrower portion of Canadian international education, making an alliance with it disadvantageous.[7] Another possibility called for the individual provinces to retain some control over their own education diplomacy. In this scenario, the CMEC would involve itself only in the most general of international activities. Each province would pursue its own regional international interests and, in some cases, provide its own representation at international conferences.[8] The downside was that the CMEC would never be in a position to emerge from the larger shadows cast by the provincial governments.

Contact with the federal government remained provisional in the organization's early years because the CMEC rejected the status quo relationship that the Standing Committee of Ministers of Education had experienced with Ottawa. The SCME's international presence had consisted primarily of limited communication with international education organizations and other national governments and the fielding of requests for recommendations regarding delegations to international events. There had been no discussion of the grand question of who controlled governance and policy-making related to Canada's education diplomacy. The new Council, however, wanted to do more.[9] In early 1973, in a meeting with the Secretary of State, the Council indicated its desire for a combined effort to address the issue.[10] They pressed for a joint meeting with the Secretary of State for External Affairs as well.[11] Such initial interprovincial assertiveness was simply seen as more sabre rattling in the battle between Ottawa and provincial authorities over jurisdiction in a number of areas. It did not convince the federal government that the transient character of its contact with the provinces and the CMEC should be altered; rather, it reinforced its "wait and see" attitude.[12] Ottawa was committed to being the preponderant actor in diplomacy and, as such, it watched the CMEC's efforts with considerable confidence about its role.

During the latter part of 1973, the Council established a task force on international relations, whose mandate was to investigate and report on education diplomacy.[13] Its focus also included the Department of External Affairs in an effort to obtain a more equal arrangement. Its final report, presented at the Fifth Meeting of the Advisory Committee of Deputy Ministers on December 5, 1973, underscored the Council's dissatisfaction with the existing arrangement. The report acknowledged the federal government's importance, but decried the international impotence of the Council in international education affairs. In the Council's view it was "the only national body representing those jurisdictions which [had] constitutional responsibility for education in Canada"; hence, it requested formal recognition of this competence and acceptance of the Council's leadership role in this area.[14] The Council thus proposed a coordinating framework for education diplomacy that would involve both itself and External Affairs. At this juncture it was simply a "mechanism for cooperation" but the search for a process to coordinate international activities had now started in earnest.[15]

In effect, however, the report extended the ad hoc collaboration between the two levels of government because the Department of External Affairs was not amenable to sharing control of diplomacy in education and was committed to the sole directorship of foreign policy. Ottawa thus continued to focus on the day-to-day activities within its relations with the CMEC, watching over the fledgling organization with unblinking vigilance.[16]

As time went by, both the Council of Ministers and the Advisory Committee of Deputy Ministers of Education (ACDME) continued their search for the best way to put an interprovincial imprimatur on education diplomacy and to establish longer-term provincially directed processes and structures.[17] Attempts to influence federal–provincial interaction in order to maximize CMEC's position evolved with each meeting and document. The minutes of the Council's meetings conveyed the reality of the arrangements between the provinces and the federal government on international events: time-limited agreements on exchanges, participation in conferences, and the distribution of related documentation continued unabated. The Canada–USSR Exchanges Agreement of 1973 was typical of this era. Memoranda accompanying this document noted new areas, such as the extension of exchanges into the field of vocational and technical education, in which the Council saw a role for itself.[18] While the CMEC agitated for the power to decide who did what in international activities, it also hesitated to undertake further financial obligations in a time of provincial retrenchment.[19] The curious duality of a small organization's confronting huge, well-funded federal ministries did much to undermine the credibility of those provincial politicians and officials who wished to be the modern-day envoys of Canadian education abroad.

While internal task forces and meetings reinforced the provisional character of diplomacy in education and did little to put its administration on a longer-term footing, other interprovincial approaches foundered as well. The Council also tried to use contact with federal ministers of foreign affairs to address education diplomacy.[20] More often than not, however, ministerial contacts, whether in person or via written correspondence, dealt perforce with the immediate financial needs of specific international activities and did not speak to the broader issues of the relationship.[21] More serious discussions were often diverted at the last minute because of other more pressing issues. This pattern engendered frustration on the part of the provincial ministers and contributed to the prolonged state of uncertainty. By the end of the period between 1967 and 1976, collaborative diplomacy in education was still based on limited agreements with Ottawa, one-time correspondence, and last-minute ministerial accords. Anticipation of the forthcoming OECD Review process in 1974 to 1976 led to mounting pressure for change, but basic agreement on a new process remained the central issue.

The OECD Review period marked a shifting of gears in diplomacy in education and in the public reappraisal of the question of national governance in education. It also marked continuing turbulence within the CMEC and the elusiveness of a longer-term accord in its relationship with Ottawa. In the aftermath of the Review, while Prime Minister Trudeau mused at a First Ministers Conference about the utility of a federal–provincial forum on higher education, the Council's Secretariat produced the document *Future Directions for the CMEC*.[22] This paper, which was designed to elicit discussion and opinions on the proper future direction of the Council, included input from provincial premiers and ministers and deputy ministers of education. The commentary of Harry Malmberg, New Brunswick's Deputy Minister of Education, gives some idea of the frustration these parties experienced with the organization. It also underlines the tentative nature of the CMEC's self-view and activities in 1976. Malmberg addressed his comments to Lucien Perras, the Secretary-General of the Council of Ministers at the time: "Perhaps the discussion on future directions for the Council of Ministers on May 12 in Montreal was as frustrating for you as it was for me. It became increasingly apparent to me during the meeting that there are ten systems of education, and people for each province identify, educationally, only with his own province. This point of view precludes any kind of national orientation."[23]

Other provincial responses were mixed. Some felt that the exercise was an excellent starting point for future discussions on the orientation of the organization, whereas others questioned the relevance of the agency. The Alberta government worried that a reorganized CMEC would have significant cost implications. British Columbia was concerned about the overall aim of the CMEC: should its primary orientation be political or solely administrative? The Manitoba Ministry of Education expressed disquiet about the fine line the CMEC had to walk between political intervention and respect for the jurisdiction of provincial governments.

Other provinces emphasized the need to improve the organization's image and argued that it should differentiate itself from provincial lobby groups on education and reflect the countrywide needs of students rather than the goals of the state.[24]

Notwithstanding the discussion on governance and structural reform within the CMEC, the Council's position on education diplomacy remained in line with the 1974 Future Directions for the CMEC Task Force report.[25] Competing priorities, such as funding for second-language education and higher education, were emerging but the Council's limited resources were inadequate to address all of them.[26]

In 1976, by the time of the twenty-sixth Council meeting in Halifax, the CMEC's collaboration with Ottawa concerning education diplomacy was still provisional.[27] The meeting, which took place between the nineteenth and twenty-second of September, was a rare departure from earlier meetings insofar as it included a session with the federal Secretary of State. The Council was keen to address several issues with the federal minister, not the least of which was the availability of ministers for meetings. Correspondence between the Council and federal officials underlined the frustrations of Council members. A letter between G. Posen and E. Greathed noted that the CMEC had been attempting to arrange a meeting with certain federal ministers for two years. The Council also wanted to meet with all the relevant ministers and address several issues simultaneously.[28]

Unfortunately, the Council's encounter with the Secretary of State illustrated the ongoing inability of the two levels of government to come to a longer-term accord on educational issues, most notably diplomacy. The federal aim in the meeting had been to establish closer links with the Council of Ministers that would enable ongoing consultation. Ottawa had wanted to focus on post-secondary education and had hoped that the CMEC would become the vehicle for communication between the two levels of government. The formalization of a federal–provincial structure in education[29] would augment agreements that Ottawa already had in place with non-governmental organizations such as the AUCC, the CAUT, and the CBIE. Much of the meeting between the CMEC and the Secretary of State, however, was spent entangled in definitions. The sides could not agree on what constituted a "national forum." The federal minister, John Roberts, and his predecessor, Hugh Faulkner, avoided defining the term, preferring to leave it to be sorted out by others. This approach perplexed the provincial education ministers, who had believed that the federal minister would come to the table with fresh ideas. Moreover, they felt that any talk of developing the federal–provincial relationship through existing "national forums" such as the CBIE should have led to the Council itself.[30] The ministers took particular exception to Roberts's statement that the Secretary of State was to be the only contact between the federal government and the CMEC. Dr. Harry Parrott of Ontario argued that the Secretary of State could act to insulate federal ministries and the provinces from each other rather than facilitating discussion between them.[31] British Columbia's Minister of Education, Patrick McGeer, suggested that a federal minister who dealt with all education questions was, by any other name, a federal minister of education.[32] Roberts disagreed with both of these views. The discussion dissolved when Roberts did not have a "clean text" copy of his proposals to distribute. That the matter remained unresolved after the meeting gave rise to many memoranda and much discussion within the CMEC.[33]

The provincial ministers danced around a central question in their meeting with the federal minister: What was to be the future nature of federal interaction with the CMEC? The consensus within the CMEC was that the Council should remain strictly an interprovincial organization. John Roberts and the federal government, on the other hand, wanted to establish a procedure whereby Ottawa could place items on the Council's agenda. The statement to which the ministers ultimately agreed—*Relations with the Federal Government*—did not flesh out the details of how federal–provincial cooperation would be resolved in the future, but instead expressed the provinces' continued desire to further interprovincial co-operation in education.[34] Relations with Ottawa would be carried out on a consultative and co-operative basis only with regard to specific programs.[35]

The provinces' desire to retain power over education, as expressed at the meeting with John Roberts, thus ensured that collaboration on international activities would remain provisional. The notion that the federal government could be a full partner with the provincial ministers in a "national forum" or through continued access to CMEC meetings was unacceptable to the provinces. The federal government's wish that the proposed forum would supersede some of the functions of the CMEC was equally untenable.[36]

The latter part of the 1970s saw a glimmer of light in federal–provincial relations in education. More collaboration and compromise between the two levels of government began to emerge. By early 1977, there were signs that collaboration on education diplomacy was solidifying. Following the summer 1976 meeting between the Secretary of State and the CMEC, the Council revisited the questions that had been raised at the meeting and strategized about how to address them more effectively. Correspondence continued with the Secretary of State and the parties agreed to maintain existing communication avenues for the time being. The federal ministers had also become more willing to participate in further discussions. This greater federal availability and enhanced recognition of the place of the CMEC led to further contact with the Secretary of State for External Affairs in the winter of 1977. By the summer, both the CMEC and the foreign ministry were discussing the administration of international education diplomacy on a more co-operative basis. Provincial reservations remained, however, as Don Jamieson, Secretary of State for External Affairs, noted in a letter to Ben Hanuschak, CMEC Chair and Minister of Education for Manitoba. Jamieson wished to spell out in greater detail the federal position on international education conferences in the face of the provinces' reservations.[37] In addition to attempting to allay the wariness of the CMEC and the provinces toward a federal–provincial accord on educational diplomacy, Jamieson addressed the thorny constitutional issue: "I believe it essential that any procedure we follow in this matter take into full account the constitutional responsibilities of the provincial governments in the field of education, the expertise of the provincial authorities and the responsibility of the Secretary of State for External Affairs for the conduct of Canada's external relations."[38] Jamieson's proposal for expanded collaboration placed much of the responsibility for the composition of delegations to international conferences in the hands of the CMEC, provided that there were ongoing consultations with the foreign ministry. He included the caveat that the provinces would have to consider several national factors among their criteria for the establishment of delegations. Delegations should reflect the diverse linguistic makeup of the country, and naturally, the two major language groups. They should also take into account both the need for efficiency and the need for economy.[39] The CMEC was favourably inclined towards Jamieson's perspective and shortly thereafter, in late September 1977, the first set of *Procedures for Canada's Participation in International Education Conferences, 1977,* was endorsed by the federal government and the provinces.[40]

As the first federal–provincial "understanding" on education diplomacy, the *Procedures* represented a substantial step towards longer-term agreement in that area.[41] Nevertheless, disagreements and provisional diplomacy continued throughout the remainder of the decade and into the early 1980s. One of the problems was the CMEC's view that it was out of the foreign policy "loop." Many of the international communications received by the federal government regarding educational diplomacy remained in Ottawa. The CMEC had successfully petitioned the Department of External Affairs to obtain an annual list of all conferences to which Ottawa received invitations but the mechanics of that process were too slow to be effective. There were concerns about the selection of delegates and the activities of those delegates once they were in the country where the international conference on education was being held.[42] On one occasion in 1980, the Department of External Affairs unilaterally struck a provincial minister off the list of delegates to the UNESCO General Conference in Sofia, Bulgaria.[43] In a summit meeting held in April 1981, the Secretary of State for External Affairs, Mark MacGuigan, and provincial ministers of education agreed to set up a temporary "working group" on education diplomacy.[44] Over a year later, in September 1982, a further understanding reached between the CMEC and External Affairs was laid out in *Participation of Delegates in International Conferences Related to Education*.[45] Although the meetings of the working group and this understanding represented important steps toward the longer-term resolution of federal–provincial co-operation in education diplomacy, problems with the mechanics of the collaborative process led to further disagreement and the need for more last-minute deals. The establishment of agreed-upon terms of reference and a more permanent consultative federal–provincial body on which to build education diplomacy would have to wait.[46] By the end of the Trudeau era in 1984, such a structure had yet to emerge, although the joint working group continued to attempt to develop one.[47] Even if a little less provisional, diplomacy in education was still marked by limited collaboration between the CMEC and the federal government.[48]

Canadian Federalism, 1970–1984

Although the changing nature of the CMEC provides a partial explanation for the incidental character of education diplomacy, another key to understanding its provisional nature can be found by studying the features of federalism in this era from a more theoretical perspective. Canadian federalism in the 1970s and early 1980s was in a state of flux: the country was on its way to becoming one of the most decentralized "quasi-feudal confederations" in the world.[49] As the roles of government changed, issues that had previously been entirely administrative in nature began to be seen as falling within the purview of politicians. Moreover, formerly nonexistent provincial powers not only sprouted up, but their reach became longer and more attuned.[50] Desiring to expand their horizons, the provinces sought a greater profile domestically, and in some cases, further involvement on the international stage. Furthermore, the appearance of new interprovincial agencies such as the CMEC and the changing nature of *executive federalism*[51] complicated what was already a crowded institutional environment.

The contingent character of international education persisted as traditional notions of what constituted "politics" and what was meant by "administration" broke down during the 1970s. The classical federalism of the past century, in which the two levels of government carried out their constitutional responsibilities in idealized isolation from each other, had passed. Whitaker characterizes the earlier Canadian federal system as an arrangement that emerged between elites.[52] Under this system, government elites did not intervene in a number of different fields, and much of the day-to-day work was left to the permanent administration. In the 1970s, however, this practice changed radically. The number of areas in which governments—and, more to the point, politicians—were active dramatically increased. Every step a government took had political costs and benefits. The stable politics of good government were giving way to a slicker calculus of polls and the need to develop a winning record for the next election.[53] Governments and political parties were also forced to re-structure their political coalitions as traditional allegiances broke down. The federal government began to seek out under-represented groups and target their interests. In the context of the Council of Ministers and international education, the curriculum represented one example of this type of change. Because of evolving OECD standards, curriculum questions had international implications that affected Canadian politics, particularly at the provincial level.[54] The overall thrust of the curriculum, therefore, was no longer just the responsibility of administrators, teachers, and curriculum specialists: political careers were increasingly on the line.

The new political reality, in addition to discouraging more established processes, also reinforced the federal–provincial divide in education. In times of necessity, banding together across provincial political ideologies to establish a common front was seen as a more effective way of dealing with federal–provincial political issues, such as diplomacy in education.[55] As Stevenson notes, conflicts between the federal and provincial governments were becoming extremely serious and could no longer be delegated to junior officials. Conflicts were emerging concurrently on a whole host of fronts—health, education, social welfare, and regional development amongst others. As the conflicts widened, they became more political in nature.[56] International education was also increasingly the subject of scrutiny by the media and the public.[57] For the provinces, nothing could be left to chance and the federal government. Ottawa was regarded with calculated mistrust. Moreover, some provinces had a tendency to retreat to their own individually oriented positions, particularly when other provinces did not agree with them on a particular issue. The politicization of educational diplomacy continued as the country's economic uncertainty dragged on.[58]

Concomitant with such politicization, the ascent of provincial power during the 1970s helped defer any permanent resolution of the struggle for power in international education. The re-regulation of federal–provincial relations proceeded through newly established and assertive provincial ministries of intergovernmental affairs. Claude Morin set the pace in the 1960s and early 1970s in Quebec as a deputy minister, contributing many of the policies that underpinned the Quiet Revolution and Quebec's international strategy.[59] Most of the other provinces followed suit and established intergovernmental affairs offices in the 1970s. Their appearance in Alberta (1972), Newfoundland (1975), Ontario (1978), British Columbia (1979), and Saskatchewan (1979) heralded a new wave of provincial influence in Canadian politics.[60] Many of the officials from intergovernmental affairs offices served as resources when interactions between governments were not going well. The presence of provincial intergovernmental affairs officials at a CMEC meeting in the mid-1970s was notable, but in the end these officials did not possess any magic cure for the ongoing difficulties in the organization's interactions with Ottawa.[61]

Moreover, the intergovernmental machinery was slow, and it operated against a backdrop of provincial ambitions for greater control over both national and international activities. The process would bog down as more political problems and obstacles arose. Diplomacy in education was one such area. The more specific the area the more likely there was to be agreement on the issues between the federal and provincial governments. Such agreement was apt to be based on the norms and understandings of professions such as social workers, engineers, foresters, and so on.[62] Once political allegiance and federal–provincial jockeying entered into the equation, however, the likelihood of agreement diminished.

The Failure to Establish Common Ground

Unfortunately, during this period there was little common ground in federal–provincial interactions regarding education diplomacy.[63] Participants from both levels of government saw themselves as diplomats and statesmen. Provincial ministers and senior officials had sophisticated knowledge of the education system, whereas the federal minister tended to focus exclusively on how international questions should be treated in the larger Canadian context.[64] The overall implication of this lack of common ground was a patchwork approach to educational issues at the international level and incommensurable views on international relations.

The nationalist and sovereignist aspirations of Quebec were also influential in impeding movement away from ad hoc collaboration in education diplomacy during this period. Although the early part of the decade saw the Liberal and federalist Bourassa government working within the Canadian system,[65] the rise of the Parti Québécois in 1976 spelled the end to that state of affairs. The spillover of Quebec nationalist fervour into the discussions of the CMEC was significant. Quebec ministers were against any federal intrusions into the field of education and, certainly, any efforts to set up "national" education-related forums. This perspective was succinctly voiced in Quebec Minister of Education Jacques Yvan-Morin's welcoming speech to the Council of Ministers' meeting in Quebec City in January 1977. Morin quietly, but firmly, advanced the sovereigntists' approach to educational issues. The Parti Québécois government embraced the CMEC as a tool to be used in enhancing its position in preparation for a push toward separation. The Quebec minister contended that the provinces should continue to press for autonomy over education and that they should also work toward increased interprovincial solidarity. He warned against allowing federal participation in decision making on educational issues. Particularly unpalatable to separatists was the notion that the interprovincial Council of Ministers of Education should be reformed to allow Ottawa to have a permanent seat.[66] Morin's presentation did not provoke any public opposition from his assembled peers, nor did it hurt his position on the Council. In the latter part of 1977, he became vice-chair and subsequently chair of the organization.

The contrast between Morin's separatist position and that of the anglophone ministers, who were more committed to Canada, illustrates the breadth of viewpoints present within the Council of Ministers. Several of the anglophone ministers, although uncomfortable with proposed arrangements for the Council that included Ottawa, had a greater acceptance of the notion of some sort of federal participation. The Ontario Ministry of Intergovernmental Affairs agreed with the CMEC's aim of increasing contacts with the federal government inasmuch as it would ensure Ontario delegations to various forums would be aware of each other's activities. This knowledge would simultaneously ensure consistency of message from the provincial perspective and monitor federal activity.[67]

Ottawa, however, remained anathema to the Quebec separatists. The new government in Quebec City wanted nothing to do with the federal capital. Quebec's alienation from Ottawa served only to guarantee that the CMEC, which itself was already provincially focused, would be even less likely to entertain initiatives that would deepen its relationship and cooperation with the federal government.[68]

The provisional character of education diplomacy was ultimately prolonged by the rise of the practice of executive federalism. Agencies dedicated to interprovincial and intergovernmental relationships multiplied exponentially during the 1970s. Some of these agencies were strictly administrative, whereas others comprised deputy ministers. Still others included politicians and administrators from both levels of government. Some were solely interprovincial in character. The very public and often combative arena of federal-provincial first ministers' conferences became a highly visible and symbolic emblem of executive federalism. The panoply of post-Second World War elite institutions served to degrade the 1867 Constitution and promote a new de facto distribution of powers in favour of both levels of government. Newly aggressive provincial administrations asserted special and exclusive interests. Moreover, interprovincial organizations contended that their territorial specificity gave them, rather than the more distant federal government, greater prerogative to represent the views of the citizenry. Lastly, it was fruitless to expect clarification from the top about education-related international activities because first ministers' conferences gave only broad directives. The annual assemblies of the Premiers and the Prime Minister had their more substantive political capital invested in addressing intractable conflicts, such as the repatriation of the Constitution from England and transfer payments.[69]

Executive federalism encouraged the advancement of politically charged special interests (e.g., energy, health care funding, etc.) much to the consternation of those seeking collaboration and cooperation on other national issues such as education. Rather than working together and acknowledging the limitations of the Constitution, both levels of government wanted to claim the matter as their own. Federal governments were very comfortable with the status quo ante, that is to say, directing foreign policy in the field with minor input from the provinces. The provinces, by contrast, wanted to take control of the matter without the financial obligations connected to it. Illustrative of the chasm between constitutional powers and provincial/federal self-interests were the governmental positions in 1977. At the January CMEC meeting, the Ministers of Education summarized the provincial viewpoint as follows: "the current situation is still unacceptable and substantial changes are needed in the existing practices of the Department of External Affairs to reflect the jurisdiction of the provinces in education."[70]

The federal government's defence of its position came in May 1977 at a meeting between officials from the CMEC and the Department of External Affairs. The issue was the perennial matter of provincial control over the composition of delegations to international education conferences. External Affairs reiterated its responsibility to dialogue directly with all Canadian citizens and groups. Despite this initially cold reception, the federal officials agreed to look further at the CMEC's proposal,[71] which they ultimately rejected for infringing on federal jurisdiction over the selection and appointment of international delegations. For the most part, the provincial and federal leaders and their deputies attempted to mediate this issue directly. In the hothouse of Canadian constitutional politics, this direct involvement had special effects on the process. The rules of the Canadian political system meant that the leaders of the two levels of government were accustomed to focusing on the power of their respective governments, rather than on more practical details or processes, such as program objectives or intergovernmental cooperation. The end result saw the work of program specialists denigrated or ignored. As Stevenson notes, "the growing distaste of both levels of government for shared-cost programs was in part a reflection of this redistribution of power and influence within their respective bureaucracies."[72] Issues of low-level importance thus became distracting grist for debates between the leaders at the highest level of the political system, drawing attention away from the more important issue of the need for effective federal–provincial co-operation in the face of a very uncertain world.

Provincial leaders in the late 1970s, although generally adherents of executive decision making, continued to identify with their own regions (the West, the Prairies, the Maritimes, Quebec, and Central Canada), stating repeatedly that their claim to control over education diplomacy was much more justified than Ottawa's. For the provinces, each of which had its own region of the globe in mind, the matter could be seen as being interprovincial in orientation. For example, it seemed to politicians in Victoria that they had a much greater connection to education-related events happening around the Pacific than did diplomats based in Ottawa.[73] Similarly, the Council of Maritime Premiers (CMP) focused on their own regional and "Northwest-Atlantic" goals.[74] Agencies such as the Maritime Provinces Higher Education Commission, an offshoot of the CMP, were much more likely to have coastal interests in mind rather than the concerns of the other Canadian provinces further to the west.[75] This regional orientation had its biggest advocate in Quebec, but the anglophone provinces also persisted in it, albeit in a quieter fashion. The combination of the CMEC's position and provincial regionalism only bedeviled even more the efforts to resolve the jurisdictional conflict over education-related international activities as time went on.

Frequent first ministers' conferences were a relatively new phenomenon in the 1970s, and direction on diplomacy in education was not something that either federal or provincial educationalists expected from them. The Prime Minister and the Premiers were already overburdened with serious issues that included the price of oil, constitutional affairs, and transfer payments. Although these conferences addressed educational issues from time to time, diplomacy in education did not have the economic traction to make it onto the agenda and end its provisional character. Diplomacy and foreign affairs in general were questions for the Department of External Affairs, not matters for federal–provincial first ministers' conferences. Diplomacy in education can be contrasted with minority-language education, which was one area of education that did surface prominently at first ministers' conferences. Unlike minority-language education, educational diplomacy did not have a visible political component; it was unheard of in the school system. Minority-language education, however, was a hot-button political issue, arising in a period when the federal government was focused on the issue of national unity in the wake of the Parti Québécois victory in Quebec.

The changing nature of executive federalism during the 1970s had a profound effect on education diplomacy. As Smiley points out, this form of political and administrative organization had some long-term consequences, including increased conflict. Jurisdictions continually sought more autonomy beyond the normal respect and deference between the two levels of government.[76] In this environment, the number of executive federal agencies burgeoned. The consequent political tensions resulted in more irritations, not only within party politics but also on the axis of federal–provincial relations. It is not surprising that the resolution of the question of educational diplomacy did not come from any of these new leadership groupings; nor did 1970s federalism provide for a longer-term solution.

Ottawa remained interested in the matter of diplomacy in education during the late 1970s and into the early 1980s. Broad changes at the global level continued to affect national education systems. The issue of Quebec nationalism and Canadian unity remained very much alive as well. The federal government, particularly the Department of External Affairs, wanted to keep its options open in an era when the prestige of the foreign ministry was continuing to decline.

Throughout the 1970s, the federal government was wary of repeating the events of the late 1960s that shook up Canada's position in education diplomacy. Institutional memories of Mitchell Sharp's pamphlet and the divisive interference exercised by France on the issue in the 1960s remained vivid in the minds of politicians in Ottawa. Given the antecedents, the automatic response to the provincial clamour for more involvement in educational diplomacy was to exercise prudence and caution. Quebec's demands, in particular, set off alarm bells at all levels. It was felt that without a federal presence, the separatist government would continue to pursue its nationalist agenda on the world stage through any possible means. Education was seen as one avenue in that crusade.

These historical memories were reinforced by the exigencies of the moment when the Parti Québécois came to power in 1976. The development of harmony between the provinces and the federal government was difficult in the late 1970s and early 1980s. The federal government had become increasingly preoccupied with a variety of important international issues and their relationship to the national well-being as illustrated in the case of health care. The speed at which a deadly disease such as Ebola could possibly cross international borders and threaten Canadians focused the attention of many, bringing the nexus between international events and domestic interests into sharper relief. A federal official explained the government's posture toward international affairs and DFAIT's expanding reach: "I want to describe why we think we are not a domestic department and conversely, why DFAIT [Department of Foreign Affairs and International Trade] is not merely the foreign ministry. All international issues must relate either to the government's agenda or to the welfare of Canadians. The biggest challenge for the foreign ministry is articulating how it relates to the domestic agenda."[77]

Temporary collaboration on international education also continued as Ottawa began to capitalize on the business opportunities accruing from schooling in the early 1980s. As described in Chapter Four, the selling of education and educational resources such as books, school supplies, and expertise, had become very big business.[78] Education was becoming linked to trade and investment as a commodity that Canadians could buy and sell. The economic chill of 1979 focused attention on these new objectives—especially, on how to package education for export. As the economic malaise continued, the evolution of the Department of External Affairs from a foreign ministry into a clearinghouse for Canadian international trade accelerated. From the early 1970s to 1981, Annual Reports of the Department consistently took the position that, in matters of education diplomacy, the foreign office was exemplary of cooperation in federal–provincial and non-governmental relations. In particular, the reports noted cooperation with the CMEC on the organization of meetings and participation in activities of the OECD, UNESCO, and the Commonwealth.[79]

In 1982, however, a change occurred. Gone were statements about co-operation with other departments and the CMEC. Taking their place were sweeping declarations linking foreign affairs, education, and significantly, trade.[80] This was the leading edge of the increasing commercialization of Canadian "culture" (including education). These international trade activities continued throughout the 1980s.[81] Bypassing federal–provincial conflicts to encourage the selling of a product through "lead" business institutions was the wave of the future.[82]

Over and above emergent "edubusiness" initiatives, Ottawa's need to be involved in education diplomacy for reasons of national unity further thwarted any permanent arrangements on jurisdiction in this area. Federal participation in international education and cultural matters acknowledged provincial prerogatives in the field but still gave a clear message that the over-arching foreign policy superstructure was under Ottawa's control and that any change in that hierarchy would not be readily, or quickly, achieved. In the early 1970s, the establishment of *L'Agence de Coopération Culturelle et Technique* and the ongoing conferences of Francophone ministers of education had prompted Ottawa to elaborate a carefully considered strategy to address these developments.[83] The federal move, in turn, spurred separatist Quebec education ministers to pressure the Council of Ministers to assert that the federal government was responsible for foreign affairs within its own areas of jurisdiction and that the provinces reserved the right to speak either individually or collectively on international education issues.[84] In the mid-1970s, the federal government worked to counter this provincial mindset through a multi-part strategy. The carrots of closer collaboration and memoranda of understandings between the two levels of government were two approaches. Although the more staid and non-separatist anglophone provincial governments rejected pure provincial individualism in favour of simpler, more functional regional and national alliances, they, too, focused on building their fiefdoms.[85] Ottawa, for its part, had to be perceived as meeting citizens' needs, while consolidating its own hold over the federation. Patchwork confederation was not an option.

Echoes and New Ideas:
The Clark Interlude and the Trudeau Restoration

A noticeable counterpoint to the Trudeau government's wish to constrain nationalism and consequently stop the use of diplomacy in education as a tool for Quebec's nationalistic purposes can be found in the brief period of Joe Clark's Progressive Conservative government from May 1979 to January 1980. Clark's approach to this issue was to conceive of Canada as a "community of communities," a reworked version of the 1880s provincial "compact" view of Confederation.[86] The first heralds of Clark's alternate view of Confederation in the world of education diplomacy were Secretary of State David MacDonald and Secretary of State for External Affairs Flora MacDonald.[87]

In a speech to the Council of Ministers' autumn 1979 meeting, David MacDonald gave clear signals of Ottawa's changed position and readiness to accede to provincial needs in education.[88] Flora MacDonald also indicated a willingness to re-examine the issue of diplomacy in education in her correspondence with the Council, thus opening the door to further provincial control over the issue. In particular, she was willing to grant the provincial education leaders much more leeway in the planning and execution of, and follow-up on, international conferences. Had Clark's Progressive Conservative government remained in power for a longer term, Canadian education diplomacy may have travelled a very different path. In the end, Flora MacDonald's legacy was to begin the establishment of a federal–provincial consultative coordinating body that would eventually oversee education diplomacy.

When the Liberals returned to power in 1980, federal willingness to accommodate the provinces in education diplomacy waned. Other events took the spotlight throughout the last phase of Pierre Trudeau's term as prime minister, which lasted until 1984. Squelching Quebec's drive for sovereignty and limiting accession to provincial demands were central to Ottawa's strategy during this period.

The provisional character of diplomacy in education continued as well; Ottawa wished to remain active in this area for practical reasons. In an era in which the prestige of foreign ministries declined because of the spread of telecommunications and more rapid transportation worldwide, among other things, the Department of External Affairs needed to keep its options open. Many new competitors, including other government ministries and private corporations, were looking for a piece of the foreign affairs action. The leadership in Ottawa felt a strong need to safeguard the prerogatives of the federal government in the face of growing provincial demands across a broad range of foreign policy issues.[89] External Affairs consequently reorganized its structure to be more effective. Combined with the pressure from the provinces to be more involved in international diplomacy, this restructuring—discussed below—retarded any long-term agreement on a permanent federal–provincial diplomatic structure. Instead, an all-too-familiar regime of temporary understandings and mechanisms arose, none of which was equipped to deal quickly with the negotiation of educational treaties among sovereign states, Canada, and provincial authorities.

Thus, the reiteration of the federal prerogative took place—not exclusively, but notably—in the area of educational treaty formation. From 1973 onwards, the CMEC had made its expectations clear concerning its desired role in the negotiation and signing of international educational agreements. The Council expected to have a presence on any negotiating team to ensure input from the provincial governments.[90] Ottawa responded to these expectations with cautious approbation: it continued to envision a consultative role for provincial authorities, with the national government's having the final say. Ultimately, federal authorities led the process and controlled the outcome. The provinces, however, could limit the impact of an international treaty in terms of the implementation of that document, because Ottawa did not have the authority to impose the implementation of a treaty on the provinces.[91] One example of the vigorous advancement of the federal prerogative in a matter of education diplomacy was the negotiation of the 1979 UNESCO *Convention on the Recognition of Studies, Diplomas and Degrees concerning Higher Education in the States belonging to the Europe Region.*[92] In this instance, the federal government stood by Mitchell Sharp's 1969 assertion that the federal government had the power to negotiate agreements and sign education treaties as held by the Judicial Committee of the Privy Council in the *Labour Conventions Reference* in 1937.[93] Ottawa was not obliged to grant provincial representation during the negotiation of educational treaties; rather, such cooperation was offered as a courtesy and in the service of practicality.

Constitutional provisions, legal precedents, and federal documents aside, the CMEC had aggressively insisted on a lead role in treaty negotiations as the 1970s progressed. The federal need to continue to defend its leadership prerogative became evident when the provinces asked that Ottawa abstain from voting on the UNESCO Convention on degrees and diplomas because they needed more time to digest its substance. The Council stressed the need for agreement between the two levels of government prior to ratification of the Convention. Abstaining from voting on the Convention, in the provinces' view, would give them the opportunity to develop a mechanism to implement it.[94] The mixed federal–provincial Canadian delegation complied and Canada abstained. Because the vote was an intermediate action, the federal government could still adhere to the Convention by signing it at a later date, which it did in 1989.[95] Ottawa could also have ratified it through the Canadian Ambassador to UNESCO.[96] Even though the provinces could delay Ottawa's signing of a treaty, they could not, however, prevent it.[97]

Following the provincially directed abstention from the UNESCO treaty vote, the CMEC and the mixed Canadian delegation threw up further obstacles to federal control. A committee was suggested to consider the question of diplomas and related federal–provincial concerns. Although partial to the recommendations of the delegation, the CMEC, under the leadership of its chair, Patrick McGeer of British Columbia, further complicated the situation by issuing its own set of demands. Notable among them was a meeting to draft an agreement between the Council and the federal government on the question of the responsibility of the provinces to consult with post-secondary institutions and professional associations.[98] McGeer also recommended the establishment of an ad hoc mechanism to deal specifically with the application of the UNESCO

Convention to Canada. The road to Canada's eventual adherence to the Convention was long and difficult as the treaty process was continually subjected to the expectations and fears of the provinces.[99] In this particular case, Ottawa took the intractable position that although the provinces could discuss a treaty and even take the lead in negotiating it, the federal government had the final word.

As mentioned, the reorganization of the Department of External Affairs during the late 1970s and early 1980s also stymied the longer-term resolution of problems of jurisdiction over educational diplomacy. Wishing to avoid surprises related to its educational diplomatic missions, the federal government had to find a way to incorporate educational diplomacy more fully into its overall diplomatic strategy. There was an ongoing concern that Canadian educational envoys could arrive in a country or at an organization such as the OECD with no prior briefing of onsite embassy staff, attend their conference, and then depart, without any post-conference debriefing. The educationalists' knowledge of foreign affairs and diplomacy was minimal and foreign ministry officials did not want problems in the host country because of beginners' blunders.[100] In an effort to avoid such situations, the External Affairs was reorganized so as to enhance its centralizing and economic character and impact.[101] In the fractious climate of federal–provincial relations, the move to centralize control over the leadership of foreign policy development ran directly counter to the decentralist ambitions of the provinces. In Allan Gotlieb's view, as Undersecretary of State at the time, a modern central agency was one that led on key issues of national interest; as such, it would produce coherent policies that could be used to guide other agencies.[102] He saw External Affairs as the central foreign policy management agency. In this role, the organization had to lead, but it also had to serve Canadians.[103] Gotlieb pushed to strengthen the role of External Affairs at all levels in Ottawa; enforcing a firm line regarding the extent of provincial activities was part of that effort.

The merger of External Affairs with the Department of Industry, Trade, and Commerce in 1982 marked the start of a much more aggressive trade policy for the Canadian government. For the first time, External Affairs had both foreign affairs expertise and economic expertise under one roof. External Affairs continued to direct policy in educational diplomacy, but because of the Department's new focus on trade, economic expectations began to take priority in educational matters.[104]

Conclusion

The future of education diplomacy in Canada remains a clouded image and an undiscovered country.[1] Why has no coherent approach to education diplomacy emerged? In many ways it is now clear that the evolution of education diplomacy in Canada reflects that of the nation itself. Starting with those in the colonies and, later, the provinces, Canada's sub-national governments have been out in front in this area and elsewhere for a long time. Quebec is, by far and away, ahead of the pack, but, as evidenced by the efforts of Ryerson and others, the practice of education diplomacy has a considerably long history. The era of *la doctrine Gérin-Lajoie* was truly a watershed, both provincially and federally. For the provinces and the CMEC, the doctrine provided a guide to what was possible. What is more, it forced the federal government to address the issue of education diplomacy squarely. With the articulation of a federal policy and direction for diplomacy in educational matters, the provincial governments remained vigilant about federal encroachment on their jurisdictional turf, just as Ottawa remained wary of provincial ambitions in the federal sphere of international relations.

At the same time, the playing field was changing. Education diplomacy was becoming increasingly intertwined with public diplomacy, and the world—beset by problems that were international in their scope and effect—was growing smaller. Public perceptions and optics were now the new norms. Provincial governments were highly attuned to this new reality as evidenced by the presentation of the OECD Report in 1976 and the provinces' response to it. Interest in and planning of a CMEC-sponsored conference on the OECD Report rose and ultimately fell with public opinion. By the end of the final era covered in this book, the education-diplomacy governmental dance partners remained locked in a struggle over who was to lead. In 2016, the dancefloor remains contested ground.

With the turning of the page on the Trudeau era in 1984, some progress had been made toward resolving the jurisdictional difficulties associated with education diplomacy, but a lack of coherence in this field continued into the latter part of the 1980s. Rudner points to the implications of this ongoing transience in the 1990s in his discussion of Canada's involvement with the Asia-Pacific Economic Cooperation forum (APEC) and education diplomacy. He argues that Canada's involvement in APEC was "greatly" complicated by the fact that education was a matter of provincial jurisdiction. He also concludes that the ambivalence in Canada's education diplomacy reflected the underlying turbulence in Canadian education policy.[2]

In the new millennium, several scholars have called for a new structure for Canada's constitutional and practical arrangements regarding education: Ungerleider; Robertson; and Hughes, Print, and Sears all argue for an explicit federal presence in education.[3] It is clear, however, that the present continues to live up to its less-than-distinguished past. *Plus ça change, plus c'est la même chose.* The familiar French expression encapsulates perfectly the dynamic that influences this issue: continuity and change.

The 2005–2006 Canadian federal election campaign saw the return to national prominence of Quebec's quest for international autonomy in education through *la doctrine Gérin-Lajoie*. The related issue during the campaign was Canada's and Quebec's co-creation of the UNESCO *Convention on Cultural Diversity* and Conservative leader Stephen Harper's comment that, under a Conservative government, Quebec would be allowed to participate in international activities according to the terms of the now historic doctrine.[4] Indeed, asymmetrical federalism once again became a topic for discussion in the early 2000s.[5] Simply stated, Gérin-Lajoie's legacy is that Quebec's diplomatic ambit for action remains wider than that of most of the other provinces. Quebec's interpretation of federalism, provincial powers, and diplomacy set an enduring precedent unequalled by any other province. The development and pronouncement of *la doctrine Gérin-Lajoie* in Quebec provided a catalyst for further education diplomacy and a collective provincial push for greater autonomy from Ottawa. It helped provincial governments and their agents understand the limits of provincial action in international relations. This was apparent in the creation of the CMEC and the self-imposed boundaries provincial ministers of education placed on their international action. Lastly, Quebec's application of this doctrine in Gabon sparked the CMEC's search for a provincial niche in international activities.

Charles Ungerleider has written about the interconnection between what goes on in the classroom and educational governance in Canada.[6] Many of the events described in this book took place in the rarified atmosphere of federal-provincial relations. At first blush, they may not have seemed of much importance "on the ground"; it is highly likely they did not matter much, if at all, to teachers who were pre-occupied with the day-to-day struggles of teaching, learning, and classroom management. Increasingly, however, Canadian classrooms were, and still are, affected by Canada's international choices. Ungerleider's axiom has become more apropos as time has passed and as education diplomacy is more than ever tying together the international and the local.

The unique constitutional arrangements in Canada that bind education and diplomacy together continue. The activities of the late 1970s described in this book, the Memorandums of Understanding of the late 1970s and early 1980s between Ottawa and CMEC, and the creation in 1986 of the Federal–Provincial Consultative Committee on Education-Related International Activities (FPCCERIA) gave momentum to a more collaborative approach to education diplomacy. The organization brings together officials from both sides to address issues of education diplomacy and Canada's international education policy generally. Although FPCCERIA is charged with addressing issues associated with education diplomacy—recent topics for discussion have included the lives of foreign students in Canada, marketing of Canadian education abroad, recruitment of foreign students overseas, and visas[7]—the record is limited as to whether its actions have actually been successful. [8]

The formulation and implementation of education diplomacy projects have been disputed repeatedly because of the conflict between federal and provincial authorities, in which each party has claimed constitutional jurisdiction over the diplomatic area in question. Moreover, many of the CMEC's corporate reports in the mid-1990s were not forthcoming about the inner workings of committees such as the FPCCERIA.[9] For example, in stark contrast to the reports of the 1980s, which listed Committee members, the Council's 1995 report merely noted the existence of FPCCERIA without providing further details.[10] The report's biannual status further limited the understanding and evaluation of the committee's role. The CMEC's current website does nothing to clarify the situation; the FPCCERIA is mentioned only in a single document containing a very brief description of its organization and activities.[11]

A recognition in the late 1990s that more had to be done in the area of collaboration on education diplomacy generated nothing more than reports.[12] In his 2001 study of Canadian international education, Farquhar saw FPCCERIA playing only an "information transfer" role during this era.[13] However, more recent developments provided some reason, however faint perhaps, to believe that some progress has been made in federal–provincial cooperation on international education issues—for example, the 2008 collaboration between the federal government and CMEC on the educational branding of Canada at the international level.[14] As Trilokekar and Shubert note, however, this cooperative venture did not pass without incident; the federal government proposed a brand, the provinces objected, and now branding is subject to FPCCERIA approval.[15] Although establishing a brand for educational marketing is admittedly a relatively easy step, there is nonetheless room for optimism that this instance of cooperation marked the beginning of further collaboration at the national and international levels. In fact, FPCCERIA is now moving toward collaboration in branding.[16] Although the CMEC is openly interfacing with Ottawa in education diplomacy as evidenced, for example, by its role in international testing and PISA (OECD's Programme for International Student Assessment), its less-than-ardent desire for permanent connections to the federal government in that regard makes future coherence less certain.[17]

The imperfect collaboration and coherence resulting from the existing constitutional arrangements are likely to persist for some time; amendment of the Canadian Constitution has proven to be not for the faint of heart, and at the beginning of the twenty-first century—whether because of Quebec succession referenda battle fatigue or some other reason—there is little taste among the public and most politicians for discussing constitutional reform. In an era of economic instability, such as the one Canada continues to experience in 2016, advocating constitutional amendment represents the kiss of death for politicians. Were the federal government to wade further into the field of education, however, there could be benefits for both sides.[18] Ungerleider provides some direction in his catalogue of possible educational responsibilities for Ottawa: "sponsoring research...developing policy papers to stimulate debate...national standards and practices.[19]" However, the provinces, for their part, continue to defend what they perceive to be theirs: jurisdiction over educational matters within their boundaries and the ability to extend that jurisdiction into the international realm and beyond. Questions remain with regard to federal–provincial agreements and the "understandings" that currently govern education diplomacy. These limited agreements could be torn up very quickly, however, should either the federal government or the CMEC decide that they were no longer relevant. None of the accords has any constitutional force. The achievement of a permanent settlement on jurisdiction, or indeed historic agreements, in education diplomacy remains problematic under the best of circumstances.

Examining other countries' arrangements could be another avenue toward reform. Both the US and New Zealand offer different approaches to systems of education governance. However, the path to reform has not been easy in the United States.[20] Despite obstacles along the way, in New Zealand there is a more positive and unified zeal around issues of education diplomacy. Indeed, the New Zealand government's strategy for education diplomacy, entitled *The International Education Agenda: A Strategy for 2007–2012*, realizes the vision and ideas brought forth by a much earlier generation.[21] In the run up to the enactment of the *International Education Act* (PL 89-598) on October 29, 1966, Charles Frankel and US President Lyndon Johnson spoke of the need for "education officers or education attachés" at US embassies around the world.[22] In 2007, the reality for New Zealand was "education counselors" at a variety of embassies worldwide and a coherent approach to international education at home.[23]

Problems in educational diplomacy could also be addressed through general reform of the CMEC, but the possibilities for structural modification of the Council remain doubtful. Recall the vehement provincial resistance to any dealings with Ottawa, particularly on the part of Quebec.[24] In past organizational reviews, proposals for a federal seat on the Council were consistently rejected. Additionally, the testiness and tense atmosphere in meetings with federal ministers have been part of the organization's institutional furniture for a long time. Resistance to full federal participation and status within the CMEC—a hallmark of the eras addressed in this book—remains substantially true today. Any impetus for change must come from the ministers of education themselves, but because they are less educationalists and more politicians of short tenure who are preoccupied with their own regions, success for such an avenue of reform seems unlikely. Since the release of *Future Directions for the* CMEC in 1976, there has been talk of change, but the CMEC still remains off the radar of most members of the public and most politicians, further reducing the prospects of deep structural change.[25] Change for the CMEC and education diplomacy, among many other issues, must also address First Nations, Metis and Inuit education, as my Nipissing colleague Ron Phillips has recently argued in 2014. [26]

Recently, multinational corporate enterprises have embraced the human capital accounting model and see "gray matter" as an exploitable resource—an ideological shift that has redefined the goals of international education.[27] Governments, too, have been drawn into the process, and education diplomacy has been one of the conduits for transmitting this model worldwide.[28] The Conservative government of Prime Minister David Cameron in the United Kingdom and President Barack Obama's Democrats in the United States have embraced this approach and the rest of the countries of the Western world will likely follow suit if they have not already done so.[29] The global transformative forces that began in the 1960s and continued into the mid-1980s—the period comprising the focus of this book—have endured. Unfortunately, many of the problems of access, gender equity, and international disparities associated with education, training, and jurisdiction have also endured. Moreover, other problems have been added to the mix, notably environmental issues and global warming. In order to exercise their democratic responsibilities, citizens need to re-examine and recast the goals of the humanities in higher education.[30] This is an incredibly daunting enterprise given the powerful grip the human-capital-driven perspective has on education systems around the globe.

The explosive growth of information technology has been yet another transition on the road to prosperity and globalization. The federal government, the provinces, and the CMEC have all set out on this supposedly gilded thoroughfare, mounting websites on the Internet and lauding the edubusiness initiatives that are being undertaken.[31] Embracing the iPad® and reaching out to the Facebook® and Twitter® generation are the latest iterations. And, even as this technological overhaul is taking place, Ottawa and the CMEC insist that Canada's accountability and testing programs must ensure that Canadian education standards rise in competition with its fellow OECD member-states. Education diplomacy has gone digital.

Despite the optimism of the new digital age, unless the system of educational governance and diplomacy that arose in the era from 1960 to 1984 is further scrutinized and reformed, nothing will change. Much time and effort will be wasted on trying to steer clear of federal–provincial crossfire or engaging in it. Continuing to address process-related issues rather than critically confronting and, indeed, working to shape, the governing philosophy of education on a national level will mean that Canadians will remain passive receptors of human-capital economics and international education standards. There will be no coherent, public, and "world-class" education system like that envisioned by Ryerson almost two centuries ago.

Even now, with all of the lessons that should have been learned from the nation's difficult history in education diplomacy, the possibilities for a more consistent approach remain merely that. As I have asserted, there continues to be very little interest in acting on the obvious and pressing need for reform. Revision of the Constitution to include education among the areas of the federal government's jurisdiction will not happen. The constitutional conundrum that characterizes Canadian education diplomacy remains unresolved and will remain so as long as the lessons of this period of history go unacknowledged and are not put to use. Governments at both levels will continue to wander, mesmerized, into the constitutional, administrative, and political mazes that comprise this area. And, if history is any indication, many parts of this labyrinth will sadly be of their own making.

A Note about References

Bringing together in this study the works from a myriad of disciplines has occupied me for the greater part of a decade and a half. Some of these works come from the field of international relations theory, whereas others are situated in the field of the history of education. Time has played a role here; some areas that early on in this study were covered only very thinly by the literature have been addressed recently by a much broader array of works as other scholars have taken up the cause. Serendipity and the thrill of the pursuit of archival treasure have also been very much part of this journey. Some thoughts on my key sources are in order.

The Council of Ministers of Education, Canada (CMEC) is a corporation under the laws of Ontario. This I can attest to. I have seen a copy of the corporate charter of the CMEC. For the historian, however, accessing corporate archives is not always easy. Fortunately, it became apparent early on in this study—in the late 1990s—that many of the records of the CMEC were also to be found in the Archives of Ontario through the Ontario Ministry of Education and the Ontario Ministry of Colleges and Universities fonds (the titles of these ministries have now changed—more than once!). Consequently, the Archives of Ontario (then on Grenville Street near Toronto Police Headquarters), particularly the Record Groups associated with the Council of Ministers, were central for this study. The Ontario Archives (now in their new location at York University) remained a very rich resource as the book evolved.

Added views and perspectives came from a variety of other archives. In the mid-1990s, the CMEC, the Canadian Education Association (CEA), and the Ontario Institute for Studies in Education at the University of Toronto (OISE/UT) were all located at 252 Bloor Street West. This concentrated cluster of education-related organizations gave me perspective on this topic. The CEA, in particular, held archives that pre-dated the CMEC, which were helpful in gaining a longer-term frame of reference for this organization. The resources of the University of Toronto Library system, the University of Toronto Archives, and particularly the John P. Robarts Research Library, were also instrumental in the pursuit of this research. The Library and Archives of Canada also contain a substantial trove of archival documents concerning the federal government and the CMEC. I only touched the tip of these resources in my research for this book.

Reading Richard Arndt's *The First Resort of Kings: American Cultural Diplomacy in the Twentieth Century* was an epiphany of sorts for me as it opened the door to a rich, nuanced discussion of cultural and education diplomacy in the twentieth century in the United States. Similarly, Evan Potter's *Branding Canada* provided a broader sense of cultural diplomacy as it was manifested in Canada.

Historians of education have also recently started to turn their attention to things international. The work of Eckhardt Fuchs, of GEI in Germany, was particularly helpful. His articles in *Paedagogica Historica* provided another window on the development of worldwide educational networks. In the same vein, a further understanding of the world of World Fairs and international education, generally, can be derived from Sylvester's work.

Closer to home, chapters in Wilson, Stamp, and Audet's *Canadian Education: A History* provided a solid foundation for the discussion of a host of issues involved in education in Canada over several decades. Ronald Manzer's 1994 book, *Public Schools and Political Ideas: Canadian Educational Policy in Historical Perspective*, illuminates the connection among policy, schooling, and political thought in Canada and is a highly relevant resource for anyone interested in the intersection of the fields of education and politics. Axelrod's *The Promise of Schooling: Education in Canada, 1800–1914* speaks to the reality of schools in nineteenth-century Upper Canada and the gap between that reality and the ideals of schooling. Gidney and Millar's work has also greatly widened our knowledge of nineteenth- and twentieth-century schooling in Ontario: *Inventing Secondary Education: The Rise of the High School in Nineteenth-Century Ontario* and, more recently, Gidney's *From Hope to Harris: The Reshaping of Ontario's Schools*. Two pieces of writing stand out in terms of providing an outside look at Canada and its education system. Both come from the pen of the former German politician, Hildegard Hamm-Brücher, and should be required reading when thinking about Canada, federalism, and international education bodies such as the OECD: "Canadian Education: A View from Abroad" in *Canadian Education in the 1980's*, edited by J. Donald Wilson, and, with her fellow OECD Examiners, Sheffield and Noah, "The OECD Review and Higher Education" in the *Canadian Journal of Higher Education*.

Concerning Quebec, in recent years there has been a series of new works that speak to international education and the role therein of Quebec and, notably, Paul Gérin-Lajoie. Paquin et al.'s *Les Relations Internationales du Québec depuis la Doctrine Gérin-Lajoie (1965–2005): Le Prolongement Externe des Compétences Internes* is highly informative as is Aird's study of André Patry: *André Patry et la Présence du Québec dans le Monde*.

The pervasive and underlying challenge for all jurisdictions in Canada is to improve education. Ungerleider's *Failing Our Kids: How We Are Ruining Our Public Schools*, a key work with that goal in mind, is instructive concerning some of the challenges facing, and possible solutions for, Canadian education in the future. Government-sponsored education remains a work in progress across Canada, from the local school level right up to the constitutional level.

The references in the notes in this book are presented as much as possible in the University of Chicago style. Legal references are in accordance with the McGill Law Journal's *Canadian Guide to Legal Citation*, 7th edition. For the reader's convenience, full bibliographical detail is provided on the first occurrence of each reference in a chapter. Thereafter a shortened version is given. Finally, the following abbreviations are used for simplicity and economy in the case of archival references, especially given their complex and repetitive nature:

ACEA Archives of the Canadian Education Association
AO   Archives of Ontario
CMEC Council of Ministers of Educaion, Canada
MCU   Ministry of Colleges and Universities (Ontario)
MOE   Ministry of Education (Ontario)

Works Cited Above

Aird, Robert. *André Patry et la Présence du Québec dans le Monde*. Montreal: VLB, 2005.

Arndt, Richard T. *The First Resort of Kings: American Cultural Diplomacy in the Twentieth Century*. Washington, DC: Potomac Books, 2005.

Axelrod, Paul. *The Promise of Schooling: Education in Canada, 1800–1914*. Toronto: University of Toronto Press, 1997.

Fuchs, Eckhardt. "Educational Sciences, Morality and Politics: International Educational Congresses in the Early Twentieth Century." *Paedagogica Historica* 40, no. 5–6 (2004): 757–84.

———. "The Creation of New International Networks in Education: The League of Nations and Educational Organizations in the 1920s." *Paedagogica Historica* 43, no. 2 (2007): 199–209.

———. "Networks and the History of Education." *Paedagogica Historica* 43, no. 2 (2007): 185–97.

Gidney, R. D. *From Hope to Harris: The Reshaping of Ontario's Schools*. Toronto: University of Toronto Press, 1999.

Gidney, R. D., and W. P. J. Millar. *Inventing Secondary Education: The Rise of the High School in Nineteenth-Century Ontario*. Montreal: McGill-Queen's University Press, 1990.

Hamm-Brücher, Hildegard. "Canadian Education: A View from Abroad." In *Canadian Education in the 1980's*, edited by J. Donald Wilson. Calgary: Detselig, 1981.

Manzer, Ronald A. *Public Schools and Political Ideas: Canadian Educational Policy in Historical Perspective*. Toronto: University of Toronto Press, 1994.

Paquin, Stéphane, Louise Beaudouin, Robert Comeau, and Guy Lachapelle, *Les Relations Internationales du Québec depuis la Doctrine Gérin-Lajoie (1965–2005): Le Prolongement Externe des Compétences Internes* (Quebec City: Presses Université Laval, 2006).

Potter, Evan H. *Branding Canada: Projecting Canada's Soft Power through Public Diplomacy*. Montreal: McGill-Queen's University Press, 2009.

Sheffield, Edward, Harold Noah, and Hildegard Hamm-Brücher. "The OECD Review and Higher Education." *Canadian Journal of Higher Education* 9, no. 2 (1979): 1–18.

Sylvester, Robert. "Mapping International Education: A Historical Survey 1893–1944." *Journal of Research in International Education* 1, no. 1 (2002): 90–125.

Ungerleider, Charles. *Failing Our Kids: How We Are Ruining Our Public Schools*. Toronto: McClelland and Stewart, 2003.

Wilson, J. Donald. "Education in Upper Canada: Sixty Years of Change." In *Canadian Education: A History*, edited by J. Donald Wilson, Robert M. Stamp, and Louis-Philippe Audet, 190–213. Scarborough, ON: Prentice-Hall, 1970.

Notes

Introduction

1   Ryan Touhey, "A New Direction for the Canada-India Relationship" (Toronto: Canadian International Council, 2009).

2   Evan H. Potter, *Branding Canada: Projecting Canada's Soft Power through Public Diplomacy* (Montreal: McGill-Queen's University Press, 2009).

3   David Johnston, "Blueprint for a Smart Nation," in Perspectives on Education: Voices of Eminent Canadians," special issue, *LEARNing Landscapes* 3, no. 2 (2010): 5–69 at 68.

4   Stephen Jones, "Cooperative Federalism? The Case of the Ministerial Council on Education, Employment, Training and Youth Affairs," *Australian Journal of Public Administration* 67, no. 2 (2008): 161–72.

5   For a more detailed definition, see page 5 *infra*.

6   Robin H. Farquhar, "Can Canada Get Its Act Together in International Education?" (paper presented at the Semi-Annual Meeting of the Management Board of the Canadian Information Centre for International Credentials, Hull, QC, 2001), 3. Robin H. Farquhar and Canadian Bureau for International Education, *Advancing the Canadian Agenda for International Education: Report of the Millennium Consultation on International Education* (Ottawa: Canadian Bureau for International Education, 2001). The question of "International Education" is a long discussion and crosses several academic disciplines, one of which is entitled "International Education."

7   For a discussion of the rise of the Confucius Institute and the different models of program execution, see Don Starr, "Chinese Language Education in Europe: The Confucius Institutes," *European Journal of Education* 44, no. 1 (2009): 65–82 at 70 and Colin Freeze, James Bradshaw, and Mark Mackinnon, "Canadian Universities, Colleges Confront Questions about Chinese Ties," *The Globe and Mail*, June 19, 2012.

8   Touhey, "A New Direction for the Canada–India Relationship."

9   The role of "education attaché" is often subsumed under the title "cultural attaché." The scope of work for an education attaché can be wide, including such tasks as establishing a website and information that directs university students

where to get support from their home country and embassy, visiting schools and developing contacts with the host country's education system over the long term, and monitoring the education system and its curriculum to widen the perspective of the host state; US Secretary of State Hillary Clinton's recent encounter with an Afghani general who thought America was all "bikinis and WWF" spoke to a clear need for curricular revision in Afghanistan: Mitchell Pullman, "Secretary Clinton's Culture Complaint," The Centre for Public Diplomacy Blog, March 22, 2011, http://uscpublicdiplomacy.org/index.php/newswire/cpdblog_detail/secretary_clintons_culture_complaint/.

10   Much of the inspiration for this prescription comes from the contemporary American, European, and Chinese models. Discussion on these issues goes back decades. Arndt's treatment is exhaustive in the American case: see Richard T. Arndt, The First Resort of Kings: American Cultural Diplomacy in the Twentieth Century (Washington, DC: Potomac Books, 2005). The works and memoirs of Philip Coombs and Charles Frankel are also important in filling out the picture: See Philip Hall Coombs, The Fourth Dimension of Foreign Policy: Educational and Cultural Affairs (New York: Harper & Row, 1964) and Charles Frankel, High on Foggy Bottom: An Outsider's Inside View of the Government (New York: Harper & Row, 1969).

11   Richard J. Evans, In Defense of History (New York: W.W. Norton, c. 1999); Martha Howell and Walter Prevenier, From Reliable Sources: An Introduction to Historical Methods (Ithaca, NY: Cornell University Press, 2001).

12   The Council of Ministers of Education, Canada (CMEC) is a corporation under the laws of Ontario. As such, it is not obligated to open its archives. Fortunately some of its documents are available from government sources such as provincial archives. Therefore, it became necessary to use all possible sources. Political scientist Cameron Thies speaks to some of the challenges of triangulating historical sources in international relations. See Cameron G. Thies, "A Practical Guide to Qualitative Historical Analysis in the Study of International Relations," International Studies Perspectives 3, no. 4 (2002): 351–72 at 367.

13   Cecilia Morgan, A Happy Holiday: English Canadians and Transatlantic Tourism, 1870–1930 (Toronto: University of Toronto Press, 2008).

14   Cooperation between states with regard to education took many forms. Another example of Canada–US Cooperation is the textbook study that took place in the 1940s led by several education groups including the American Council on Education, the Canada and Newfoundland Education Association, the Canadian Teachers' Federation, and the National Conference of Canadian Universities. The purpose of the analysis was to determine if each country's texts dealt adequately with the other nation's history. The report offered recommendations "for the improvement of national history textbooks as instruments of international goodwill between Canada and the United States." See The American Council on Education and The Canada–United States Committee on Education, "A Study of National History Textbooks Used in the Schools of Canada and the United States," Canadian Education 2 (June 1947): 2.

15   For an examination of some of the other issues linked to education, notably citizenship, see Alan Sears, "Possibilities and Problems: Citizenship Education in a Multinational State: The Case of Canada," in Globalization, the Nation-State and the Citizen: Dilemmas and Directions for Civics and Citizenship Education, ed. Alan Reid, Judith Gill, and Alan Sears, 191–205 (New York: Routledge, 2010).

16 Samy Mesli, "Le Développement de la 'Diplomatie Éducative' du Québec," *Globe: Revue Internationale d'Études Québécoises* 12, no. 1 (2009): 115–31 at 116.

17 For a discussion of this in contemporary international relations, see Jeffrey A. Engel, "A Better World . . . but Don't Get Carried Away: The Foreign Policy of George H. W. Bush Twenty Years On," *Diplomatic History* 34, no. 1 (2010): 25–46.

18 Eckhardt Fuchs, "The Creation of New International Networks in Education: The League of Nations and Educational Organizations in the 1920s," *Paedagogica Historica* 43, no. 2 (2007): 199–209.

19 Linda Constant, "Art and Cultural Diplomacy in the International Exhibition: Documenta 1 and Prospect 1" (MPAS thesis, University of Southern California, 2009).

20 The Canadian Bureau of International Education (CBIE) is an active domestic partner in this regard. See, for example, Tony McKittrick, "Supporting the Short-Term International Student: The Canadian–Australian Connection," (paper presented at the 17th Australian International Education Conference, Melbourne, Australia, October 21–24, 2003), 4.

21 Philip Jones, "Globalisation and the UNESCO Mandate: Multilateral Prospects for Educational Development," *International Journal of Educational Development* 19, no. 1 (1999): 17–25.

22 *Constitution Act, 1982*, being Schedule B to the *Canada Act 1982* (UK), 1982, c 11. In 1982 the *British North America Act*, 1867, 30 & 31 Vict, c 3 was renamed the *Constitiution Act, 1867*. See *Constitution Act, 1867* (UK), 30 & 31 Vict, c 3, reprinted in RSC 1985, App II, No 5.

23 The term "education diplomacy" or "*diplomatie éducative*" is seeing increasing usage in the literature and government practice: Mark Cullen, "Harnessing the Potential for International Education" (Auckland: Government of New Zealand, 2010); Alex Oliver, "AEI: Educational Diplomacy Scapegoat?" *The Interpreter*, June 22, 2010, http://www.lowyinterpreter.org/post/2010/06/22/AEI-educational-diplomacy-scapegoat.aspx?; and Mesli, "Le Développement de la 'Diplomatie Éducative' du Québec." "Diplomacy in education" is synonymous with "education diplomacy." "Education-Related International Activities," a term coined by the Council of Ministers of Education (CMEC), seeks to differentiate between diplomacy, which was seen as a strictly federal government activity, and those international activities run by provincial governments.

24 Robert Arnove and Ruth Hayhoe, "A Reflection on the Achievements of One of China's Most Influential Scholars of Comparative Education, Professor Wang Chengxu, at 100," *Frontiers of Education in China* 6, no. 1 (2011): 158–65 at 164.

25 Paul Sharp, "For Diplomacy: Representation and the Study of International Relations," *International Studies Review* 1, no. 1 (1999): 33–57 at 44; Peter Forlin and Chris Forlin, "Constitutional and Legislative Framework for Inclusive Education in Australia," *Australian Journal of Education* 42, no. 2 (1998): 204–17.

26 It is also the realm of the idealistic first-year undergraduate political science major. Roy Macridis's work is a representative and historical text from the undergraduate curriculum: Roy Macridis, ed., *Foreign Policy in World Politics* (Englewood Cliffs, NJ: Prentice-Hall, 1976).

27 See Stuart Murray, Paul Sharp, Geoffrey Wiseman, David Criekemans, and Jan Melissen, eds., "The Present and Future of Diplomacy and Diplomatic Studies,"

International Studies Review 13, no. 4 (2011): 709–28. See, particularly, the essay by Criekemans entitled "Exploring the Relationship between Geopolitics, Foreign Policy and Diplomacy" (713–16), which provides a very succinct distinction between foreign policy and diplomacy.

28   Jean Orieux, *Talleyrand: The Art of Survival* (New York: Knopf, 1974).

29   Chas. W. Freeman Jr., *Diplomat's Dictionary*, 2d ed. (Washington, DC: United States Institute of Peace (USIP), 2010), 55.

30   James Der Derian, *On Diplomacy: A Genealogy of Western Estrangement* (London: B. Blackwell Publishers, 1987), 73.

31   James Der Derian, "Diplomacy," in The *Oxford Companion to Politics of the World*, 2d ed., ed. Joel Kreiger and Margaret E. Crahan (Oxford: Oxford University Press, 2001), 222.

32   *On Diplomacy: A Genealogy of Western Estrangement*, 76.

33   Norman Hillmer and J. L. Granatstein, *Empire to Umpire: Canada and the World into the Twenty-first Century*, 2d ed. (Toronto: Thomson Nelson, 2008), 5.

34   Herbert C. Kelman, "Interactive Problem Solving as a Tool for Second Track Diplomacy," in *Second Track/Citizens' Diplomacy: Concepts and Techniques for Conflict Transformation*, ed. John Davies and Edward (Edy) Kaufman (London: Rowman & Littlefield, 2003), 81–106 at 84.

35   Paul Sharp, "Making Sense of Citizen Diplomats: The People of Duluth, Minnesota, as International Actors," *International Studies Perspectives* 2, no. 2 (2001): 131–50.

36   Jim Yardley, "India–Pakistan Game Breaks Out on Way to Diplomatic Thaw," *The New York Times*, March 30, 2011, A4.

37   The term remains contested. See Nicholas Cull, "Public Diplomacy: Seven Lessons for Its Future from Its Past," *Place Branding and Public Diplomacy* 6, no. 1 (2010): 11–17 and Jan Melissen, ed. *The New Public Diplomacy: Soft Power in International Relations* (Basingstoke, UK: Palgrave Macmillan, 2005).

38   Potter, *Branding Canada: Projecting Canada's Soft Power through Public Diplomacy*, 128–51.

39   Notable examples include Richard Arndt, *The First Resort of Kings: American Cultural Diplomacy in the Twentieth Century* (Washington, DC: Potomac Books, 2005), which chronicles the activities of the United States Information Service and the Department of State as they addressed the period from World War II forward. Also, Nicholas Cull provides an exhaustive analysis of the United States Information Agency detailing public diplomacy in the United States during the era of the Cold War in Nicholas John Cull, *The Cold War and the United States Information Agency: American Propaganda and Public Diplomacy, 1945–1989* (Cambridge; New York: Cambridge University Press, 2008). Grace Ai-Ling Chou examines cultural diplomacy as a subset of public diplomacy influencing Hong Kong in the 1950s in Grace Ai-Ling Chou, "Cultural Education as Containment of Communism: The Ambivalent Position of American NGOs in Hong Kong in the 1950s," *Journal of Cold War Studies* 12, no. 2 (2010): 3–28.

40   For those from the field of International Relations and in organizations such as the International Studies Association (ISA) in the United States, "international education" often means a program of studies at the undergraduate level culminating in a third year abroad.

41 Some institutions are embedded in government; quasi-governmental organizations are imbued with some functions and aspects of government, whereas NGOs are outside government. See List of Abbreviations for a listing of some of these organizations.

42 Lawrence M. Bezeau, "Federal Involvment," in *Educational Administration for Canadian Teachers*, 2d ed. (Toronto: Copp Clark, c. 1995), 63–77.

43 For the higher education perspectives, see Glen Jones, ed., *Higher Education in Canada: Different Systems, Different Perspectives* (London: Garland Publishing, 1997) (see, particularly, David M. Cameron, "The Federal Perspective").

44 I wish to draw attention to the work of some of my Nipissing University colleagues in this area. John Long's work examines Treaty Nine and the situation of First Nations in northeastern Ontario. Ron Phillips's work, notable for this book, looks at the absence of a federal minister of education (and, arguably, a First Nations minister) to speak to First Nations education. The redressing of the lack of such a presence at the CMEC table is long overdue, with negative effects for First Nations children. Mike DeGagné and co-authors Shelagh Rogers, Jonathan Dewar, and Glen Lowry have selected the testimonies of residential school survivors to provide a reader and foundation for dialogue for Canadians. See John Long, *Treaty No. 9: Making the Agreement to Share the Land in Far Northern Ontario in 1905* (Montreal/Kingston: McGill-Queen's University Press, 2010); Ron Sydney Phillips, "The Absentee Minister of Education of Canada: The Canadian Federal Government's Constitutional Role in First Nations Education," *McGill Journal of Education* 46, no. 2 (2011): 231–45; Shelagh Rogers, Mike DeGagné, Jonathan Dewar, and Glen Lowry, eds., *Speaking My Truth: Reflections on Reconciliation & Residential School* (Ottawa: Aboriginal Healing Foundation, 2012).

45 In addition to those already mentioned, a variety of other works address the federal government's stake and role in education. See, e.g., Donald Fisher et al., *Canadian Federal Policy and Postsecondary Education* (Vancouver: The Centre for Policy Studies in Higher Education and Training, University of British Columbia, 2006); Ernest D. Hodgson, *Federal Intervention in Public Education* (Toronto: Canadian Education Association, 1976); Andrew Hughes and Alan Sears, "Citizenship Education: Canada Dabbles While the World Plays On," *Education Canada* 46, no. 4 (2006): 6–9; Reva Joshee, "Federal Policies on Cultural Diversity and Education, 1940–1971" (PhD diss., University of British Columbia, 1995); Reva Joshee and Lauri Johnson, eds., *Multicultural Education Policies in Canada and the United States* (Vancouver: UBC Press, 2007); and Charles Ungerleider, *Failing Our Kids: How We Are Ruining Our Public Schools* (Toronto: McClelland and Stewart, 2003).

46 Potter, *Branding Canada: Projecting Canada's Soft Power through Public Diplomacy.*

47 Rosemary R. Gagan, *A Sensitive Independence: Canadian Methodist Women Missionaries in Canada and the Orient, 1881–1925* (Montreal: McGill-Queen's Press, 1992).

48 David Morrison, *Aid and Ebb Tide: A History of CIDA and Canadian Development Assistance* (Waterloo, ON: Wilfrid Laurier University Press, 1998).

49 Roopa Desai Trilokekar, Glen A. Jones, and Adrian Shubert, eds., *Canada's Universities Go Global* (Toronto: J. Lorimer & Company, 2009).

50 Jane Knight, "A Shared Vision? Stakeholders' Perspectives on the Internationalization of Higher Education in Canada," *Journal of Studies in International Education* 1, no. 1 (1997): 27–44.

51   Mesli, "Le Développement de la 'diplomatie éducative' du Québec, 131.

52   Paul Wells, "Harper and the Death (for Now) of Executive Federalism," *MacLean's*, November 10, 2008, http://www.macleans.ca/politics/ottawa/stephen-harper-and-the-death-for-now-of-executive-federalism/.

Chapter One

1   This chapter appeared previously in a shorter and different form as a peer-reviewed journal article: see John Allison, "From Journeymen Envoys to Skilled Diplomats: Change in Canada's Education-Related International Activities, 1815–1968," *Diplomacy and Statecraft* 17, no. 2 (2006): 237–59. Reprinted by permission of Taylor & Francis, LLC (http://www.tandfonline.com).

2   State formation in Canada is covered in a variety of works—notably Bruce Curtis's efforts: Bruce Curtis, *True Government by Choice Men? Inspection, Education, and State Formation in Canada West* (Toronto: University of Toronto Press, 1992); Bruce Curtis, *The Politics of Population: State Formation, Statistics, and the Census of Canada, 1840–1875* (Toronto: University of Toronto Press, 2002). See also Anthony Di Mascio, "Educational Discourse and the Making of Educational Legislation in Early Upper Canada," *History of Education Quarterly* 50, no. 1 (2010) 34–54.

3   The role of education in the crafting of the *British North America Act, 1867* is examined by Andy Khan, "The Legal Context of Canadian Education," *The Australian and New Zealand Journal of Law and Education* 2, no. 1 (1997): 25–58.

4   Arndt's discussion of "the first resort of kings" speaks more fully of the role of cultural diplomacy in the more distant past: Richard Arndt, *The First Resort of Kings: American Cultural Diplomacy in the Twentieth Century* (Washington, DC: Potomac Books, 2005), 9.

5   Benedict Anderson, *Imagined Communities: Reflections on the Origins and Spread of Nationalism* (London: Verso, 1991).

6   The story of Talleyrand illustrates the remarkable continuity during this era. Many of the chief ministers involved in foreign relations had known each other for decades. See Jean Orieux, *Talleyrand: The Art of Survival* (New York: Knopf, 1974).

7   Hedley Bull and Adam Watson, eds., *The Expansion of International Society* (Oxford: Clarendon Press; New York: Oxford University Press, 1984), 6.

8   John J. Mearsheimer, *The Tragedy of Great Power Politics* (New York: W. W. Norton, 2003), 236.

9   The dominance of churches goes only so far; this was the case in Upper Canada and the UK, but not the case in other states such as those of continental Europe and the United States. See Bruce Curtis, *True Government by Choice Men? Inspection, Education, and State Formation in Canada West* (Toronto: University of Toronto Press, 1992) and Andy Green, *Education and State Formation: The Rise of Education Systems in England, France, and the USA* (Hampshire, UK: Macmillan, 1990).

10   Roger Magnuson provides excellent background on the state of education in New France: Roger Magnuson, "The Elusive Lay Schoolmasters of New France," *Historical Studies in Education* 2, no. 1 (Spring 1990): 73–94; Roger Magnuson, *Education in New France* (Montreal: McGill-Queen's University Press, 1992).

11 Magnuson, *Education in New France*, 64.

12 Louis-Philippe Audet, "The French Heritage," in *Canadian Education: A History*, ed. J. Donald Wilson, Robert M. Stamp, and Louis-Philippe Audet (Scarborough, ON: Prentice-Hall, 1970), 2–23 at 13.

13 B. Speirs and R. Reynolds, eds., *Inventory 2 Records of the Ministry of Education, Vol. I*, 1970, AO, 6.

14 Bernard Hyams, "The Colonial Office and Educational Policy in British North America and Australia before 1850," *Historical Studies in Education* 2, no. 2 (1990): 323–38.

15 See note 2, above.

16 Ryerson's role in early education diplomacy in Ontario was similar to the proto-diplomatic role fulfilled by Sir John Rose in early Confederation Canada: see the text to note 33 in the Introduction.

17 Clara Thomas, *Ryerson of Upper Canada* (Toronto: Ryerson Press, 1969), 71.

18 Ibid., 80. See, also, Ronald A. Manzer, *Public Schools and Political ideas: Canadian Educational Policy in Historical Perspective* (Toronto: University of Toronto Press, 1994), 81.

19 Several references are made to Upper Canada, Canada West, and Ontario. These political/governmental titles are used to describe the area roughly constituting modern-day Ontario. "Upper Canada" was used between 1791 and 1841 to describe a somewhat smaller geographical area, whereas "Canada West" was used between 1841 and 1867. The region became known as the Province of Ontario under the terms of the *British North America Act, 1867* and the *Canada Act 1982*.

20 Speirs and Reynolds, *Inventory 2 Records of the Ministry of Education* Vol. I, 6.

21 Michael S. Cross, "DUNCOMBE, CHARLES," in *Dictionary of Canadian Biography*, vol. 9, University of Toronto/Université Laval, 2003–, accessed May 8, 2015, http://www.biographi.ca/en/bio/duncombe_charles_9E.html.

22 J. Donald Wilson, "Education in Upper Canada: Sixty Years of Change," in *Canadian Education: A History*, 190–213 at 208–209. See, also, Charles Duncombe, *Report Upon the Subject of Education made to the Parliament of Upper Canada, 25th February, 1836* (Toronto: M. Reynolds, 1836), 9–13, passim.

23 Susan Houston, "Politics, Schools and Social Change in Upper Canada," in *Education and Social Change: Themes from Ontario's Past*, ed. Michael B. Katz and Paul H. Mattingly (New York: New York University Press, 1975), 29. See, also, Ryerson's first report on schools: Egerton Ryerson, "Report on a System of Public Elementary Instruction for Upper Canada," ed. Department of Education (Montreal: Lovell & Gibson, 1847), iv and J. Donald Wilson, "The Ryerson Years in Canada West," in *Canadian Education: A History*, 214–40.

24 Horace Mann and others travelled extensively as well: see Jonathan Messerli, *Horace Mann: A Biography* (New York: Knopf, 1972), 379–400, passim. Victor Cousins of France also travelled to Prussia: see Victor Cousin and Sarah Taylor Austin, "Report on the State of Public Instruction in Prussia/Rapport sur l'état de l'instruction publique dans quelques pays de l'Allemagne et particulièrement en Prusse," (London: E. Wilson Publishers, 1834).

25 Thomas, *Ryerson of Upper Canada*, 77.

26   John Hilliker and Donald Barry do an excellent job of describing the early diplomatic
     prerogatives of the colonies (or lack thereof) and also the evolving bureaucracy: see
     John Hilliker and Donald Barry, *Canada's Department of External Affairs*, vol. 1, *The
     Early Years: 1909–1946* (Montreal and Kingston: McGill-Queen's University Press,
     1995), 3–5.

27   Alison Prentice and Susan Houston, *Schooling and Scholars in Nineteenth-Century
     Ontario* (Toronto: University of Toronto Press, 1988), 113–14.

28   Department of Education and J. George Hodgins, eds., *Documentary History of
     Education in Upper Canada: Vol. 5: 1843–1845*,6 (Toronto: Warwick Brothers &
     Rutter, 1897), 245.

29   Ryerson did not exclusively import Pestalozzian pedagogy; it also came with
     students and teachers who studied it in Switzerland and then came to Canada.
     Ryerson was, however, the first leader of a school system in Ontario to run across
     this methodology.

30   Markus Mosslang and Torsten Riotte, eds., *The Diplomats' World: A Cultural History
     of Diplomacy, 1815–1914* (Oxford; New York: Oxford University Press, 2008), 8–9.

31   Discussions of diplomatic culture run through the literature. See Simon Marginson,
     "Federal/State Relations in Education and the 2006 Work Relations Case," in
     *Institute of Public Administration Australia (IPAA) & Academy of Social Sciences
     Australia (ASSA) Policy Roundtable on Federalism* (Canberra: ASSA, 2007), 409–10.
     More generally, see Bull and Watson, *The Expansion of International Society*.

32   Department of Education and Hodgins, *Documentary History of Education in Upper
     Canada: Vol. 5: 1843–1845*,6, 237–38. See, also, Thomas, *Ryerson of Upper Canada*,
     98–99.

33   Matthew S. Seligmann, "'While I am in it I am not of it": A Naval Attaché's
     Reflections on the Conduct of British Diplomacy and Foreign Policy, 1906–1908,"
     in Mosslang and Riotte, *The Diplomats' World*, 433–60.

34   Ibid., 438–39.

35   For an interesting discussion of the changing "languages of diplomacy," see Robert
     Sylvester, "Framing the Map of International Education (1969–1998)," *Journal of
     Research in International Education* 4, no. 2 (2005): 123–51.

36   J. A. Black, *A History of Diplomacy* (London: Reaktion Books, 2010), 164. Fuchs
     also writes about the significance of networks in Eckhardt Fuchs, "Networks and the
     History of Education," *Paedagogica Historica* 43, no. 2 (2007): 185–97.

37   Wilson, "The Ryerson Years in Canada West," in *Canadian Education: A History*,
     219–40 at 219–20.

38   Patrick Walsh, "Education and the 'Universalist' Idiom of Empire: Irish National
     School Books in Ireland and Ontario," *History of Education* 37, no. 5 (2008): 645–
     60 at 648.

39   Ibid., 653–54.

40   Ibid., 654–55.

41   1850, 1855, and 1867 were the other three dates.

42   Egerton Ryerson, Chief Superintendent, to the Earl of Clarendon, Secretary of
     State for Foreign Affairs, July 1855, MOE Files, RG2, E-1, Envelope 9, AO.

43   Thomas, *Ryerson of Upper Canada*, 199–220.

44   Charles Edward Phillips, *The Development of Education in Canada* (Toronto: Gage, 1957), 353.

45   J. K. Jobling, "Jean-Baptiste Meilleur Architect of Lower Canada's School System," in *Profiles of Canadian Educators*, ed. Robert S. Patterson, John W. Chalmers, and John W. Friesen (Toronto: D. C. Heath, 1974), 102.

46   This has improved over the years with increased government co-operation in education.

47   For an examination of world fairs and their use for the purposes of state propaganda, see Nicholas Cull, "Overture to an Alliance: British Propaganda at the New York World's Fair, 1939–1940," *The Journal of British Studies* 36, no. 3 (1997): 325–54.

48   The United States Bureau of Education, *Report of the Commissioner of Education Made to the Secretary of the Interior for the Year 1876* (Washington, DC: United States Government Printing Office, 1877), ccxxii.

49   Phillips, *The Development of Education in* Canada, 356.

50   Joseph Schull, *Ontario since 1867* (Toronto: McClelland and Stewart, 1978), 84. See, also, A. Margaret Evans, *Sir Oliver Mowat* (Toronto: University of Toronto Press, 1992), 295.

51   George Hodgins, Historiographer, to Richard Harcourt, Minister of Education, July 17, 1903, MOE Files, RG2, E-1, Folder 3, Envelope 9, AO.

52   Mary Gregory, Chair of Education Society, Bradford, to George Hodgins, Historiographer, July 15, 1903, MOE Files, RG2, E-1, Folder 3, Envelope 9, AO, Toronto.

53   Manoly R. Lupul, "Educational Crisis in the New Dominion to 1917," in *Canadian Education: A History*, 266–289 at 267.

54   Ibid., 268–69.

55   Paul Axelrod, *The Promise of Schooling: Education in Canada, 1800–1914* (Toronto: University of Toronto Press, 1997), 30–31.

56   Ibid., 31.

57   J. R. Miller, *Shingwauk's Vision: A History of Native Residential Schools* (Toronto: University of Toronto Press, 1996). See, also, Ron Sydney Phillips, "The Absentee Minister of Education of Canada: The Canadian Federal Government's Constitutional Role in First Nations Education," *McGill Journal of Education* 46, no. 2 (2011): 231–45 and John S. Long, *Treaty No. 9: Making the Agreement to Share the Land in Far Northern Ontario in 1905* (Montreal: McGill-Queen's University Press, 2010).

58   Donald Fisher et al., *Canadian Federal Policy and Postsecondary Education*, 3; René Morin and Department of National Defence, Canada, *DND Dependants' Schools, 1921–1983* (Ottawa: Directorate of History, National Defence Headquarters, 1986).

59   Fisher et al., *Canadian Federal Policy and Postsecondary Education*, 3.

60   G. E. Malcolm MacLeod and Robert E. Blair, *The Canadian Education Association: The First 100 Years, 1891–1991* (Toronto: Canadian Education Association, 1992), 3. For more information on the NEA, see Edgar Bruce Wesley, *NEA, The First Hundred Years: The Building of the Teaching Profession* (New York: Harper, 1957). McLean speaks about the later 1920s efforts to create a Canadian National Bureau of Education in her article. See; McLean, Lorna R. "Education, identity, and

citizenship in early modern Canada." *Journal of Canadian Studies/Revue d'études canadiennes* 41, no. 1 (2007): 5-30.

61   Sylvester speaks to the development of World Fairs' role: see Robert Sylvester, "Mapping International Education: A Historical Survey 1893-1944," *Journal of Research in International Education* 1, no. 1 (2002): 90–125 at 97. Fuchs also mentions it in passing: see Eckhardt Fuchs, "The Creation of New International Networks in Education: The League of Nations and Educational Organizations in the 1920s" *Paedagogica Historica* 43, no. 2 (2007): 199–209 and Eckhardt Fuchs, "Educational Sciences, Morality and Politics: International Educational Congresses in the Early Twentieth Century," *Paedagogica Historica* 40, no. 5–6 (2004): 757–84 at 782–84. See, also, Aaron Benavot and Phyllis Riddle, "The Expansion of Primary Education, 1870–1940: Trends and Issues," *Sociology of Education* 61, no. 3 (1988): 191–210 at 193–94.

62   Robert M. Stamp, "Education and the Economic and Social Milieu: The English-Canadian Scene from the 1870's to 1914," in *Canadian Education: A History*, 290–313 at 306.

63   Schull, *Ontario since 1967*, 75.

64   David Dyment, "The Ontario Government as an International Actor," *Regional and Federal Studies* 11, no. 1 (2001): 55–79 at 56.

65   Adam Watson, "New States in the Americas," in Bull and Watson, eds., *The Expansion of International Society*, 131.

66   Freeman K. Stewart, *Interprovincial Co-operation in Education* (Toronto: Gage, 1957), 15.

67   Peter Waite, "Between Three Oceans: Challenges of a Continental Destiny (1840–1900)," in *The Illustrated History of Canada*, ed. Craig Brown (Toronto: Lester Publishing, 1987), 277–376 at 373.

68   Stewart, *Interprovincial Co-operation in Education*, 16. Moss also addresses Empire Day and the implications for physical activities and drill: Mark Moss, *Manliness and Militarism: Educating Young Boys in Ontario for War* (Toronto: University of Toronto Press, 2001), 94–96.

69   Stewart, *Interprovincial Co-operation in Education*, 25.

70   Joseph Pope's role and the run-up to the creation of a department are documented by Hilliker and Barry: *Canada's Department of External Affairs*, vol. 1, *The Early Years: 1909–1946*, 20–32, passim.

71   Wifrid Laurier had an expansive view of the new department and Pope's activities. See Carmen Miller, "Sir Joseph Pope: A Pragmatic Tory" in *Architects and Innovators: Building the Department of Foreign Affairs and International Trade, 1909–2009/Architectes et Innovateurs: Le Développement du Ministère des Affaires Étrangères et du Commerce International, 1909–2009*, ed. Greg Donaghy and Kim Richard Nossal (Kingston, ON: School of Policy Studies, Queen's University, 2009), 11–28 at 22 and F. H. Soward, *The Department of External Affairs and Canadian Autonomy, 1899–1939* (Ottawa: Canadian Historical Association, 1972), 9.

72   John Hilliker and Donald Barry, "The PM and the SSEA in Canada's Foreign Policy: Sharing the Territory, 1946–1968," *International Journal* 50, no. 1 (1995): 163–88 at 163.

73 Joseph Pope, Under-Secretary of External Affairs, to Mr. Wallis, Department of Education, June 23, 1915, MOE Central Registry Files, RG2, P-3, Box 12, AO. One of the first contacts between the two organizations was a letter confirming the delivery of passports to ministers in the Ontario government who had been unexpectedly called to New York City. Others later included a letter to Arthur Meighen from an American industrialist about private schools. In his secondary capacity as Secretary of State for External Affairs, Meighen transferred the letter to the Ontario Department of Education.

74 "C'est une Église puissante, triomphante, et qui n'hésite pas à intervenir dans tous les domaines où elle croit la foi menacée...malgré ces limites, l'Église catholique demeure au Québec une force importante...pour une bonne part dans le quasi-monopole qu'elle exerce sur certains services indispensables à la collectivité comme ...l'éducation." Paul André Linteau, François Ricard, René Durocher, and Jean-Claude Robert, *Histoire du Québec Contemporain*, vol. 2, *Le Québec depuis 1930* (Montreal: Boréal, 1989), 611.

75 Louis-Philippe Audet, "Educational Development in French-Canada after 1875," in *Canadian Education: A History*, 337–359 at 341.

76 Ibid., 340. John Ralston Saul states that Msgr. Bruchési, the Archbishop, faked Rome's involvement: John Ralston Saul, *Reflections of a Siamese Twin: Canada at the End of the Twentieth Century* (Toronto: Viking Penguin, 1997), 309. Lacoursière also points to the unusual role of Msgr. Bruchési in this matter: Jacques Lacoursière, *Histoire Populaire du Québec* (Sillery, QC: Les éditions du Septentrion, 1997), 18–20.

77 Stamp, "Education and the Economic and Social Milieu: The English Canadian Scene from the 1870's to 1914," 305.

78 Ibid.

79 J. R. Vincent, "Racial Equality," in *The Expansion of International Society*, 239.

80 Archives of Saskatchewan, e-mail to author, November 1997. See, also, Kelly Alcorn, "Border Crossings: US Contributions to Saskatchewan Education, 1905–1937" (PhD diss., University of Kentucky, 2008), 33.

81 Alcorn, "Border Crossings," 85.

82 Joseph Pope, Under-Secretary of State for External Affairs to A. H. Colquhoun, Deputy Minister of Education, February 23, 1917, MOE Central Registry Files, RG2, P-3, Box 43, AO.

83 Fuchs discusses the increasing prevalence of congresses during the early twentieth century and how the Great War prevented the early establishment of the International Bureau of Education: Fuchs, "Educational Sciences, Morality and Politics," 775.

84 The organization went through several name changes: it was the Dominion Education Association, the Canadian Education Association, the Canada and Newfoundland Education Association, and, again, the Canadian Education Association.

85 Canadian Education Association, *The Proceedings of the Tenth Convention* (Ottawa: James Hope and Sons, 1918), 9.

86 Ibid., 136.

87 Norman Hillmer, "O. D. Skelton: Innovating for Independence," in Donaghy and Nossal, eds., *Architects and Innovators*, 59–73.

88   Bogdan Suchodolski and International Bureau of Education, *The International Bureau of Education in the Service of Educational Development* (Paris: UNESCO, 1979), 61.

89   The IBE was initially established as a private organization in 1925. Through new statutes governments became members after 1929. See International Bureau of Education and Clementina Acedo, *IBE Strategy: 2008–2013* (Geneva: IBE, 2008), 11.

90   Suchodolski and International Bureau of Education, *The International Bureau of Education in the Service of Educational Development*, 69.

91   IBE Secretariat, e-mail message to the author, Fall, 1997.

92   Organisation for Economic Cooperation and Development, *Reviews of National Policies for Education: Canada* (Paris: Organisation for Economic Cooperation and Development, 1976), 25.

93   W. H. Measures, External Affairs, to A. H. Colquhoun, October 18, 1933, MOE Central Registry Files, RG2, P-3, Box 181, AO.

94   For an excellent treatment of this posture in the matter of European Jews, see Harold Troper and Irving Abella, *None is Too Many* (Toronto: Lester Publishing, 1983).

95   Suchodolski and International Bureau of Education, *The International Bureau of Education in the Service of Educational Development*, 79.

96   Gillies talks about the experiences of Allied prisoners of war: Midge Gillies, *The Barbed Wire University: The Real Lives of Allied Prisoners of War in the Second World War* (London: Aurum, 2011), 271–90.

97   Suchodolski and International Bureau of Education, *The International Bureau of Education in the Service of Educational Development*, 80. The idea of the internment university came to fruition primarily on Swiss soil: IBE Secretariat, e-mail to the author. See, also, A. C. Breycha-Vauthier, "Reading for Prisoners of War as Seen from Geneva," *The Library Quarterly* 11, no. 4 (1941): 442–47. The role of books in prisoner of war camps is described in David Shavit, "'The Greatest Morale Factor Next to the Red Army': Books and Libraries in American and British Prisoners of War Camps in Germany during World War II," *Libraries & Culture* 34, no. 2 (1999): 113–34. Rolf looks at the education of British POWs in David Rolf, "The Education of British Prisoners of War in German Captivity, 1939–1945," *History of Education* 18, no. 3 (1989): 257–65, whereas Mears considers the plight of American internees in Dwight S. Mears, "Interned Or Imprisoned? The Successes and Failures of International Law in the Treatment of American Internees in Switzerland, 1943–45" (PhD diss., University of North Carolina at Chapel Hill, 2010).

98   Suchodolski and International Bureau of Education, *The International Bureau of Education in the Service of Educational Development*, 82.

99   Mona Gleason, *Normalizing the Ideal: Psychology, Schooling, and the Family in Postwar Canada* (Toronto: University of Toronto Press, 1999), 120.

100   Roger Hall, William Westfall, and Laurel Sefton McDowell, *Patterns of the Past: Interpreting Ontario's History* (Toronto: Dundurn Press, 1988), 358.

101   Charles M. Johnston, "The Children's War: The Mobilization of Ontario Youth during the Second World War," in *Patterns of the Past: Interpreting Ontario's History*, 361.

102   Phillips, *The Development of Education in Canada*, 356.

103 Suchodolski and International Bureau of Education, *The International Bureau of Education in the Service of Educational Development*, 107.

104 This was the beginning of the "Golden Era" of Canadian foreign policy. See John English, *The Worldly Years: The Life of Lester Pearson* (Toronto: Alfred A. Knopf Canada, 1992), 8.

105 CNEA, "The Proceedings of the Twenty-Second Convention of the Canada and Newfoundland Education Association" (paper presented at the Convention of the Canada and Newfoundland Education Association, Toronto, ON, 1944), 21.

106 MacLeod and Blair, *The Canadian Education Association: The First 100 Years, 1891–1991*, 103.

107 The Hope Report came out during a period when conservative views dominated. It was not implemented because it took too radical a position on issues of school funding among other things. See *Report of the Royal Commission on Education in Ontario, 1950* [Hope Report] (Toronto: King's Printer, 1950). See also R. D. Gidney, *From Hope to Harris: The Reshaping of Ontario's Schools* (Toronto: University of Toronto Press, 1999), 23–24.

108 J. W. Friesen and D. McGaw, "John G. Althouse Eclectic Educator," in *Profiles of Canadian Educators*, ed. Robert S. Patterson, John W. Chalmers, and John W. Friesen (Toronto: D.C. Health, 1974), 386–405 at 400.

109 Karen Mundy offers a broader examination of the development and historical periodization of UNESCO: Karen Mundy, "Educational Multilateralism in a Changing World Order: Unesco and the Limits of the Possible," *International Journal of Educational Development* 19, no. 1 (1999): 27–52.

110 Linda Goldthorp, "Reluctant Internationalism: Canadian Approaches to UNESCO, 1946–1987" (PhD diss., University of Toronto, 1990), 40. Robertson later became Clerk of the Canadian Privy Council between 1963 and 1975: see Government of Canada, Privy Council, "Clerk of the Privy Council/Former Clerks of the Privy Council," accessed June 4, 2015, http://www.clerk.gc.ca/eng/clerks-greffiers.asp?pageId=117.

111 Goldthorp, "Reluctant Internationalism," 50.

112 Stewart, *Interprovincial Co-operation in Education*, 54.

113 Ibid., 127–28. McNally was a teacher, school inspector, and deputy minister of education in Alberta, Chancellor of the University of Alberta, and the secretary and president of the CEA. For more on his life, see University of Alberta, "University of Alberta: George Fred McNally (1946–1952)," http://www.ualbertacentennial.ca/organization/chancellors/mcnally.html.

114 Canadian Education Association, "U.N.E.S.C.O.," *Newsletter* 32 (1947): 1.

115 Ibid.

116 Freeman Stewart, "The History of the Canadian Education Association, 1882–1960" (master's thesis, University of Toronto, 1950), 156.

117 Ibid., 130.

118 "As a result of a memo, the Ministers of Education meeting there [Victoria, B.C.] agreed to provide a special grant to the CEA to enable it to send a representative to international education conferences, usually the International Bureau of Education conference in Geneva. Representation began in 1952, leading to more active and extended relations with the External Affairs department." MacLeod and Blair, *The Canadian Education Association: The First 100 Years, 1891–1991*, 104.

119   Ibid., 129.

120   G. Fred McNally, *The Story of G. Fred McNally* (Don Mills, ON: J.M. Dent and Sons, 1964), 108.

121   Stewart, "The History of the Canadian Education Association, 1882–1960," 160.

122   Kathryn Gladys Heath, *Ministries of Education: Their Functions and Organization* (Washington, DC: US Department of Health, Education and Welfare, 1962), 199.

123   Ibid., 110–11.

124   Audrey Doerr, "Education and Constitutional Reform: An Overview," in *Federal-Provincial Relations: Education Canada*, ed. George Ivany and Michael Manley-Casimir (Toronto: OISE, 1981), 46. See, also, Canada, *Report — Royal Commission on National Development in the Arts, Letters and Sciences 1949–1951* (Ottawa: King's Printer, 1951), 132–33.

125   Doerr, "Education and Constitutional Reform," 49.

126   Hugh Stevenson, "Federal Presence in Canadian Education, 1939–1980," in *Federal–Provincial Relations: Education Canada*, 3–22 at 6.

127   Ibid., 4.

128   Robert M. Stamp, "Government and Education in Post-War Canada," in *Canadian Education: A History*, 444–470 at 464.

129   Stevenson, "Federal Presence in Canadian Education, 1939–1980," 12.

130   Ibid.

131   Ibid.

132   Kim Richard Nossal, *The Politics of Canadian Foreign Policy* (Scarborough, ON: Prentice-Hall, 1989), 131.

133   For the immigration side of this equation, see Harold Troper, "Canada's Immigration Policy since 1945," *International Journal* 48, no. 2 (1993): 255–81.

134   Hilliker and Barry, "The PM and the SSEA in Canada's foreign policy," 288–315, passim. Several other evaluations followed the Glassco Commission.

135   Ibid., 204.

136   Canada, Royal Commission on Government Organization, *Report*, vol. 4 (Ottawa: Queen's Printer, 1962), 141 [Glassco Commission].

137   Stewart, *Interprovincial Co-operation in Education*, 130.

138   Glassco Commission *Report*, vol. 3, 78.

139   George Papadopoulos, *Education 1960–1990: The OECD Perspective* (Paris: OECD Publications, 1994) gives an overview of the OECD perspective on this.

140   John Hilliker and Donald Barry, *Canada's Department of External Affairs*, vol. 2, *Coming of Age: 1946–1968* (Montreal and Kingston: McGill-Queen's University Press, 1995), 177.

141   Ibid., 180.

142   Nossal, *The Politics of Canadian Foreign Policy*, 135.

143   Hilliker and Barry, *Canada's Department of External Affairs*, vol. 2, 399.

144   Nossal, *The Politics of Canadian Foreign Policy*, 141.

145   J. L. Granatstein and Robert Bothwell, *Pirouette: Pierre Trudeau and Canadian Foreign Policy* (Toronto: University of Toronto Press, 1990), 223.

146 See Goldthorp, "Reluctant Internationalism."

147 Canada, Department of External Affairs, *Report on the Department of External Affairs, 1951* (Ottawa: Author, 1951), 52.

148 F. K. Stewart, "UNESCO and Canada's Relations with It," *Canadian Education* 13, no. 1 (1957): 45–53.

149 A full slate of international activities continued throughout these years and there was ongoing contact between External Affairs and the Canadian Education Association. The reason for the absence of information on cultural diplomacy in the annual report during these years is not clear.

150 The Diefenbaker years also saw conflicting activities regarding education in the Department of External Affairs. Sidney Smith (Secretary of State for External Affairs, 1957–1959) was the "educationalist" foreign minister, whereas Howard Green (Secretary of State for External Affairs, 1959–1963) had alienated many with his bungling of the 1959 Oxford England Commonwealth Conference on Education: see "Education in the Commonwealth," *The Globe and Mail*, Thursday, July 30, 1959, 6.

151 Canada, Department of External Affairs, *Report on the Department of External Affairs, 1963* (Ottawa: Author, 1964), 44.

152 Canada, Department of External Affairs, *Report on the Department of External Affairs, 1965* (Ottawa: Author, 1966), 47.

153 Trilokekar also discusses the establishment of the Academic Relations Division and the implications it had for higher education during this era: see Roopa Desai Trilokekar, "Federalism, Foreign Policy and the Internationalization of Higher Education: A Case Study of the International Academic Relations Division, Department of Foreign Affairs and International Trade, Canada" (EdD diss., University of Toronto, 2007), 48.

154 Canada, Department of External Affairs, *Report on the Department of External Affairs, 1968* (Ottawa: Author, 1969), 46.

155 Although education diplomacy remained within the purview of the Education Liaison Desk, the desk was under the control of the Cultural Relations Section, a part of the Information Division which answered to the Bureau of Public Affairs. Confusing this bureaucratic picture even further was the existence of the Cultural Affairs Division within the Department of External Affairs. See Trilokekar, "Federalism, Foreign Policy and the Internationalization of Higher Education," 94.

156 Canada, Department of External Affairs, *Report on the Department of External Affairs, 1969* (Ottawa: Author, 1970), 61.

157 Hilliker and Barry, "The PM and the SSEA in Canada's Foreign Policy," 381.

158 François Rocher and Miriam Smith, eds., *New Trends in Canadian Federalism* (Peterborough, ON: Broadview Press, 1995), 8.

159 Alain Gagnon, "The Political Uses of Federalism," in *New Trends in Canadian Federalism*, 34.

160 Stephen Brooks, "Federal–Provincial Relations: The Decline of the New Centralism," in *Canadian Public Policy: Globalization and Political Parties*, ed. Andrew F. Johnson and Andrew Stritch (Toronto: Copp-Clark, 1997), 275–93 at 278.

161 Alvin Finkel, *Social Policy and Practice in Canada: A History* (Waterloo, ON: Wilfrid Laurier University Press, 2006), 135.

162 Ibid.

163 Rocher and Smith, *New Trends in Canadian Federalism*, 10.

164 J. L. Finlay and D. N. Sprague, *The Structure of Canadian History* (Scarborough: Prentice-Hall, 1984), 444.

165 G. Bruce Doern and Richard W. Phidd, *Canadian Public Policy: Ideas, Process and Structure* (Toronto: Methuen, 1983), 232.

166 See S. N. Eisenstadt, *Modernization: Protest and Change* (Englewood Cliffs, NJ: Prentice-Hall, 1966) and Daniel Bell, *The Coming of Post-Industrial Society: A Venture in Social Forecasting* (New York: Basic Books, 1973).

167 Alan Bullock and Oliver Stallbrass, eds., *The Fontana Dictionary of Modern Thought* (London: Collins, 1977), 670.

168 The "East," the "South," and the "Far East" had additional influences and problems as well.

169 John Kenneth Galbraith, *The New Industrial State* (Boston: Houghton Mifflin, 1978), 299.

170 Ibid.

171 This is what followers of Braudel and the Annales school described as the *histoire événementielle*. See Ernst Breisach, *Historiography: Ancient, Medieval, & Modern* (Chicago: University of Chicago Press, 1983), 372–73.

172 John Kenneth Galbraith, *The Good Society: The Humane Agenda* (Boston: Houghton Mifflin, 1996), 19.

173 Hugh A. Stevenson, "Crisis and Continuum: Public Education in the Sixties," in *Canadian Education: A History*, 471–508 at 497.

174 Gerald Nason, "The Canadian Teacher's Federation: A Study of Its Historical Development, Interests, and Activities from 1919 to 1960" (EdD diss., University of Toronto, 1964), 185–200, passim.

175 Freeman K. Stewart, *The Canadian Education Association 1957–1977* (Toronto: Canadian Education Association, 1982), 29.

176 Carmen F. Moir, "Priorities and Purposes" (presidential address, CEA Convention, Calgary, AB, 1977).

177 Greg Donaghy, "Coming Off the Gold Standard: Reassessing the 'Golden Age' of Canadian Diplomacy" (paper presented to the symposium "A Very Modern Ministry: Foreign Affairs and International Trade Canada," University of Saskatchewan, Saskatoon, SK, September 28, 2009).

178 English, *The Worldly Years: The Life of Lester Pearson*, 4.

179 Hedley Bull and Adam Watson, "Conclusion" in *The Expansion of International Society*, 425–35 at 430.

180 For a fuller discussion of the era of the Concert of Europe (1812–1914) and the principal personalities of this period, see Henry Kissinger, *A World Restored: Metternich, Castlereagh and the Problems of Peace, 1812–1822* (London: Phoenix, 2000).

181 Stewart, *The Canadian Education Association 1957–1977*, 40.

182 Ibid., 44.

183 Ibid.

Chapter Two

1 The literature on Quebec's international relations, particularly la doctrine *Gérin-Lajoie*, has blossomed in recent years. Much of this ground has been covered well by Québécois scholars. For example, see Stéphane Paquin, Louise Beaudouin, Robert Comeau, and Guy Lachapelle, *Les Relations Internationales du Québec depuis la Doctrine Gérin-Lajoie (1965–2005): Le Prolongement Externe des Compétences Internes* (Quebec City: Presses Université Laval, 2006); Stéphane Paquin and Louise Beaudouin, eds., *Histoire des Relations Internationales du Québec* (Montreal: VLB, 2006); and Robert Aird, *André Patry et la Présence du Québec dans le Monde* (Montreal: VLB, 2005). For the perspective of Pierre Trudeau on Quebec's evolving international profile, see John English, *Citizen of the World: The Life of Pierre Elliott Trudeau*, vol. 1, *1919–1968* (Toronto: Vintage Canada, 2007), 412, 434–35.

2 *Attorney-General for Canada v Attorney-General for Ontario*, [1937] AC 326.

3 Aird, *André Patry et la Présence du Québec dans le Monde*, 60 and Robin Gendron, *Towards a Francophone Community* (Montreal: McGill-Queen's University Press, 2006), 105. See, also, T. A. Heins, *Canadian–American Environmental Relations: A Case Study of the Ontario-Michigan Municipal Solid Waste Dispute* (Waterloo, ON: University of Waterloo, 2007) and Hugo Cyr, *Canadian Federalism and Treaty Powers: Organic Constitutionalism at Work* (Brussels: Peter Laing, 2009), 72 for further discussion of the *Labour Conventions* case.

4 The diplomacy of sub-national governments is often termed "para-diplomacy." For the sake of consistency I will continue with "education diplomacy." One should note, however, the well-developed literature on para-diplomacy in Canada. See, for example, Richard Vengroff and Jason Rich, "Foreign Policy by Other Means: Paradiplomacy and the Canadian Provinces," in *Handbook of Canadian Foreign Policy*, ed. Patrick James, Nelson Michaud, and Marc J. O'Reilly (Lanham, MD: Lexington Books, 2006), 105–32.

5 Louis-Philippe Audet, "Education in Canada East and Quebec: 1840–1875," in *Canadian Education: A History*, ed. J. Donald Wilson, Robert M. Stamp, and Louis-Philippe Audet (Scarborough, ON: Prentice-Hall, 1970), 167–89 at 177 and 183 and Jean Hamelin and Pierre Poulin, "CHAUVEAU, PIERRE-JOSEPH-OLIVIER," in *Dictionary of Canadian Biography*, vol. 11, University of Toronto/ Université Laval, 2003–, accessed May 19, 2015, http://www.biographi.ca/en/bio/ chauveau_pierre_joseph_olivier_11E.html.

6 Claude Ryan, "Quebec's Cultural Diplomacy," in *Canadian Culture: International Dimensions*, ed. Andrew Fenton Cooper (Waterloo, ON: Centre on Foreign Policy and Federalism, 1985), 59–68 at 60.

7 Conrad Black, *Duplessis* (Toronto: McClelland and Stewart, 1977), 491 and 532.

8 Nicole Neatby, *Carabins ou Activistes? L'idéalisme et la Radicalisation de la Pensée Étudiante à l'Université de Montréal au Temps du Duplessisme* (Montreal: McGill-Queen's University Press, 1999), 60–61.

9 A. K. McDougall, *John P. Robarts: His Life and Government* (Toronto: University of Toronto Press, 1986), 128.

10 This expression comes from the United States Secretary of State, Dean Acheson. See Dean Acheson, *Present at the Creation: My Years in the State Department* (New York: W. W. Norton, 1987).

11 G. E. Malcolm MacLeod and Robert E. Blair, *The Canadian Education Association: The First 100 Years, 1891–1991* (Toronto: Canadian Education Association, 1992), 28–33.

12 Ibid., 1.

13 Ibid., 107.

14 Ibid., 106.

15 Alison Prentice, *The School Promoters* (Toronto: McClelland and Stewart, 1977), 55.

16 Minutes of the Seventh Meeting of the Advisory Committee of Deputy Ministers of Education (ACDME) Sub-Committee on Priorities and Programs Elementary/ Secondary Education, December 8, 1987, RG2-40, Box 2, B103128, CMEC Meetings, AO.

17 Freeman K. Stewart, *The Canadian Education Association 1957–1977* (Toronto: Canadian Education Association, 1982), 106.

18 Minutes of the First Meeting, June 19–20, 1961, Standing Committee of Ministers of Education 1961–1969 Files, ACEA, Toronto.

19 Gendron's recent work, which looks at the development of *la francophonie* and French Africa, approaches this question from the viewpoint of *la francophonie*: see Gendron, *Towards a Francophone Community*, 103–104.

20 Ibid., 104.

21 Stewart, *The Canadian Education Association 1957–1977*, 96.

22 Canadian Education Association, "1963 Convention: Proceedings and Addresses" (paper presented at the CEA Convention, Toronto, ON, 1963), 30.

23 Gendron, *Towards a Francophone Community*, 105.

24 Ibid.

25 Minutes of the Canadian Education Association Standing Committee of Ministers of Education, September 21–22, 1965, RG32-1-1, B103223, File: Canadian Education Association Standing Committee of Ministers, 1965, ACEA.

26 The IBE remained a classic example of the problems of federalism and diplomacy in education. Canada was not a member because education was a provincial responsibility. Only national governments could join—and Ottawa would not. The subject was mooted again in the 1960s at the third meeting of the SCME: see Minutes of the Third Meeting, September 18–19, 1962, ACEA.

27 Canada, Department of External Affairs, *Report on the Department of External Affairs, 1964* (Ottawa: Author, 1964), 46. See, also, Canadian Education Association, "1967 Convention: Proceedings and Addresses" (paper presented at the CEA Convention, Toronto, ON, 1967), 98. The "English tradition" also changed with time: see Margaret Doxey, "Canada and the Commonwealth," in *Making a Difference? Canada's Foreign Policy in a Changing World Order*, ed. John English and Norman Hillmer (Toronto: Lester Publishing, 1992), 34–53.

28 Paul-André Linteau, François Ricard, René Durocher, and Jean-Claude Robert, *Histoire du Québec Contemporain*, vol. 2, *Le Québec depuis 1930* (Montreal: Boréal, 1989).

29 Ibid., 599. See, also, Arthur Tremblay, Robert Blais, and Marc Simard, *Le Ministère de l'Éducation et le Conseil Supérieur: Antécédents et Création, 1867–1964* (Quebec: Presses Université Laval, 1989), 389.

30 Quebec, Department of Education, *Report of the Department of Education, 1964–1965* (Quebec: Author, 1965), 111.

31 James MacGregor Burns, *Transforming Leadership: A New Pursuit of Happiness* (New York: Grove Press, 2003).

32 Jean-Marc Léger, "De Gaulle et l'accession du Québec à la scène internationale," http://agora.qc.ca/reftext.nsf/Documents/Charles_de_Gaulle--De_Gaulle_et_l%E2%80%99accession_du_Quebec_a_la_scene_internationale_par_Jean-Marc_Leger. See, also, Gendron, *Towards a Francophone Community*, 90.

33 Dale C. Thomson, *Vive le Québec Libre* (Toronto: Deneau, 1988), 140. See, also, Samy Mesli, "La Coopération Franco-Québécoise en Éducation: Les Échanges de Jeunes Maîtres (1965–1982)," in *Histoire des Relations Internationales du Québec*, 87–98 at 87–89.

34 Quebec, "Entente entre le Québec et la France sur un Programme d'Échanges et de Coopération dans le Domaine de l'Éducation," accesssed May 27, 2015, http://www.mrif.gouv.qc.ca/content/documents/fr/ententes/1965-01_Original.pdf.

35 Quebec, *Report of the Department of Education, 1964–1965*, 114.

36 Paul Gérin-Lajoie and Dale Thomson treat this meeting differently in their works. Gérin-Lajoie describes it this way in his memoirs: "Au cours de l'été, j'informe de nos intentions le secrétaire d'État aux Affaires extérieures du Canada, Paul Martin, qui ne soulève aucun problème de fond." Paul Gérin-Lajoie, Combats d'un Révolutionnaire Tranquille: Propos et Confidences (Montreal: Centre Éducatif et Culturel, 1989), 323. Thomson states that Gérin-Lajoie "obtained his [Martin's] acquiescence." Thomson, *Vive Le Québec Libre*, 128. Donaghy also treats Paul Martin Sr.'s role in his 2015 work. See; Donaghy, G. Grit: The Life and Politics of Paul Martin Sr. (Vancouver: UBC Press, 2015), p. 240, 282.

37 Robert Stewart, "The Constitutional Nature of Federal Participation in Canadian Education," (PhD diss., Carleton University, 1991), 194–95.

38 John Hilliker and Donald Barry, *Canada's Department of External Affairs*, vol. 2, *Coming of Age: 1946–1968* (Montreal and Kingston: McGill-Queen's University Press, 1991), 394.

39 An additional agreement signed in November 1965 was less than the federal government wanted: Gabrielle Mathieu, *Les Relations Franco-Québécoises: De 1976 à 1985* (Quebec: Université Laval, Centre Québécois de Relations Internationales, 1992 Cahiers du CQRI, no. 8), 32.

40 "End of February 1965 I found myself in Paris with Gérin-Lajoie who was going to sign Quebec's first international treaty with a sovereign country." Claude Morin, *Mes Premiers Ministres* (Montreal: Boréal, 1991), 163 (my translation).

41 Gérin-Lajoie, *Combats d'un Révolutionnaire Tranquille*, 324–25. Indeed, a brief look at the Government of Quebec Ministry of International Relations website bears out Gérin-Lajoie's view: see Quebec, "International agreements — MRIF — Ministère des Relations internationales et de la Francophonie," accessed on May 22, 2015, http://www.mrif.gouv.qc.ca/en/Ententes-et-Engagements/Ententes-internationales.

42 Gendron, *Towards a Francophone Community*, 116 and Gérin-Lajoie, *Combats d'un Révolutionnaire Tranquille*, 325.

43 Gérin-Lajoie, *Combats d'un Révolutionnaire tranquille*, 325.

44 Morin, *Mes Premiers Ministres*, 195.

45   Minutes of the Canadian Education Association Standing Committee of Ministers of Education, September 21–22, 1965.

46   Morin, *Mes Premiers Ministres*, 196.

47   Cadieux was deputy-minister at the Department of External Affairs: Thomson, *Vive le Québec Libre*, 149–51.

48   Allan Gotlieb, "Only One Voice Speaks for Canada," *The Globe and Mail*, October 5, 2005, A23.

49   Gérin-Lajoie, *Combats d'un Révolutionnaire tranquille*, 326.

50   At this point the government of Ontario under Premier John Robarts had undertaken "Operation School Supplies": see David Dyment, "The Ontario Government as an International Actor," *Regional and Federal Studies* 11, no. 1 (2001): 55–79 at 64–65 and David M. Dyment, "The Reluctant Traveller: Understanding the International Activities of a Non-protodiplomatic Component Government: The Case of the Ontario Government from 1945 to 1995" (PhD diss., University of Montreal, 1996), 167–68.

51   Dyment, "The Ontario Government as an International Actor, 66.

52   Minutes of the Canadian Education Association Standing Committee of Ministers of Education, September 21–22, 1965.

53   Stewart, *The Canadian Education Association 1957-1977*, 55.

54   International Bureau of Education, "Recommendation No. 63 to the Ministries of Education concerning Health Education in Primary Schools" (paper presented at the 30th Session of the International Conference on Public Education, Geneva, 1967).

55   L. H. Bergstrom, *Report of the Canadian Delegation to the Thirtieth International Conference on Public Education, Geneva, July 6–15, 1967*, Standing Committee of Ministers of Education, RG-32-1-1, B147388, AO.

56   Meeting of the Standing Committee of Ministers of Education, September 26, 1967, CMEC Files 1967–1971, MOE, RG2-40, Accession 84-1090, Box 1, AO.

57   Montreal Star Staff, "Masse Stands In," *Montreal Star*, September 27, 1967.

58   Bill Davis, Minister of Education for Ontario, to Paul Martin, Secretary of State for External Affairs, November 8, 1967, RG32-1-1, MCU Central Registry Files, Barcode 388989, Box M-0409, Book 4, AO .

59   Paul Martin, Secretary of State for External Affairs, to William Davis, Minister of Education for Ontario, November 21, 1967, RG32-1-1, Barcode 388989, Box 4, September 14, 1968, AO.

60   Davis to Martin, November 8, 1967.

61   E. J. Quick, Acting Secretary of the Council of Ministers of Education, to Marcel Cadieux, Under-Secretary of State for External Affairs, September 3, 1968, RG32-1-1, Barcode 388989, Box 4, AO.

62   Canada, Department of External Affairs, *Working Paper on Selection of Delegates for International Education Conferences during the Period 1965–1968* (Ottawa: Author, 1968), 1.

63   Ibid., 2–3.

64   Minutes of Council Executive Meeting September 16–17, 1968, RG32-1-1, Barcode 388989, Book 3, AO. Italics added.

65   Ibid.

66   Ibid.

67   Ferguson writes on the subject of historical counterfactuals: see Niall Ferguson, ed., *Virtual History: Alternatives and Counterfactuals* (New York: Basic Books, 1999).

68   Indeed, "the times they are a-changin.'" September 2010 witnessed an unprecedented summit between the CMEC and the government of China. See Council of Ministers of Education Canada, "Canada's Ministers of Education Hold Historic Meeting with the People's Republic of China," news release, September 24, 2010, http://www.cmec.ca/278/Press-Releases/Press-Releases-Detail/Canada-s-Ministers-of-Education-Hold-Historic-Meeting-with-the-People-s-Republic-of-China.html?id_article=266.

69   J. F. Bosher, *The Gaullist Attack on Canada, 1967-1997* (Montreal: McGill-Queen's Press, 1998), 27.

70   Thomson, *Vive le Québec Libre*.

71   Henry Kissinger, *Diplomacy* (Toronto: Simon and Schuster, 1994), 611–19, passim.

72   John Ralston Saul, *Reflections of a Siamese Twin: Canada at the End of the Twentieth Century* (Toronto: Viking Penguin, 1997), 375–79.

73   For an examination of the activities of *Alliance Française*, see J. M. Mitchell, *International Cultural Relations* (London: Allen & Unwin, 1986), 119.

74   Jean Lacouture, *De Gaulle*, vol. 2, *The Ruler 1945-1970* (New York: Norton, 1991), 447. See, also, Éric Amyot, *Le Québec entre Pétain et de Gaulle: Vichy, la France Libre et les Canadiens français, 1940-1945* (Paris: Fides, 1999), 135.

75   Gérin-Lajoie underlines the significance of this moment *culturally* in his preface to Paquin, Beaudouin, Comeau, and Lachapelle, *Les Relations Internationales du Québec depuis la Doctrine Gérin-Lajoie (1965-2005)*, 17.

76   Thomson, *Vive le Québec Libre*, 93.

77   Claude Morin, *L'Art de l'Impossible: La Diplomatie Québécoise depuis 1960* (Montreal: Boréal, 1989), 83.

78   Quebec, Department of Education, *Report of the Department of Education, 1966–1967* (Quebec: Author, 1967), 120.

79   Anne Rouanet and Pierre Rouanet, *Les Trois Derniers Chagrins du Général de Gaulle* (Paris: B. Grasset, 1980), 78–79 and J. L. Granatstein and Robert Bothwell, *Pirouette: Pierre Trudeau and Canadian Foreign Policy* (Toronto: University of Toronto Press, 1990), 134.

80   The Gabon incident is covered extensively in the literature. As noted earlier, Gendron, *Towards a Francophone Community*, amongst others, cites this case. It is also covered as a case study by Don Munton and John J. Kirton, *Canadian Foreign Policy: Selected Cases* (Scarborough, ON: Prentice-Hall Canada, 1992), who cite John P. Schlegel, *The Deceptive Ash: Bilingualism and Canadian Foreign Policy in Africa: 1957–1971* (Washington, DC: University Press of America, 1978). Kirton also covers the Gabon affair in his text on Canadian foreign policy during the Pearson and Trudeau eras: John J. Kirton, *Canadian Foreign Policy in a Changing World* (Toronto: Thomson Nelson, 2007), 86 and 131. Gabon is also discussed in Douglas Yates, *The Rentier State in Africa: Oil Rent Dependency and Neocolonialism in The Republic of Gabon* (Trenton, NJ: Africa World Press, 1996). For Canadian involvement during the Mulroney era, see Stevie Cameron, *On the Take* (Toronto: Seal Books, 1995), 359–69.

81   Gendron, *Towards a Francophone Community*, 64–65.

82   Ibid., 105–10.

83   More will be said in later chapters about the changing nature of international education organizations.

84   This organization, originally known as *Conférence des Ministres de l'Éducation des Pays ayant le Français en Partage*, and now known as *Conférence des Ministres de l'Éducation des États et Gouvernements de la Francophonie*, has its secretariat in Dakar. The organization's website provides a history of its development: CONFEMEN, "Historique," accessed May 25, 2015, http://www.confemen.org/page-d-exemple/historique/.

85   Thomson, *Vive le Québec Libre*, 268.

86   Morin, *L'Art de l'Impossible: La Diplomatie Québécoise depuis 1960*, 113.

87   Gendron, *Towards a Francophone Community*, 130.

88   Stéphane Paquin, "Les Relations Internationales du Québec sous Johnson et Bertrand 1966–1970," in Paquin and Beaudoin, *Histoire des Relations Internationales du Québec*, 39–55 at 45. John English deals extensively with de Gaulle's speech and the reaction of the Pearson government in his biography of Lester Pearson: see John English, *The Worldly Years: The Life of Lester Pearson, 1949–1972* (Toronto: Alfred A. Knopf Canada, 1992), 319–45, passim.

89   Morin, *L'Art de l'Impossible*, 116.

90   Thomson, *Vive le Québec Libre*, 268.

91   Ibid.

92   Kim Richard Nossal, *The Politics of Canadian Foreign Policy* (Scarborough, ON: Prentice-Hall, 1989), 272.

93   Louis Sabourin, "Canada and Francophone Africa," in *Canada and the Third World*, ed. Peyton V. Lyon and Tariq Y. Ismael (Toronto: Macmillan, 1976), 133–161 at 144.

94   Morin, *L'Art de l'Impossible*, 121.

95   Arthur Tremblay, Deputy Minister of Education, and Julien Aubert: see Gendron, *Towards a Francophone Community*, 133.

96   Jean-Guy Cardinal, "Réponses au Devoir," in *L'Union (Vraiment) Nationale* (Montreal: Les Éditions du Jour, 1969), 69–70.

97   Morin, *L'Art de L'Impossible*, 127 and Gendron, *Towards a Francophone Community*, 135.

98   Granatstein and Bothwell, *Pirouette: Pierre Trudeau and Canadian Foreign Policy*, 131 and Donald J. Riseborough, *Canada & the French,*, ed. Donald Riseborough (New York: Facts on File, 1975), 94.

99   Granatstein and Bothwell, *Pirouette*, 154–56.

100   Quebec's ongoing efforts to further its international agenda are well documented in Paquin et al., *Les Relations Internationales du Québec depuis la doctrine Gérin-Lajoie (1965-2005)*.

101   Morin, *L'Art de l'Impossible*, 135.

102   Ibid.

Chapter Three

1 Mitchell Sharp, Paul Martin, and Canada, the Department of External Affairs, *Federalism and International Conferences on Education: A Supplement to Federalism and International Relations* (Ottawa: Queen's Printer, 1968).

2 Thomas J. Courchene, David W. Conklin, and Gail C. A. Cook, eds., *Ottawa and the Provinces: The Distribution of Money and Power* (Ontario Economic Council, 1985), 6.

3 Matthew Hayday, *Bilingual Today, United Tomorrow: Official Languages in Education and Canadian Federalism* (Montreal: McGill-Queen's University Press, 2005); Reva Joshee, "Federal Policies on Cultural Diversity and Education, 1940–1971" (PhD diss., University of British Columbia, 1995); Alan Sears, "Scarcely Yet a People: State Policy in Citizenship Education: 1947–1982" (PhD diss., University of British Columbia, 1996); and Alan Sears, "Instruments of Policy: How the National State Influences Citizenship Education in Canada," *Canadian Ethnic Studies* 29, no. 2 (1997): 1–21.

4 See English's work on Pierre Trudeau's perspective in this era: John English, *Citizen of the World: The Life of Pierre Elliott Trudeau*, vol. 1, *1919–1968* (Toronto: Vintage Canada, 2007), 412, 434–35 and John English, *Just Watch Me: The Life of Pierre Elliott Trudeau, 1968–2000* (Toronto: Vintage Canada, 2010), 22.

5 Mitchell Sharp, *Which Reminds Me...:A Memoir* (Toronto: University of Toronto Press, 1994), 188.

6 The booklet came out on May 8, 1968 and the commentary in the English Canadian press centred exclusively on the Gabon affair (discussed later in this chapter), election coverage, and Quebec. See Anthony Westell, "Stanfield says Prime Minister escalating Quebec conflict," *The Globe and Mail*, May 10, 1968, 11.

7 Sharp, Martin, and Canada, *Federalism and International Conferences on Education*, 12.

8 Ibid., 10.

9 Although this was true for the most part, the problems involving the creation of CAME and Mackenzie King, as well as those that Howard Green had with the first meeting of the Commonwealth Education Conference, revealed another side of the relationship.

10 *Federalism and International Conferences on Education*, 18.

11 For a long time, the chief superintendents of education were the individuals who travelled. Ministers also travelled, but the leading deputies were more often sent to involve themselves in international events.

12 Increasingly there was also the view that the problems with the French were a "Gaullist" phenomenon, not representative of Franco-Canadian relations. De Gaulle would not live forever.

13 *Federalism and International Conferences on Education*, 36.

14 Ibid., 54.

15 J. Stefan Dupré et al., *Federalism and Policy Development: The Case of Adult Occupational Training in Ontario* (Toronto: University of Toronto Press, 1973), 91–92.

16 Ibid., 93.

17 Ibid.

18   Robert M. Stamp, "Government and Education in Post-War Canada," in *Canadian Education: A History*, ed. J. Donald Wilson, Robert M. Stamp, and Louis-Philippe Audet (Scarborough, ON: Prentice-Hall, 1970), 444–70 at 455.

19   SC 1942-43, c 34.

20   Stamp, "Government and Education in Post-War Canada," 456.

21   SC 1960-61, c 6.

22   Gordon DiGiacomo, *Federal Occupational Training Policy: A Neo-Institutional Analysis*, Working Paper 2(8) (Kingston, ON: Institute for Intergovernmental Relations, Queen's University, 2001), accessed July 22, 2015, http://www.queensu.ca/iigr/WorkingPapers/Archive/2001.html.

23   Stamp, "Government and Education in Post-War Canada," 458.

24   Canada, Department of Labour, *Annual Report, 1965* (Ottawa: Queen's Printer, 1966), 30.

25   Ibid., 29.

26   Ibid., 32.

27   Ibid.

28   *Federal Occupational Training Policy: A Neo-Institutional Analysis.*

29   Ibid., 50.

30   Discussion of this question continued in the 1960s. See "Lowe Urges Federal Education Office," *The Globe and Mail*, May 13, 1968, 1.

31   Robert Adie and Paul Thomas, *Canadian Public Administration: Problematical Perspectives* (Scarborough, ON: Prentice-Hall, 1987), 433–35.

32   The act had ten different programs. See s 3(1) of the *Technical and Vocational Training Assistance Act* for a list of requirements for the agreements.

33   Canada, *Annual Report, 1965*, 32.

34   That is to say vocation training was meant for adolescents and post-matriculation students, whereas adult occupational training was to be retraining for career changes.

35   Dupré et al., *Federalism and Policy Development*, 89.

36   SC 1966–67, c 94.

37   Stamp, "Government and Education in Post-War Canada," 463.

38   Dupré et al., *Federalism and Policy* Development, 108.

39   Ibid., 123.

40   This is an ongoing theme in Canadian industry. The Business Council on National Issues (BCNI) was critical of the societal view of vocational training, but uncharacteristically also bemoaned the concentration on white-collar occupations rather than the shop floor in the corporate training environment. See Michael E. Porter, *Canada at the Crossroads: The Reality of a New Competitive Environment* (Ottawa: Business Council on National Issues, 1991), 171.

41   Dupré et al., *Federalism and Policy* Development, 128.

42   Ibid.

43 The annual report from the Ministry of Education announcing the establishment of the training branch focused on curricular standards and grades for various courses: Ontario, *Report of the Minister, 1963* (Toronto: Legislative Assembly of Ontario, 1963), xii.

44 Ontario, Department of Labour, *Annual Report of the Department of Labour, 1965–1966* (Toronto: Queen's Printer, 1966), 23.

45 Dupré et al., *Federalism and Policy Development*, 75.

46 Ibid., 82.

47 There is little evidence of the behind-the-scenes struggles in annual reports of the provincial labour ministry. Rather the Ontario Department of Labour waxed poetic about its new programs: Ontario, Department of Labour, *Annual Report of the Department of Labour, 1966–67* (Toronto: Queen's Printer, 1967), 4–6. By contrast, the Ministry of Education reports show the twists and turns in vocational training. Compare the education ministry's 1963 report with its 1967 report: see Ontario, Ministry of Education, *Report of the Minister, 1967* (Toronto: Legislative Assembly of Ontario, 1967), 15–16.

48 That came only with time. When the ILO was established in 1919, Canada was not present. Rather it was represented in Versailles by the British delegation.

49 Canada, Department of Labour, *Annual Report, 1968* (Ottawa: Queen's Printer, 1969), 31.

50 Ibid., 30.

51 International Labour Organization, *ILO History*, accessed May 24, 2015, http://www.ilo.org/global/about-the-ilo/history/lang--en/index.htm.

52 George Papadopoulos, *Education 1960–1990: The OECD Perspective* (Paris: OECD Publications, 1994), 13.

53 Ibid., 27.

54 Canada, Department of Labour, "Training Methods for Older Workers," *The Labour Gazette* LXV, no. 6 (1965): 517.

55 Kim Richard Nossal, *The Politics of Canadian Foreign Policy* (Scarborough, ON: Prentice-Hall, 1989), 133.

56 More often than not, the level of education of immigrants has been a deciding factor in their admissibility to Canada and their success after arrival. See Ninette Kelley and Michael J. Trebilcock, *The Making of the Mosaic: A History of Canadian Immigration Policy*, 2nd ed. (Toronto: University of Toronto Press, 2010).

57 John Hilliker and Donald Barry, *Canada's Department of External Affairs*, vol. 1, *The Early Years: 1909–1946* (Montreal and Kingston: McGill-Queen's University Press, 1995), 336.

58 Sharp, Martin, and Canada, *Federalism and International Conferences on Education*, 12.

59 Rutherford and Metzler to MacNamara, April 4, 1950, RG7-61, Box No. 8, Folder "I", ILO, Vocational Training, AO.

60 R. J. Cudney, Deputy Provincial Secretary, to Alice Buscombe, Statistician, Department of Labour, October 19, 1953, Records of the Department of Labour, RG7-61, Box No. 7, Folder "I", ILO, Movement of Trainees File, AO.

61 G. A. Johnston, *The International Labour Organisation: Its Work for Social and Economic Progress* (London: Europa, 1970), 315.

62   International Labour Organization, *Canada and the International Labour Organization,*
      1919–1969: 50 Years of Social Progress (Geneva: International Labour Organization,
      1969), 3–5.

63   Canada, *Report of the Committee of Inquiry into the Unemployment Insurance Act*
      (Ottawa: Queen's Printer, 1962).

64   SC 1940, c 44.

65   The Manpower Centres plan, however, did not work well in reality. See Dupré et
      al., *Federalism and Policy Development*, 224–25.

66   Canada, *Report of the Committee of Inquiry into the Unemployment Insurance Act,*
      167–68.

Chapter Four

1   Much has been said about the economic crises of the 1970s and the neo-liberal
      response articulated late in that decade. See, for example, David Harvey, *A Brief*
      History of Neoliberalism (Oxford; New York: Oxford University Press, 2005).

2   Historians and economists have argued that the consequences of the Vietnam War
      will be with the world for some time to come. Veterans' benefits are but one obvious
      example of this. It is possible that they will continue to be paid out well into the
      2040s, with a total cost of up to 295 percent of the original cost of the war. See
      Joseph E. Stiglitz and Linda J. Bilmes, *The Three Trillion Dollar War: The True Cost of*
      the Iraq Conflict (New York: W. W. Norton, 2008), 71 and Robert Warren Stevens,
      Vain Hopes, Grim Realities: The Economic Consequences of the Vietnam War (New
      York: New Viewpoints, 1976), 175. See, also, Jeffrey W. Helsing, *Johnson's War/*
      Johnson's Great Society: The Guns and Butter Trap (Westport, CT: Praeger, 2000),
      215 for an analysis of the inflationary aftereffect of the war.

3   Antiwar demonstrations that included university communities are another
      important link between the two at a different level. Douglas A. Ross, *In the Interests*
      of Peace: Canada and Vietnam, 1954-1973 (Toronto: University of Toronto Press,
      1984), 306.

4   Robert Gilpin, *The Political Economy of International Relations* (Princeton: Princeton
      University Press, 1987), 90. For the broader picture, see Roland Axtmann,
      Globalization and Europe: Theoretical and Empirical Investigations (London;
      Washington: Pinter, 1998), 18.

5   Joseph A. Califano Jr., *The Triumph and Tragedy of Lyndon Johnson* (New York;
      Toronto: Simon and Schuster, 1991), 48.

6   American education diplomacy took some of the biggest hits. See Richard Arndt,
      The First Resort of Kings: American Cultural Diplomacy in the Twentieth Century
      (Washington, DC: Potomac Books, 2005).

7   Anthony Campagna, *The Economic Consequences of the Vietnam War* (New York:
      Praeger, 1991), 52–53.

8   Theodore M. Vestal, *International Education: Its History and Promise for Today*
      (Westport, CT: Praeger, 1994), 140.

9   Seymour Melman, *The Permanent War Economy: American Capitalism in Decline*
      (New York: Simon and Schuster, 1974).

10   Cy Gonik, *Inflation or Depression: An Analysis of the Continuing Crisis of the Canadian Economy* (Toronto: James Lorimer, 1975), 117.

11   The other notable factor is the demographic situation. The demographic shift of the baby boom had a profound effect on the economics of education within Canada. Doug Owram gives a nuanced account of the baby boom generation in Canada and its influence on public policy. As the passage of baby boomers through the school system was coming to an end in the late 1960s, the military excursions continued to buoy the global economy—for a time. Doug Owram, *Born at the Right Time: A History of the Baby-Boom Generation* (Toronto: University of Toronto Press, 1996).

12   In his critique of the spending policies of all post-war administrations, Jansson slams Lyndon Johnson's administration for its profligate waste: Bruce S. Jansson, *The Sixteen-Trillion-Dollar Mistake: How the U.S. Bungled Its National Priorities from the New Deal to the Present* (New York: Columbia University Press, 2001), 172.

13   Stevens, *Vain Hopes, Grim Realities*, 92, 113.

14   Politicization was also a factor in the evolution of international monetary policy. See J. Finlayson, "Canadian International Economic Policy: Context, Issues and a Review of Some Recent Literature," in *Canada and the International Political/Economic Environment*, ed. Denis Stairs, Gilbert R. Winham, and Royal Commission on the Economic Union and Development Prospects for Canada (Toronto: University of Toronto Press, 1985), 9–84 at 21.

15   Niall Ferguson discusses this in the context of the end of the Bretton Woods trading system and monetary systems more generally: Niall Ferguson, *The Ascent of Money: a Financial History of the World* (New York: Penguin Press, 2008), 308.

16   As a result of its unfavorable balance of payments and increasing inflation, the United States felt that it was necessary to change its relationship with the international economic system. The Nixon Administration's adjustment to the relationship caused a shock wave that reverberated throughout the decade. In August 1971, a decision was taken to abandon the fixed conversion exchange system based on the dollar. In associated measures, a 10 percent tariff was levied on all goods entering the United States. Previously, the American economic system had dominated the post-war world and financed its endeavours in American dollars. See Finlayson, "Canadian International Economic Policy: Context, Issues and a Review of Some Recent Literature," 21. Gilpin makes the same observation: Gilpin, *The Political Economy of International Relations*, 136.

17   William J. Reese, *America's Public Schools: From the Common School to "No Child Left Behind"* (Baltimore, MD: Johns Hopkins University Press, 2005), 217–19.

18   Wilfred J. Brown, "The Educational Toll of the 'Great Recession,'" in Barry D. Anderson, Wilfred J. Brown, Stephen B. Lawton, Pierre Michaud, and Eric W. Ricker, *The Cost of Controlling the Costs of Education in Canada* (Toronto: OISE, 1983), 1–22 at 1.

19   The OPEC crisis meant the end of "cheap energy": Andy Green, *Education, Globalization, and the Nation State* (New York: St. Martin's Press, 1997), 12.

20   Campagna, *The Economic Consequences of the Vietnam War*, 118.

21   Donald V. Smiley, "The Economic Dimension of Canadian Federalism," in *Canada in Question: Federalism in the Eighties*, 3rd ed., ed. Donald Smiley (Toronto: McGraw-Hill Ryerson, 1980), 158–213 at 170.

22   George Papadopoulos, *Education 1960–1990: The OECD Perspective* (Paris: OECD Publications, 1994), 141.

23   Although there was increased emphasis on Canadian–American relations, there remained a curious "disconnect" in public between the critical examination of American foreign policy and American international economic policy. Vietnam was not seen as a crucial factor in all the economic changes. See Ross, *In the Interests of Peace: Canada and Vietnam, 1954-1973*, 327–28.

24   Canada, Department of External Affairs, *Annual Review* (Ottawa: Queen's Printer, 1973), 27 provides an overview of the move towards the "Third Option"; Canada, Department of External Affairs, *Annual Review* (Ottawa: Queen's Printer, 1974), 2–3, offers a highlighted discussion of the global state of affairs. External Affairs' world had suddenly become a busy place!

25   J. L. Granatstein and Robert Bothwell, *Pirouette: Pierre Trudeau and Canadian Foreign Policy* (Toronto: University of Toronto Press, 1990), 87.

26   Dennis Dibski, "Financing Education," in *Social Change and Education*, 3rd ed., ed. Ratna Ghosh and Douglas Ray (Toronto: Harcourt Brace, 1995), 66–80 at 76. See, also, Anderson et al., *The Cost of Controlling the Cost of Education Canada*. In some cases, educational authorities also started to contract the educational state.

27   This agreement was established in Geneva in 1948 to regulate trade between industrialized nations. It went through several "Rounds" culminating in the establishment of the World Trade Organization on January 1, 1995. See World Trade Organization, "Fiftieth Anniversary of the Multilateral Trading System," press brief, http://www.wto.org/english/thewto_e/minist_e/min96_e/chrono.htm.

28   Gilpin, *The Political Economy of International Relations*, 195.

29   Ibid., 196.

30   Finlayson, "Canadian International Economic Policy: Context, Issues and a Review of Some Recent Literature," 34.

31   Ibid.

32   Gilpin, *The Political Economy of International Relations*, 213.

33   Eric Hobsbawm, *Age of Extremes: The Short Twentieth Century, 1914–1991* (London: Michael Joseph, 1994), 403–33. See, also, Stephen Paul Heyneman, "Economic Crisis and the Quality of Education," *International Journal of Educational Development* 10, no. 2/3 (1990): 115–29 at 117–18.

34   Brown, "The Educational Toll of the 'Great Recession,'" 1–2.

35   In Canadian schools, expenditures were now transferred as a percentage from education to other areas (i.e., policing, social welfare, healthcare, etc.) despite increasing real-term dollar figures. Brown notes that elementary and secondary education systems were hit the hardest. Government spending on the K–12 school system declined from 14.33 per cent of the budget through 10.48 per cent in 1975 to 9.91 per cent in 1980. The impact was immediately visible in the school system. Ibid., 9. In his studies of national economies in crisis, Frederick Hunt concludes that educational policy in times of economic downturn moves towards the practical and technologically oriented studies. In his view, business studies and civics are considered citizen building, whereas the creative arts and humanities are seen as supplementary or eliminated entirely: F. J. Hunt, *The Incorporation of Education: An International Study in the Transformation of Educational Priorities* (London; New York: Routledge and Kegan Paul, 1987), 133.

36 Alfred D. Chandler and Bruce Mazlish, eds., *Leviathans: Multinational Corporations and the New Global History* (Cambridge; New York: Cambridge University Press, 2005).

37 In a manner much more open than that displayed by today's transnational corporations, the Hudson Bay Company was deeply involved in schooling in the nineteenth century. It established schools in Manitoba and British Columbia prior to Confederation. The ultimate supervision of these schools was at the company's headquarters in London. Manoly R. Lupul, "Education in Western Canada before 1873," in *Canadian Education: A History*, ed. J. Donald Wilson, Robert M. Stamp, and Louis-Philippe Audet (Scarborough, ON: Prentice-Hall, 1970), 241–64. For the early educational role of First Nations women in the society in which the Company operated, see Sylvia Van Kirk, "The Role of Native Women in the Fur Trade Society of Western Canada, 1670–1830," *Frontiers: A Journal of Women Studies* 7, no. 3 (1984): 9–13 at 11.

38 Roach discusses the role of contemporary multinational corporations in education. See Brian Roach, "A Primer on Multinational Corporations," in *Leviathans: Multinational Corporations and the New Global History*, 19–44 at 38.

39 Philip Brown and Hugh Lauder, "Education, Globalization, and Economic Development," in *Education: Culture, Economy, and Society*, ed. A. H. Halsey, Hugh Lauder, Phillip Brown, and Amy Stuart Wells (Oxford: Oxford University Press, 1997), 172–92 at 172–73.

40 Raymond Vernon, "Sovereignty at Bay: Twenty Years After," in *Multinationals in the Global Political Economy*, ed. Lorraine Eden and Evan H. Potter (New York: St. Martin's Press, 1993), 19–24.

41 Susan Strange, "Big Business and the State," in *Multinationals in the Global Political Economy*, 101–107 at 102.

42 Vernon, "Sovereignty at Bay: Twenty Years After, 21.

43 This section draws heavily from Lorraine Eden's work.

44 Lorraine Eden, "Bringing the Firm Back In: Multinationals in International Political Economy," in *Multinationals in the Global Political Economy*, 25–58 at 46. The term is also prevalent in other literature that deals with transnational corporations and education. See Green, *Education, Globalization, and the Nation State*, 174.

45 The movement towards comparative achievement statistics is very much oriented towards developing a picture of education in the West. Although the statistics are meant to encourage convergence, they are often used to point to the superior educational performance of other states, not taking into account other relevant differences.

46 Eden, "Bringing the Firm Back In," 46 and Hobsbawm, *Age of Extremes*, 277.

47 Eden, "Bringing the Firm Back In," 46.

48 Alan M. Rugman, "Drawing the Border for a Multinational Enterprise and a Nation-State," in *Multinationals in the Global Political Economy*, 84–100 at 94.

49 Green, *Education, Globalization, and the Nation State*, 161. More recently, Green and his colleagues have focused on social cohesion as well: see Andy Green, John Preston, and Jan Germen Janmaat, *Education, Equality and Social Cohesion* (Basingstoke, UK; New York: Palgrave Macmillian, 2006), 2.

50 This is to suggest that corporations came to communities rather than the other way around: see Paul Axelrod, *Scholars and Dollars* (Toronto: University of Toronto Press, 1982), 50–51.

51 Graham Taylor and Peter Baskerville, *A Concise History of Business in Canada* (Toronto: Oxford University Press, 1994), 439.

52 Stevenson alludes to the increasing power of the corporate world in education: see Hugh A. Stevenson, "Crisis and Continuum: Public Education in the Sixties," in *Canadian Education: A History*, 471–508 at 497–98.

53 The role of the multinational in Canada has been much discussed: see Anthony Winson, "School Food Environments and the Obesity Issue: Content, Structural Determinants, and Agency in Canadian High Schools," *Agriculture and Human Values* 25, no. 4 (2008): 499–511 at 500; Marina McCarron, "Marketing in Educational Publishing: A Case Study of Textbook Sales between Competing Publishers" (MPub thesis, Simon Fraser University, Burnaby, BC, 2005), 46; Kari Levitt, *Silent Surrender: The Multinational Corporation in Canada* (Montreal: McGill-Queen's University Press, 2002); Gregory Marchildon and Duncan McDowall, eds., *Canadian Multinationals and International Finance* (London: Routledge, 2013); and Taylor and Baskerville, *A Concise History of Business in Canada*, 447.

54 Leslie Sklair, *Sociology of the Global System: Social Change in Global Perspective*, 2d ed. (Baltimore, MD: The Johns Hopkins University Press, 1995), 71.

55 Hobsbawm, *Age of Extremes*, 298.

56 John Rowland Young, "Demographic Changes and Educational Development," in *Social Change and Education*, 3rd ed., 54–65 at 61.

57 This brought up the recurring issue of transferability and equivalence of qualifications.

58 There was also the opposite concern in the mid-1970s. A large influx of foreign faculty members, particularly Americans, quickly raised fears that universities would be taken over by them, their ideas, and their influences. See Robin Mathews and James A. Steele, eds., *The Struggle for Canadian Universities: A Dossier* (Toronto: New Press, 1969), 1–11; David S. Churchill, "An Ambiguous Welcome: Vietnam Draft Resistance, the Canadian State, and Cold War Containment," *Histoire sociale/Social History* 37, no. 73 (2004): 1–26, http://hssh.journals.yorku.ca/index.php/hssh/article/view/4372/3570 at 25; Brooke Anderson, "The Elephant in the (Class)room: The Debate over Americanization of Canadian Universities and the Question of National Identity," *Studies by Undergraduate Researchers at Guelph*, 4, no. 2 (2011), https://journal.lib.uoguelph.ca/index.php/surg/article/view/1315/0.

59 This acknowledges that the barriers to mobility—primarily financial and ideological—also continued to be very high for the majority of immigrants during this era. See Harold Troper, "Canada's Immigration Policy since 1945," *International Journal* 48, no. 2 (1993): 255–81 at 272-74.

60 Gary Becker, a professor and economist at the University of Chicago, argues that human capital is a means of production in which additional investment in humans increases output. One can invest in human capital through education, training, and health care. See Gary S. Becker, *Human Capital: A Theoretical and Empirical Analysis, with Special Reference to Education* (Chicago, IL: University of Chicago Press, 2009).

61   Mark Olssen, John Codd, and Anne-Marie O'Neill, *Education Policy: Globalization, Citizenship and Democracy* (London: Sage, 2004), 148. See other human capital theorists as well: Theodore W. Schultz, *The Economic Value of Education* (New York: Columbia University Press, 1963); Edward F. Denison, *The Sources of Economic Growth in the United States and the Alternatives before Us* (New York: The Committee for Economic Development, 1962).

62   Green, *Education, Globalization, and the Nation State*, 173.

63   There were, without question, a lot of different factors at work in these events—the state's not following the international organization's prescriptions being only one of them. The US and the UK withdrew from UNESCO because of the fiscal mismanagement they saw in the organization and the politicization of its programs, amongst other reasons: see Chester E. Finn Jr., "The Rationale for the American Withdrawal," *Comparative Education Review* 30, no. 1 (1986): 140–47 at 140–41.

64   Martha Finnemore, *National Interests in International Society* (Ithaca, NY: Cornell University Press, 1996), 36–57 passim.

65   Connie L. McNeely, *Constructing the Nation-State: International Organization and Prescriptive Action* (Westport, CT: Greenwood Press, 1995), 35.

66   Finnemore, *National Interests in International Society*, 48, note 22.

67   SEAMEO was more active and assertive in its role in the beginning, whereas ASEAN took on a greater role in education in the latter part of the 1970s: Southeast Asian Ministers of Education Secretariat, *Resource Book on SEAMEO* (Bangkok: SEAMES, 1981), 25–26. See, also, ASEAN, *ASEAN: An Overview* (Jakarta: ASEAN Secretariat, 1995), 1–2, 24.

68   David Ashton and Johnny Sung, "Education, Skill Formation and Economic Development: The Singaporean Approach," in *Education: Culture, Economy and Society*, 207–18 at 209.

69   Ibid.

70   David Ashton and Francis Green, *Education, Training and the Global Economy* (Cheltenham, UK: Edward Elgar, 1996), 151–56.

71   Singapore is a complex example that combines the very hard-nosed political calculus of its founder Lee Quan Yew, a strict almost Confucian society, and an incredible capacity to work: Rolf Vente and Chow Kit Boey, *Education and Training for Industrial Development in Singapore and Other ASEAN Countries* (Singapore: Nomos, 1984), 91.

72   Ashton and Sung, 209.

73   Ibid., 211.

74   The flowering of SEAMEO regional resource centres took place in the late 1960s and early 1970s: *Resource Book on SEAMEO*, 25–27.

75   Vente and Boey, *Education and Training for Industrial Development*, 102.

76   David Crone, "The Diversification Strategy of the ASEAN States: Implications of Canadian Economic Ties with Southeast Asia," in *Canada and International Trade: Conference Papers*, vol. 2, *Canada and the Pacific Rim*, ed. Institute of International Relations and Institute for Research on Public Policy, University of British Columbia (Montreal: Institute for Research on Public Policy, 1985), 711–44 at 718–19.

77   See Chapter Three.

78   Scholarship on OECD Education Policies is only now starting to examine in a
     more in-depth fashion the role this organization plays in education worldwide.
     Papadopoulos is the early canonical source, but others scholars have since emerged.
     See Papadopoulos, *Education 1960–1990: The OECD Perspective*, 11; Kjell
     Rubenson, "OECD Education Policies and World Hegemony," in *The OECD and
     Transnational Governance*, ed. Rianne Mahon and Stephen McBride (Vancouver:
     UBCPress, 2009), 242–59; Miriam Henry, Bob Lingard, Fazal Rizvi, and Sandra
     Taylor, *The OECD, Globalisation and Education Policy* (Oxford: Pergamon Press,
     2001); and Olssen, Codd, and O'Neill, *Education Policy: Globalization, Citizenship
     and Democracy*.

79   Scott Sullivan, *From War to Wealth: Fifty Years of Innovation* (Paris: OECD, 1997),
     32.

80   Ibid., 34.

81   Ibid., 49.

82   Papadopoulos, *Education 1960–1990: The OECD Perspective*, 15.

83   Canada participated in one of these reviews early on. It was focused specifically
     on higher education, science, and technology. See Organisation for Economic
     Cooperation and Development, *Training and Demand for High-Level Scientific and
     Technical Personnel in Canada* (Paris: OECD, 1966).

84   Papadopoulos, *Education 1960–1990: The OECD Perspective*, 25.

85   Sullivan, *From War to Wealth: Fifty Years of Innovation*, 70–71.

86   Henry et al., *The OECD, Globalisation and Education* Policy, 85.

87   The economic development mission statement from the OECD's charter is restated
     before the preface to each of the Reviews: see, for example, Organisation for
     Economic Cooperation and Development, *Reviews of National Policies for Education:
     The Netherlands* (Paris: OECD, 1991), 2.

88   Maurice Kogan, *Education Policies in Perspective: An Appraisal of OECD Country
     Educational Policy Reviews* (Paris: OECD, 1979), 30.

89   Henry et al. speak of the normative nature of the language in OECD reports, which
     they describe as "degree zero" writing: *The OECD, Globalisation and Education*
     Policy, 14.

90   Kogan, *Education Policies in Perspective: An Appraisal of OECD Country Educational
     Policy Reviews*, 36–37.

91   Ibid., 37.

92   The emphasis on politics was not so much an overt policy, but rather inherent in
     the focus on governance.

93   Kogan, *Education Policies in Perspective: An Appraisal of OECD Country Educational
     Policy Reviews*, 38.

94   Ibid.

95   Heyneman, "Economic Crisis and the Quality of Education," 128.

96   Karen Mundy, "Educational Multilateralism and World (Dis)Order," *Comparative
     Education Review* 42, no. 4 (1998): 448–78 at 462–472. Mundy also discusses the
     actions international organizations take to limit their exposure to the challenges
     posed by developing countries and to cultivate Western economies. "Defensive"
     approaches helped advanced capitalist countries to compete; "disciplinary"
     approaches spread cross-national neoliberal policies across Western societies.

Chapter Five

1   C. E. Phillips, *The Development of Education in Canada* (Toronto: W. J. Gage and Company, 1957), xi.

2   Ibid., ix.

3   Ibid., xii.

4   Since the 1950s, critics of the Canadian education system, warts and all, had been actively chipping away at the Whiggish view of Canadian history of education exemplified by Phillips. For example, see Hilda Neatby, *So Little for the Mind* (Toronto: Clark, Irwin, 1953).

5   Again, the issues of which bubble and when it burst can be disputed. As described earlier, the spending bubble certainly came to an end with the forces of the war and events elsewhere.

6   Efforts to revise and change the process were being undertaken concomitantly with the OECD process. Serious revision of the execution of education-related international activities, however, was not an outcome of negotiations for change in this turbulent era.

7   Maurice Kogan, *Education Policies in Perspective: An Appraisal of OECD Country Educational Policy Reviews* (Paris: OECD, 1979).

8   Sears notes the contradictions in the following memo on the federal government's participation in education in 1971:

"(a) federal policies should respect the provision of the constitution leaving to the provinces the authority to operate their education systems.(b) Policies should be developed in agreement with the provinces.(c) Policies should be such that all provinces may participate. (d) Policies should be designed so that federal purposes may be accomplished and the federal presence easily recognized."

Alan Sears, "Instruments of Policy: How the National State Influences Citizenship Education in Canada," *Canadian Ethnic Studies* 29, no. 2 (1997): 1–21 at 2.

9   J. Donald Wilson, "Education In Upper Canada: Sixty Years of Change," in *Canadian Education: A History*, ed. J. Donald Wilson, Robert M. Stamp, and Louis-Philippe Audet (Scarborough, ON: Prentice-Hall, 1970), 190–213; Alison Prentice and Susan Houston, *Schooling and Scholars in Nineteenth-Century Ontario* (Toronto: University of Toronto Press, 1988), 123.

10   Roger Magnuson, *The Two Worlds of Quebec Education during the Traditional Era, 1760–1945* (London, ON: The Althouse Press, 2005), 51; Bruce Curtis, *True Government by Choice Men? Inspection, Education, and State Formation in Canada West* (Toronto: University of Toronto Press, 1992), 5; Kerry Kennedy, ed., *Citizenship Education and the Modern State* (Oxford: RoutledgeFalmer, 1997), 13.

11   The *School Support (Independent) Act*, RSBC 1979, c 378. See Lawrence Downey, "The Aid-to-Independent-Schools Movement in British Columbia," in *Schools in the West: Essays in Canadian Educational History*, ed. Nancy M. Sheehan, J. Donald Wilson, and David C. Jones (Calgary, AB: Detselig Enterprises Limited, 1986), 305–23.

12   Paul Axelrod, *The Promise of Schooling: Education in Canada, 1800–1914* (Toronto: University of Toronto Press, 1997), 35–36.

13   It has been persuasively argued, however, that it bore little resemblance to that
     which is understood today to be secondary education. See R. D. Gidney and W. P.
     J. Millar, *Inventing Secondary Education: The Rise of the High School in Nineteenth-*
     Century Ontario (Montreal, QC: McGill-Queens University Press, 1990).

14   Roger Magnuson, *A Brief History of Quebec Education* (Montreal: Harvest House,
     1980), 128–30.

15   Lawrence M. Bezeau, "Federal Involvement," in *Educational Administration for*
     Canadian Teachers, 2d ed. (Toronto: Copp Clark, c. 1995).

16   However, the last residential school, Gordon Residential School in Saskatchewan,
     did not close until 1996. For details on the Gordon Residential School, see
     Patricia Treble and Jane O'Hara, "Residential Church School Scandal" in *The*
     Canadian Encyclopaedia, online: http://www.thecanadianencyclopedia.ca/en/article/
     residential church-school-scandal/. See, also, J. R. Miller, *Shingwauk's Vision: A*
     History of Native Residential Schools (Toronto: University of Toronto Press, 1996),
     377 and 404–405.

17   As noted in the previous chapter, Confrontation Meetings were meetings with
     country-nominated and OECD- selected officials, usually politicians and scholars
     of *other* countries, who evaluated the target country's education system. National
     officials would usually be present because, in most cases, there was a national
     ministry of education.

18   Fazal Rizvil and Bob Lingard, "Globalization and the Changing Nature of the
     OECD's Educational Work," in *Education, Globalization, and Social Change*, ed.
     Hugh Lauder, Phillip Brown, Jo-Anne Dillabough, and A. H. Halsey (Oxford:
     Oxford University Press, 2006), 247–60 at 247–48.

19   It is significant to note that not everyone sees the OECD indicators project as
     unproblematic and positive. It also has very direct consequences for policy and
     governance. See Julia Resnik, "International Organizations, the 'Education–
     Economic Growth' Black Box, and the Development of World Education Culture,"
     Comparative Education Review 50, no. 2 (2006): 173–95. For UNESCO's educational
     statistics, see Stephen P. Heyneman, "The Sad Story of UNESCO's Education
     Statistics," *International Journal of Educational Development* 19, no. 1 (1999): 65–74.

20   There is a host of questions that a Canadian national ministry of education could
     address: see Charles Ungerleider, *Failing Our Kids: How We Are Ruining Our Public*
     Schools (Toronto: McClelland and Stewart, 2003), 279–80.

21   See Sears, "Instruments of Policy: How the Federal State Influences Citizenship
     Education in Canada," 2.

22   An interesting analysis of provincial similarities and differences can be found in
     Ben Levin, *Governing Education* (Toronto: University of Toronto Press, 2005), 65–
     66.

23   "The Quiet Revolution" is the term commonly used to describe the period of
     modernization, social change, and evolution in Quebec between 1960 and 1966
     under the Lesage government. See Paul André Linteau, François Ricard, René
     Durocher, and Jean-Claude Robert, *Histoire du Québec Contemporain*, vol. 2, *Le*
     Québec depuis 1930 (Montreal: Boréal, 1989), 307.

24   *Background Paper for the CMEC Executive Task Force Meeting, Montreal, September*
     11, 1972, CMEC Files 1972–1974, MCU, RG2-40, Accession 84-1090, Box 1, AO.

25   Participation in the UNESCO and Commonwealth processes of writing annual
     reports was not, in the same way, critical of the "national" system.

26   *Background Paper for the CMEC Executive Task Force Meeting.*

27   Mitchell Sharp, Secretary of State, to François Cloutier, Chairman of the Council, November 8, 1973, in Fifth Meeting of the Advisory Committee of Deputy Ministers of Education, December 5, 1973, CMEC Files 1972–1974, MOE, RG 2-40, Accession 84-1090, Box 1, Folder 2, AO.

28   Ibid. Although unidentified, the writer was undoubtedly a senior official in the Ministry of Colleges and Universities.

29   Fifth Meeting of the Advisory Council of Deputy Ministers of Education, December 5, 1973, Summary of Discussions, CMEC Files 1972-1974, MOE, RG2-40, Accession 84-1090, Box 1, Folder 2, AO.

30   James S. Hrabi, "The OECD Review of Education Policies in Canada: An Analysis and Some Impressions," in Canadian Education Association, *Reactions to the OECD Review — Canada: 1976 Conference of the Canadian Education Association Halifax, Nova Scotia* (Toronto: CEA, 1976), 1–18 at 2.

31   Minutes of the Twentieth Meeting of the Council of Ministers of Education, September 10–11, 1974, CMEC Files 1972–1974, MOE, RG2-40, Accession 84-1090, Box 2, Folder 1, AO.

32   Council of Ministers of Education, Canada, *Annual Report 1975–1976* (Toronto: CMEC, 1976), 8.

33   Canada, Council of Ministers of Education (Canada), and Organisation for Economic Cooperation and Development, *Review of Educational Policies in Canada*, vol. 4, *Ontario* (Paris: OECD, 1975), 166.

34   Canada, Council of Ministers of Education (Canada), and Organisation for Economic Cooperation and Development, *Review of Educational Policies in Canada*, vol. 6, *Western Region* (Paris: OECD, 1975), 97.

35   The Atlantic Region report, for example, drew attention to the interregional cooperation of the four maritime provinces and the benefits of an educated citizenry that, for the first time in a long while, was not leaving these provinces in large numbers: Canada, Council of Ministers of Education (Canada), and Organisation for Economic Cooperation and Development, *Review of Educational Policies in Canada*, vol. 5, *Atlantic Region* (Paris: OECD, 1975), 4 and 13–14.

36   The Committee was established after the two levels of government agreed to undertake the OECD Review in 1973. It was comprised of representatives from the Atlantic and Western regions, Ontario, and Quebec, as well as two representatives from the federal government. See Canada, Council of Ministers of Education (Canada), and Organisation for Economic Cooperation and Development, *Review of Educational Policies in Canada*, vol. 1, *Foreword and Introduction* (Paris: OECD, 1975), 3.

37   Minutes of the Twentieth Meeting of the Council of Ministers of Education, September 10–11, 1974.

38   Harold Noah, Examiner and Rapporteur for the Canadian Review, noted in a post-Confrontation Meeting discussion of the process some of the criteria for picking Examiners. Examiners should represent a "good spread in terms of nationality," and, "in no circumstances, may an examiner be a national of the country under examination." Edward Sheffield, Harold Noah, and Hildegard Hamm-Brücher, "The OECD Review and Higher Education," *Canadian Journal of Higher Education* 9, no. 2 (1979): 1–18 at 7–8.

39 The Examiners toured the country between May 31 and June 30, 1975. OECD *Review of Education Policies in Canada: Schedule for Visit of External Examiners,* CMEC Files 1972–1974, MCU, RG32-78, Accession 17719, Box 3, Folder 6, AO.

40 Hildegard Hamm-Brücher was somewhat familiar with federal–state chicanery in the German context. Her attitude towards the federal–provincial policy relationship in Canada was one of distaste. See, Sheffield, Noah, and Hamm-Brücher, "The OECD Review and Higher Education," 16. Hamm-Brücher also discusses the two levels of government in her later reflection on the Canadian process. See, Hamm-Brücher, Hildegard. "Canadian Education: A View from Abroad." In *Canadian Education in the 1980's,* edited by Donald Wilson. Calgary: Detselig Enterprises Limited, 1981.

41 One proposal that had been aired earlier was the idea of "regional examinations." Because of the highly fractionated nature of Canadian education, it was thought that Examiners could conduct their examinations during their inspection visit to Canada, thus being able to focus on "concerns specific to a particular region." Regional examinations were later abandoned as being too complicated, unmanageable, and time consuming. The Ontario Deputy Minister of Education also expressed concern that they would provide fodder for the press, who would be critical of the Ontario education system. Minutes of the Twentieth Meeting of the Council of Ministers of Education, September 10–11, 1974; James Auld to Thomas Wells, July 23, 1974, CMEC Files 1972–1974, MOE, RG32-78, B205677, AO.

42 Sheffield, Noah, and Hamm-Brücher, "The OECD Review and Higher Education," 14.

43 Minutes of the Twenty-First Meeting of the Council of Ministers of Education, Canada, January 23–24, 1975, CMEC Files 1972–1976, MCU, RG32-78, Accession 17719, Box 3, Folder 1, AO.

44 Allan MacEachen, Secretary of State for External Affairs, to Thomas Wells, Chairman of the Council of Ministers of Education, Canada and Minister of Education for the Province of Ontario, July 29, 1975, CMEC Files 1972–1976, MCU, RG32-78, Accession 17719, Box 3, Folder 2, AO.

45 Minutes of the Eleventh Meeting of the Advisory Council of Deputy Ministers of Education, November 13–14, 1975, CMEC Files 1972–1976, MOE, RG2-40, Accession 84-1090, Box 1, Folder 2, AO.

46 Ibid.

47 Ibid.

48 Ibid.

49 The exact composition of the Paris Review delegation is to be found in the Review Document. Organisation for Economic Cooperation and Development, *Reviews of National Policies for Education: Canada* (Paris: Organisation for Economic Cooperation and Development, 1976) 11–12.

50 The question of coordinated responses had been mooted earlier in September 1974 at the twentieth CMEC Council meeting. The Council raised, discussed, and rejected the possibility of the earlier-mentioned "regional examinations." Although regional examinations would put a more Canadian face on the process, the complexity of managing them in several different areas of the country ultimately led to their elimination. Management of the message at the Paris meeting also proved to be a key issue. Minutes of the Twentieth Meeting of the Council of Ministers of Education, September 10–11, 1974.

51 Hrabi, "The OECD Review of Education Policies in Canada: An Analysis and Some Impressions," 7–10.

52 Organisation for Economic Cooperation and Development, *Reviews of National Policies for Education: Canada*, 122.

53 Ibid., 75.

54 Ibid., 93.

55 Ibid., 96.

56 Ungerleider sees no constitutional impediment to a federal ministry of education in Canada: Ungerleider, *Failing Our Kids: How We Are Ruining Our Public Schools*, 279.

57 Hrabi, "The OECD Review of Education Policies in Canada: An Analysis and Some Impressions," 17.

58 The role of federalism and education has been examined over the years in Australia and the United States among other federal states. See, for example, Stephen Jones, "Cooperative Federalism? The Case of the Ministerial Council on Education, Employment, Training and Youth Affairs," *Australian Journal of Public Administration* 67, no. 2 (2008): 161–72; Roopa Desai Trilokekar, "Federalism, Foreign Policy and the Internationalization of Higher Education: A Case Study of the International Academic Relations Division, Department of Foreign Affairs and International Trade, Canada" (EdD, University of Toronto, 2007).

59 The Examiners' probes referred to dealt with the paucity of national control in education. Canadian Education Association, *Reactions to the OECD Review*, 12.

60 The Chair of the CMEC and head of delegation, Ben Hanuschak, explicitly expressed this view in addressing the Confrontation Meeting. Mike Heron, "The OECD Review of Education Policies in Canada: A Teacher Perspective," in *Reactions to the OECD Review*, 37–42 at 39.

61 Organisation for Economic Cooperation and Development, *Reviews of National Policies for Education: Canada*, 129.

62 Ibid., 131–35, passim.

63 Ibid., 135.

64 Ibid., 136.

65 Ibid.

66 Minutes of the Twenty-Fifth Meeting of the Council of Ministers of Education, Canada, June 18, 1976, CMEC Files 1972–1976, MOE, RG2-40, Accession 84-1090, Box 3, AO.

67 Canada, Department of External Affairs, *The OECD Report on Education Policies in Canada* (Ottawa: Department of External Affairs, 1976).

68 Council of Ministers of Education, Canada, *Annual Report 1975–1976*, 9.

69 Ibid., 13.

70 Although the Review engaged the education and, to a lesser extent, the foreign policy communities, there was less interest in the process by society in general. The Republican convention in the United States and the federal–provincial first ministers meetings on other questions dominated the political affairs press in the summer of 1976.

71 Jeff Sallot, "Educators Defend Canadian System," *The Globe and Mail*, August 18, 1976, A8.

72 Canadian Press, "Planning Lack Threat to Schools, Study Says," *Toronto Star*, August 18, 1976, B17.

73 See Chapter Three.

74 Editorial, "L'OCDE note l'absence d'une conception de l'avenir du pays," *Le Devoir*, August 20, 1976, *cahier* 2, 9.

75 In the course of their visit to Canada, at no time did the Examiners meet with any business organizations nor did they receive business briefs. See *OECD Review of Education Policies in Canada: Schedule for Visit of External Examiners.*

76 School financial officials talked about educational finance, but the business productivity question was not raised. Ibid.

77 This type of reaction continued throughout the period and up to the present. Economist Michael Porter makes a plea for the improvement of intergovernmental policy coordination in the field of education, among others, in his analysis of Canada's competitiveness. Michael E. Porter, *Canada at the Crossroads: The Reality of a New Competitive Environment* (Ottawa: Business Council on National Issues, 1991), 87.

78 Geoffrey Hale speaks to the challenges of business working with government in Canada in the 1970s and how in many senses during this decade the federal government lost the respect of parts of the business community because of its handling of particular issues. Geoffrey Hale, *Uneasy Partnership: The Politics of Business and Government in Canada* (Peterborough, ON: Broadview Press, 2006), 143.

79 Canadian Education Association, "Proceedings 1976: A Report of the 53rd Convention of the Canadian Education Association" (paper presented at the 53rd Convention of the Canadian Education Association, Toronto, ON, 1976), 7. See, also, Matthew Hayday, *Bilingual Today, United Tomorrow: Official Languages in Education and Canadian Federalism* (Montreal: McGill-Queen's University Press, 2005).

80 Canadian Education Association, "Proceedings 1976," 7.

81 Canadian Education Association, "Proceedings 1977: A Report of the 54th Convention of the Canadian Education Association" (paper presented at the 54th Convention of the Canadian Education Association, Toronto, ON, 1977), 12.

82 Australia, by contrast, had both a body similar to the Council of Ministers— the Australian Education Council (AEC), which had been in operation since 1936—and a federal Department of Education (created in 1972). The federal department oversees international education, and the Secretary of Education sits as a full member of the AEC. E. A. Holdaway, "Federal Initiatives in Education in Australia," *Education Canada* 16, no. 3 (1976): 4–13 at 6–8.

83 Maurice R. Berube, *American Presidents and Education* (Westport, CT: Greenwood Press, 1991), 49–52.

84 Association of Universities and Colleges of Canada, *A Brief to the Prime Minister of Canada and to the Premiers of the Provinces of Canada* (Toronto: AUCC, 1976), 15–16.

85 Sheffield, Noah, and Hamm-Brücher, "The OECD Review and Higher Education," 16.

86 Ibid.

87 Holdaway, "Federal Initiatives in Education in Australia," 4.

88   Hrabi, "The OECD Review of Education Policies in Canada: An Analysis and Some Impressions," 16–17.

89   Ibid., 13.

90   Ibid., 15.

91   Jean-Marie Beauchemin, "Educational Policies in Canada: Review of the Organisation for Economic Co-operation and Development (OECD)," in *Reactions to the OECD Review*, 28–36 at 30.

92   Ibid.

93   Martha Finnemore, *National Interests in International Society* (Ithaca, NY: Cornell University Press, 1996), 12.

94   Beauchemin, "Educational Policies in Canada: Review of the Organisation for Economic Co-operation and Development (OECD)," 31.

95   Ibid., 35.

96   The Review was also the subject of examination and discussion at numerous non-governmental conferences.

97   John Egantoff, "The OECD Review of Education Policies in Canada: General Observations and a Course of Action," in *Reactions to the OECD Review*, 43–47 at 44.

98   Minutes of the Eleventh Meeting of the Advisory Council of Deputy Ministers of Education, November 13–14, 1975.

99   "Dr. Parrott Responds to OECD Review of Education Policy in Canada," news release, CMEC Files 1972–1974, MCU, RG32-78, Accession 17719, Box 3, Folder 6, AO.

100   Ibid.

101   Head and Trudeau's review of the era makes little mention of education. Ivan Head and Pierre Trudeau, *The Canadian Way: Shaping Canada's Foreign policy, 1968–1984* (Toronto: McClelland and Stewart, 1995).

102   Other aspects of the Canadian role in the OECD, such as representation on the Education Committee, continued uninterrupted.

103   The words "Government of Canada" do little to indicate the document's true origin. In some government document collections it is included with documents from the Prime Minister's Office. The document states explicitly that financial support for the *Statement* came from the Department of External Affairs, rather than the Secretary of State: "The preparation and the publication of this report have been made possible through the financial assistance of the Department of External Affairs and that of the provincial departments responsible for education." Council of Ministers of Education, Canada, *A Statement by Canadian Authorities for the OECD Appraisal of Country Educational Policy Reviews* (Toronto: CMEC, 1978), i.

104   Organisation for Economic Cooperation and Development, *Reviews of National Policies for Education: Canada.*

105   For example, unlike in the case of the OECD Examiners' report, there was no press release.

106   Organisation for Economic Cooperation and Development, *Reviews of National Policies for Education: Canada*, 27.

107   Council of Ministers of Education, Canada, *A Statement by Canadian Authorities for the OECD Appraisal of Country Educational Policy Reviews*, 25.

108   Ibid.

109   Ibid., 1.

110   Hildegard Hamm-Brücher, "Canadian Education: A View from Abroad," in *Canadian Education in the 1980's*, ed. J. Donald Wilson (Calgary: Detselig, 1981), 45–51 at 47.

111   Council of Ministers of Education, Canada, *A Statement by Canadian Authorities for the OECD Appraisal of Country Educational Policy Reviews*, 14. Ottawa and the provinces also addressed OECD concerns about the lack of federal involvement in the CMEC. This was one criticism with which the federal government agreed! Contrast this with Pierre Trudeau's musings on a more structured federal involvement in education. See Douglas Fisher, "Ottawa Eyes Education Role," *Edmonton Journal*, June 21, 1976, 7.

112   Council of Ministers of Education, Canada, *Statement*, 11.

113   Despite divided opinions, Macdonald wrote in a letter to Ryerson that education should be under the control of the central government. Robert M. Stamp, "Government and Education in Post-War Canada," in *Canadian Education: A History*, 444–470 at 452.

114   Council of Ministers of Education, Canada, *Statement*, 12.

115   Ibid., 15.

116   In the latter part of the 1970s, the groups desiring change were predominately special interest groups and some lower-level school and school board officials.

117   Council of Ministers of Education, Canada, *Statement*, 12.

118   For the OECD leadership, changes to the Review process were less important than initiatives to develop new ways of looking at educational problems. George Papadopoulos, *Education 1960–1990: The OECD Perspective* (Paris: OECD Publications, 1994), 141–42.

119   By the late 1970s, this organization and other organs of the OECD were testing different ideas for dealing with the economic downturn. Although undertaking the *Statement* process was important, it was part of a broader move to re-examine the ways in which the OECD looked at education. Papadopoulos, *Education 1960–1990: The OECD Perspective*, 142–43.

120   Canada continued to be represented on the Education Committee throughout this period.

121   The end of the 1970s witnessed huge changes in international politics once more. Head and Trudeau, *The Canadian Way: Shaping Canada's Foreign policy, 1968–1984*, 209.

Chapter Six

1   This chapter appeared previously in a shorter and different form as a peer-reviewed journal article: see John Allison, "Walking the Line: Canadian Federalism, the Council of Ministers of Education, and the Case of International Education, 1970–1984," *Journal of Educational Administration and History* 39, no. 2 (2007): 113–28. Reprinted by permission of Taylor & Francis, LLC (http://www.tandfonline.com).

Head and Trudeau's book, *The Canadian Way*, perhaps would have been better entitled *The Ottawa Way*—at least provincial leaders would think so! Ivan Head and Pierre Trudeau, *The Canadian Way: Shaping Canada's Foreign policy, 1968–1984* (Toronto: McClelland and Stewart, 1995), ix.

2 Kim Richard Nossal evaluated Graham Allison's "bureaucratic politics" model as it might be applied to the Canadian circumstance. See Kim Richard Nossal, "Allison through the (Ottawa) Looking Glass: Bureaucratic Politics and Foreign Policy in a Parliamentary System," *Canadian Public Administration* 22, no. 4 (1979): 610–26.

3 The change was dramatic. The first meeting between Premier Ernest Manning of Alberta and C. D. Howe, federal Minister of Trade and Commerce, which did not take place until 1952 after both had been in powerful positions for over seventeen years, underlines this point. Donald Smiley, *Canada in Question: Federalism in the Eighties* (Toronto: McGraw-Hill Ryerson, 1980), 92.

4 Triolokekar addresses this issue as it applies to higher education and scholarships among other things: Roopa Desai Trilokekar, "Federalism, Foreign Policy and the Internationalization of Higher Education: A Case Study of the International Academic Relations Division, Department of Foreign Affairs and International Trade, Canada" (EdD diss., University of Toronto, 2007), 237.

5 Both Joshee and Sears closely examine federal involvement in education from the 1940s to the 1980s, including extensive analysis of the national government's collaborative work with the provinces and ways to circumvent the provinces when necessary. See Reva Joshee, "Federal Policies on Cultural Diversity and Education, 1940–1971" (PhD diss., University of British Columbia, 1995); Alan Sears, "Scarcely Yet a People: State Policy in Citizenship Education: 1947–1982" (PhD diss., University of British Columbia, 1996); and Alan Sears, "Instruments of Policy: How the National State Influences Citizenship Education in Canada," *Canadian Ethnic Studies* 29, no. 2 (1997): 1–21.

6 Minutes of the Twelfth Meeting of the Advisory Committee of Deputy Ministers of Education, CMEC Files, 1974–1978, MCU, RG32-78, Accession 17719, Box 4, AO.

7 Non-governmental organizations were increasingly entering the field.

8 The last option re-surfaced in an innocuous paragraph in CMEC's 1973 Task Force Report on International Education Events. Echoing the 1968 conferences in Gabon and Paris, which Quebec attended on its own, provinces sometimes individually stepped onto the international stage where, for its part, France continued to provoke the assertion of provincial influence. *Involvement of the Council of Ministers of Education, Canada in International Education Events*, January 10, 1974, CMEC Files 1974–1978, MCU, RG32-78, Accession 17719, Box 4, AO.

9 Meeting of the Standing Committee of Ministers of Education, September 26, 1967, CMEC Files 1967–1971, MOE, RG2-40, Accession 84-1090, Box 1, AO.

10 Secretary of State Hugh Faulkner met with the Council. Minutes of the Meeting between the Council and Federal Government Representatives, February 20, 1973, CMEC Files 1972–1974, MOE, RG2-40, Accession 84-1090, Box 1, AO.

11 Ibid.

12 Nossal discusses this in general terms—the threat to federal primacy was gauged and the response calibrated accordingly: Kim Richard Nossal, *The Politics of Canadian Foreign Policy* (Scarborough, ON: Prentice-Hall, 1989), 273.

13   Fifth Meeting of the Advisory Council of Deputy Ministers of Education, December 5, 1973, Summary of Discussions, CMEC Files 1972–1974, MOE, RG2-40 Accession 84-1090, Box 1, Folder 2, AO.

14   Task Force on Council Involvement in International Education Events, *Results of October Tenth Meeting*, November 1973, CMEC Files 1972–1976, MOE, RG2-40, Accession 84-1090, Box 1, AO.

15   *Task Force Draft Report on Council Involvement in International Education Events*, November 1973, CMEC Files 1972–1976, MOE, RG2-40, Accession 84-1090, Box 1, AO.

16   Mitchell Sharp's document continued to set the framework for education-related international activities: Mitchell Sharp, Paul Martin, and Canada, Department of External Affairs, *Federalism and International Conferences on Education: A Supplement to Federalism and International Relations* (Ottawa: Queen's Printer, 1968).

17   The ACDME was established in September 1972 as an adjunct to the more primarily political Council of Ministers and to streamline Secretariat activities. *Selected List of Council Activities 1968–69 to 1975–76*, CMEC Files 1974–1978, MCU, RG32-78, Accession 17719, Box 4, AO. See, also, Council of Ministers of Education, Canada, *Annual Report 1972–1973* (Toronto: CMEC Secretariat, 1973), 2.

18   Ministry of Treasury, Economics, and Intergovernmental Affairs, *Policy and Planning Coordination Office Memorandum on Task Force on Council Involvement in International Education Events*, November 28, 1973, CMEC Files 1972–1974, MOE, RG2-40, Accession 84-1090, Box 1, AO.

19   The reluctance to take on further financial commitments can be attributed to several factors. Primary amongst them was the changing importance of education generally as the 1970s progressed. Also of importance was the recognition on the part of provincial authorities that having an international presence came at a high financial cost. Kim Richard Nossal, "Anything but Provincial: The Provinces and Foreign Affairs," in *Provinces: Canadian Provincial Politics*, ed. Christopher Dunn (Peterborough, ON: Broadview Press, 1996), 503–18 at 506.

20   Meetings between the two levels of government were infrequent. Mitchell Sharp met with the CMEC in June 1973. Following this meeting, the issue was primarily addressed in correspondence. *Summary of Discussions and Correspondence Relative to the Role of the Council in International Education Activities*, CMEC Files 1981, MOE, RG2-40, Accession 22321, Box 81/4, AO.

21   As noted in the last chapter, contacts between the CMEC and the Minister of External Affairs also dealt with daily issues in the diplomacy of education such as the OECD Review.

22   Douglas Fisher, "Ottawa Eyes Education Role," *Edmonton Journal*, June 21, 1976, 7.

23   Harry Malmberg, Deputy Minister of Education, New Brunswick, to Lucien Perras, Executive Director, Council of Ministers of Education, Canada, May 17, 1976, CMEC Files 1974–1978, MCU, RG32-78, Accession 17719, Box 4, AO.

24   Agenda Item 2, Minutes of the Thirteenth Meeting of the Advisory Committee of Deputy Ministers of Education, December 5, 1973, CMEC Files 1972–1976, MOE, RG2-40, Accession 84-1090, Box 1, AO.

25   *Future Directions of the Council of Ministers of Education*, CMEC Files 1974–1978, MCU, RG32-78, Accession 17719, Box 4, AO.

26   Matthew Hayday, *Bilingual Today, United Tomorrow: Official Languages in Education and Canadian Federalism* (Montreal: McGill-Queen's University Press, 2005), 65–66.

27   This gathering was a meeting of the full Council, as opposed to some of the earlier meetings, which were of the Deputy Ministers (the ACDME).

28   G. S. Posen, Director, Federal–Provincial and Interprovincial Affairs Secretariat, to Mr. E. D. Greathed, Executive Director, Office of Intergovernmental Affairs, CMEC Files 1975–1977, MCU, RG32-78, Accession 17719, Box 3, AO.

29   Ibid.

30   Meeting of the CMEC with Sec. of State on September 20, 1976, CMEC Files 1975–1977, MCU, RG32-78, Accession 17719, Box 3, AO.

31   Ibid.

32   Ibid.

33   Ibid.

34   *Proposed Text for a CMEC Statement on Relations with the Federal Government*, CMEC Files 1975–1977, MCU, RG32-78, Accession 17719, Box 3, AO.

35   Ibid.

36   Minutes of the Twenty-Fourth Meeting of the Council of Ministers of Education, September 19, 1976, CMEC Files 1975–1977, MCU, RG32-78, Accession 17719, Box 3, AO.

37   Don Jamieson, Secretary of State for External Affairs, to Ben Hanuschak, Chairman of the Council of Ministers of Education and Minister of Education for Manitoba, August 22, 1977, CMEC Files 1975–1977, MCU, RG32-78, Accession 17719, Box 3, AO.

38   Ibid.

39   Ibid.

40   Council of Ministers of Education, Canada, *Understandings between the Council of Ministers of Education, Canada and the Department of External Affairs* (Toronto: CMEC Secretariat, 1988), 3.

41   One of the interesting asides to come out of the regulation of international diplomatic delegations to education conferences is contained in the following entry in the online curriculum vitae of Lorne McGuigan (Minister of Education in New Brunswick, 1974–78): "Appointment by the Minister of External Affairs. (34 countries attended)." Clearly, participating in education diplomacy has a cachet. See Commission on Legislative Democracy, *Commission on Legislative Democracy — Other Commissioners*, Government of New Brunswick, accessed October 5, 2010, http://www.gnb.ca/0100/other-e.asp#mcguigan.

42   The CMEC continued to be skeptical that the federal government during this period would adhere to understandings with the organization. Minutes of the Twenty-Eighth Meeting of the Council of Ministers of Education, Canada, September 25–27, 1977, CMEC Files 1978, MOE, RG2-40, Accession 17999, Box 78/2, AO.

43   CMEC *Summary Record of Discussions: Meeting Between the Council of Ministers of Education and the Honourable Mark MacGuigan…item 4, p. 5, CMEC Files 1981, MOE, RG2-40, Accession 22321, Box 81/1, AO.

44   Ibid.

45 Council of Ministers of Education, Canada, *Understandings between the Council of Ministers of Education, Canada and the Department of External Affairs*, 5.

46 Only with further efforts did the CMEC and the Department of External Affairs establish FPCCERIA in March 1986. This Committee was designed to put in place, once and for all, a mechanism whereby the contingent character of diplomacy in education would be replaced by something more permanent and able to adjust to developments on an ongoing basis.

47 Discussions carried on until 1984 and the election of a new federal government. Minutes of the Thirty-Sixth Meeting of the Advisory Committee of Deputy Ministers of Education, December 7–8, 1983, CMEC Files 1983, MOE, RG2-40, Accession 29327, Box 1, AO.

48 Council of Ministers of Education, Canada, *Understandings*, 15–16.

49 Garth Stevenson, *Unfulfilled Union: Canadian Federalism and National Unity* (Toronto: Gage, 1989), ix.

50 For more on the variety of nations, see E. J. Hobsbawm, *Nations and Nationalism since 1780: Programme, Myth, Reality* (Cambridge: Cambridge University Press, 1990), 32.

51 *Executive federalism* may be defined as the relations between elected and appointed officials of the two orders of government in federal–provincial interactions and among the executives of the provinces in interprovincial interactions: Smiley, *Canada in Question: Federalism in the Eighties*, 91.

52 Reg Whitaker, "Democracy and the Canadian Constitution." In *A Sovereign Idea: Essays on Canada as a Democratic Community*, edited by Reg Whitaker (Montreal: McGill-Queen's University Press, 1992), 205–32.

53 Although foreign affairs did not get the treatment received by domestic issues, increasing attention was being paid to international issues both in the media and through polling: Nossal, *The Politics of Canadian Foreign Policy*, 116.

54 Not much of this importance was evident in the early days; obviously the OECD Review was more highly visible in this regard. There is closer scrutiny now of provincial education systems by international agencies, notably through such vehicles as the Programme for International Student Assessment (PISA) and the collection of education statistics. The setting of the policy agenda is evident in documents such as the following OECD report: Organisation for Economic Cooperation and Development, *The Introduction of the New Information Technologies in Education: Policy Trends and Developments in Member Countries* (Paris: CERI, 1984).

55 Stevenson, *Unfulfilled Union*, 192.

56 Ibid.

57 The political necessity of involvement at the international level was and is often tied to contingent issues over which Premiers have no control, but on which they must take a stand, and to issues of perceived economic and local importance: Nossal, "Anything but Provincial: The Provinces and Foreign Affairs," 513.

58 Hobsbawm, *Nations and Nationalism since 1780*, 81. Heather-Jane Robertson continues this history in a more contemporary context with a discussion of the economic side of this question: Heather-Jane Robertson, *No More Teachers, No More Books* (Toronto: McClelland and Stewart, 1999), 28–29.

59 See Chapter 3.

60   Kathy Brock, "The End of Executive Federalism?" in *New Trends in Canadian Federalism*, ed. François Rocher and Miriam Smith (Peterborough, ON: Broadview Press, 1995), 91–108 at 97–98. These moves were followed in 1993 by one of the few actions of Prime Minister Kim Campbell's short-lived government—a shift in protocol to require the federal–provincial relations office to report directly to the Prime Minister. Although Campbell does not mention this in her autobiography, she does discuss federal–provincial relations. Kim Campbell, *Time and Chance: The Political Memoirs of Canada's First Woman Prime Minister* (Toronto: McClelland and Stewart, 1997), 330–31.

61   Posen to Greathed.

62   Smiley, *Canada in Question: Federalism in the Eighties*, 96.

63   This is to say nothing of domestic educational issues. As one example, few politicians and educationalists seemed to want to agree on the national standardization of teaching qualifications, which is still an ongoing question. It was only recently, in 2009, that a labour mobility agreement moved Canada in the direction of national standards. See Dick Henley and Jon Young, "Trading in Education: The *Agreement on Internal Trade*, Labour Mobility and Teacher Certification in Canada," *Canadian Journal of Educational Administration and Policy* 91 (February 23, 2009).

64   Ministers had more political acumen; officials knew how to administer the system, while teachers, parents, and students dealt with the day-to-day challenges of being educated in, working in, and working with the school system. As noted earlier, the overall effectiveness of ministers and deputies over the longer term was limited by the revolving door nature of the education portfolio. Also, as Simeon rightly implies in the title of his long-term work on Canadian federalism, within Canadian politics "diplomacy" was necessary simply to keep the ship of state afloat. See Richard Simeon, *Federal-Provincial Diplomacy: The Making of Recent Policy in Canada* (Toronto: University of Toronto Press, 2006).

65   Paul André Linteau, François Ricard, René Durocher, and Jean-Claude Robert, *Histoire du Québec Contemporain*, vol. 2, *Le Québec depuis 1930* (Montreal: Boréal, 1989), 653–54.

66   *Opening Statement of Jacques-Yvan Morin, Minister of Education of Quebec, to the Twenty-Seventh Meeting of the Council of Ministers of Education, Canada, January 13, 1977*, CMEC Files 1977, RG2-40, Accession 17227, Box 77/1, AO.

67   Posen to Greathed.

68   Ibid.

69   This section draws on the scholarship of Donald Smiley. See *Canada in Question: Federalism in the Eighties*, 91–116.

70   Minutes of the Twenty-Seventh Executive Committee Meeting of the Council of Ministers of Education, Canada, June 19–21, 1977, CMEC Files 1977, RG2-40, Accession 17227, Box 77/1, AO.

71   Meeting between CMEC Secretariat Staff and Officials at the Department of External Affairs, Ottawa, May 31, 1977, CMEC Files 1977, RG2-40, Accession 17227, Box 77/1, AO.

72   Stevenson, *Unfulfilled Union*, 193.

73   The implementation of the OECD Pacific Circle Project was one example that the Department of External Affairs and the CMEC dealt with in the latter part of the 1970s. Ultimately it was run out of the University of Victoria, School of Education.

This project was of much greater import and immediacy in Victoria than in either Toronto or Ottawa because of its proximity. Indeed, by 1983, the governmental financial commitment to the project had devolved to institutional support only. The CMEC was involved in a "watching stance" capacity. Special Meeting of the Pacific Rim Nations CERI Representatives, May 27, 1977, CMEC Files, 1977–1978, MOE, RG2-40, Accession 17999, Box 78/2, AO; Minutes of the Thirty-Second CMEC Meeting, January 22–23, 1979, CMEC Files, 1979, MOE, RG2-40, Accession 1892, Box 79/3, AO; and Minutes of the Forty-Second CMEC Meeting, January 24–25, 1983, CMEC Files, 1983, MOE, RG2-40, Accession 29327, Box 1, AO.

74   The Council of Maritime Premiers (CMP), established in 1971, was comprised of the first ministers of the provinces of Nova Scotia, New Brunswick, and Prince Edward Island (Newfoundland chose not to participate). The organization had quite an extensive secretariat. Similarly, the CMP (in contemporary times, the Council of Atlantic Premiers) focused on their own regional and "Northwest-Atlantic" goals. Agencies such as the Maritime Provinces Higher Education Commission, an offshoot of the CMP, were much more likely to have coastal interests in mind rather than the concerns of the Canadian provinces further to the west. See Council of Atlantic Premiers, accesssed June 5, 2015, http://www.cap-cpma.ca/default. asp?mn=1.98.

75   Smiley, *Canada in Question: Federalism in the Eighties*, 105. The *Maritime Provinces Higher Education Commission Act*, sets out that the organization should "develop programs" outside the region for purposes of higher education. See Maritime Premiers Higher Education Commission, *Maritime Provinces Higher Education Commission Act*, Office Consolidation, accessed February 17, 2015, http://www. mphec.ca/resources/MPHEC%20Act%20Office%20Consolidation%202006.pdf.

76   Smiley, ibid., 116.

77   Alan B. Nymark, Jean-Marc Metivier, David Lee, et al., "Many Masters: How Others See the Head of Mission," in *Diplomatic Missions: The Ambassador in Canadian Foreign Policy*, ed. Robert Wolfe (Kingston, ON: School of Policy Studies, Queen's University, 1998), 175–84 at 175–77.

78   The whole area of educational publishing in the K–12 market is illustrative of this commercialization. See Stephen Jones, "Cooperative Federalism? The Case of the Ministerial Council on Education, Employment, Training and Youth Affairs," *Australian Journal of Public Administration* 67, no. 2 (2008): 161–72.

79   Canada, Department of External Affairs, *The Department of External Affairs Annual Review, 1981* (Ottawa: Supply and Services, 1981), 103.

80   Canada, Department of External Affairs, *The Department of External Affairs Annual Report, 1982–1983* (Ottawa: Supply and Services, 1983), 35.

81   The Department's 1985–1986 annual review states, "Cultural and educational industries are emerging as major economic sectors. The Department has increased efforts to support their international marketing activity....To remain competitive, Canada must promote the sale of goods and services in the education field such as training programs and packages, text-books, education films, etc." Canada, Department of External Affairs, *The Department of External Affairs Annual Review, 1985–1986* (Ottawa: Supply and Services, 1986), 56. For a 1990s view of this phenomenon, see Martin Rudner, "Canada and International Education in the Asia Pacific Region," in *Canada Among Nations 1997: Asia Pacific Face Off*, ed. Fen Osler Hampson, Maureen Appel Molot, and Martin Rudner (Ottawa: Carleton University Press, 1997), 211–31 at 212.

82   Nonetheless, the division of powers makes everyone tiptoe around education and international relations. Rudner argues that the impediments of federalism continue to shackle education-related activities even after they have supposedly been resolved through standing organizations such as FPCCERIA: Rudner, "Canada and International Education in the Asia Pacific Region," 218.

83   Ottawa continued to send representatives to Francophone education conferences together with Quebec, New Brunswick, and in some cases, Ontario. Things became more tricky in terms of recognition issues at the heads of state and government (*sovereign* states and governments) meetings of the *Francophonie* in the 1980s. Head and Trudeau, *The Canadian Way*, 291.

84   *Changes Suggested by Quebec to the Proposal Concerning Procedures of the Participation of the Provinces in International Education Conferences*, June 1977, CMEC Files 1977, RG2-40, Accession 177227, Box 77/1, AO.

85   Ibid.

86   Stevenson, *Unfulfilled Union*, 53–60 and Canada, Royal Commission on Bilingualism and Biculturalism, and Ramsay Cook, *Provincial Autonomy, Minority Rights and the Compact Theory, 1867–1921* (Ottawa: Queen's Printer, 1965).

87   The brief period of Conservative rule was characterized by struggles for power within External Affairs, of which there was no clear winner: John Kirton, "Elaboration and Management of Canadian Foreign Policy," in *From Mackenzie King to Pierre Trudeau: Forty Years of Canadian Diplomacy, 1945–1985*, ed. Paul Painchaud (Quebec: Les Presses de l'Université Laval, 1989), 55–80 at 71.

88   *Opening Remarks by Secretary of State David MacDonald*, Meeting with the Council of Ministers of Education, Canada, October 22, 1979, CMEC Files 1979, RG2-40, Accession 18921, Box 79/3, AO.

89   The need to safeguard federal prerogatives was commonly felt, but pursued in different ways. Trudeau initially saw little need for the foreign ministry.

90   *CMEC Task Force Draft Report on Council Involvement in International Education Events*, November 1973.

91   Robert Stewart, "The Constitutional Nature of Federal Participation in Canadian Education" (PhD diss., Carleton University, 1991), 193. Hugo Cyr also addresses this question in his book on treaty making and the federation, arguing that the Council (CMEC) represents one example of a developing tool of "federal democracy" that can achieve coherence in international relations, treaty formation and diplomacy, alongside the federal role. See Hugo Cyr, *Canadian Federalism and Treaty Powers: Organic Constitutionalism at Work* (Brussels: Peter Lang, 2009), 160–62.

92   UNESCO, Office of international Standards and Legal Affairs, *Convention on the Recognition of Studies, Diplomas and Degrees concerning Higher Education in the States belonging to the Europe Region,* accessed June 2, 2015, http://portal.unesco.org/en/ev.php-URL_ID=13516&URL_DO=DO_TOPIC&URL_SECTION=201.html.

93   *Canada (AG) v Ontario (AG)*, [1937] A.C. 326. "The case decided that the Parliament of Canada could not legislate in areas of provincial jurisdiction simply as a result of the Canadian Government's entering into international agreements. However, the judges…explicitly recognized that the Canadian Government could enter into treaties on all subjects." Sharp, Martin, and Canada, *Federalism and International Conferences on Education*, 10.

94   Patrick McGeer, Chairman of the Council of Ministers of Education, Canada and Minister of Education for British Columbia, to Flora MacDonald, Secretary of

State for External Affairs, December 7, 1979, CMEC Files 1980, MOE, RG2-40, Accession 20135, Box 80/2, AO.

95   The Canadian Information Centre for International Credentials (CICIC), *The Council of Europe/UNESCO Convention on the Recognition of Qualifications Concerning Higher Education in the European Region Fact Sheet No 3*, The Canadian Information Centre for International Credentials (CICIC), accessed November 8, 2009, http://www.cicic.ca/623/factsheet-no3.canada. The actual text of the Convention details Canadian federal concerns under a section entitled "Declarations and Reservations." See UNESCO, *Convention on the Recognition of Studies, Diplomas and Degrees concerning Higher Education in the States belonging to the Europe Region.*

96   *Canada and the Signing of International Treaties*, June 10, 1980, CMEC Files 1980, MOE, RG2-40, Accession 20135, Box 80/2, AO.

97   Ibid.

98   McGeer to MacDonald.

99   *Canada and the Signing of International Treaties*. See, also, Annmarie Jacomy-Millette, "Les Activités Internationales des Provinces Canadiennes," in *From Mackenzie King to Pierre Trudeau: Forty Years of Canadian Diplomacy 1945-1985*, 81–104 at 98.

100 Council of Ministers of Education, Canada, *Understandings between The Council of Ministers of Education, Canada and the Department of External Affairs*, 7.

101 Kirton, "Elaboration and Management of Canadian Foreign Policy," 68–69.

102 Allan Gotlieb, *Canadian Diplomacy in the 1980's: Leadership and Service* (Toronto: Centre for International Studies, 1979), 8.

103 Ibid., 8–9.

104 Kirton, "Elaboration and Management of Canadian Foreign Policy," 76.

Chapter Seven

1   Indeed, the clouds deepen. See Paul Martin, "Canada's Image Abroad: Fade to Black," *University Affairs*, June 6, 2012 http://www.universityaffairs.ca/opinion/in-my-opinion/canadas-image-abroad-fade-to-black/, accessed on Monday June 8, 2015.

2   Martin Rudner, "Canada and International Education in the Asia Pacific Region," in *Canada Among Nations 1997: Asia Pacific Face Off*, ed. Fen Osler Hampson, Maureen Appel Molot, and Martin Rudner (Ottawa: Carleton University Press, 1997), 211–31 at 218.

3   Robertson's analysis is succinct; we need a national "vehicle" now. See Heather-Jane Robertson, "An Idea Whose Time Keeps Coming," *Phi Delta Kappan* 87, no. 5 (2006): 410–12; Andrew S. Hughes, Murray Print, and Alan Sears, "Curriculum Capacity and Citizenship Education: A Comparative Analysis of Four Democracies," *Compare* 40, no. 3 (2010): 293–309; and Charles Ungerleider, *Failing Our Kids: How We Are Ruining Our Public Schools* (Toronto: McClelland and Stewart, 2003).

4   Graham Fraser, "New Life in Old Quebec Doctrine," *CIGI-Online*, December 30, 2005, https://www.cigionline.org/articles/2005/12/new-life-old-quebec-doctrine.

5   Alain-G. Gagnon, "Taking Stock of Asymmetrical Federalism in an Era of Exacerbated Centralization," in *Contemporary Canadian Federalism: Foundations, Traditions, Institutions*, ed. Alain-G. Gagnon (Toronto: University of Toronto Press, 2009), 255–72.

6   Ungerleider, *Failing Our* Kids.

7   Council of Ministers of Education Canada. "CMEC > Programs and Initiatives > International > Overview." CMEC, 2007, http://www.cmec.ca/148/Programs-and Initiatives/International/Overview/index.html, accessed on Monday June 8th, 2015

8   Roopa Desai Trilokekar, "Federalism, Foreign Policy and the Internationalization of Higher Education: A Case Study of the International Academic Relations Division, Department of Foreign Affairs and International Trade, Canada" (EdD diss., University of Toronto, 2007), 175–78.

9   As a corporation under the laws of Ontario the CMEC is not in any way an officially government-created or constitutionally mandated body. Its "corporate" report is, in actual fact, just that.

10   Council of Ministers of Education, Canada, CMEC – *International*, 16.

11   Council of Ministers of Education, Canada, CMEC, accessed June 8, 2015, http://www.cmec.ca/148/Programs-and-Initiatives/International/Overview/index.html.

12   Robin H. Farquhar and Canadian Bureau for International Education, *Advancing the Canadian Agenda for International Education: Report of the Millennium Consultation on International Education* (Ottawa: Canadian Bureau for International Education, 2001).

13   Ibid., 11.

14   Council of Ministers of Education, Canada, CMEC – *International*.

15   Roopa Trilokekar and Adrian Shubert, *Governments and International Education: The Canadian Case*, Institute of International Education (IIE Network), accessed June 8, 2015, http://web.archive.org/web/20071206165950/http://iienetwork.org/page/108517/.

16   Manitoba Chambers of Commerce, *Canada's Ministers of Education Advance "Learn Canada 2020" Priorities*, Manitoba Chambers of Commerce, accessed June 8, 2015, https://web.archive.org/web/20100929052849/http://www.mbchamber.mb.ca/2010/09/canadas-ministers-of-education-advance-learn-canada-2020-priorities/.

17   Although the "Understandings" are now online, the Council gives little indication of the conundrum that foreign policy poses. See Council of Ministers of Education, Canada, *Understandings between the Council of Ministers of Education, Canada and the Department of External Affairs*, CMEC, accessed June 8, 2015, http://www.cmec.ca/Publications/Lists/Publications/Attachments/159/ententes.en.PDF. For more information on Canada's role in PISA and international testing and a critical analysis of coverage of PISA results in Canada, see Michelle Stack, "Testing, Testing, Read All about It: Canadian Press Coverage of the PISA Results," *Canadian Journal of Education* 29, no. 1 (2006): 49–69.

18   The alternative of a constitutional struggle between the two levels of government is not one worth contemplating; it would make Palaeolithic *berserkirs* look like kids at play. Rick Fields, *The Code of the Warrior: In Myth, History and Everyday Life* (New York: Harper Perennial, 1991), p.62.

19   Ungerleider, *Failing Our Kids*, 277–81.

20   Finn notes the advancements and reversals in US cultural and educational diplomacy since the 1960s: see Helena K. Finn, "The Case for Cultural Diplomacy: Engaging Foreign Audiences," *Foreign Affairs* 82, no. 6 (2003): 15–20.

21   New Zealand, Ministry of Education, International Division, *The International Education Agenda: A Strategy for 2007–2012* (Wellington, NZ: Ministry of Education, International Division, 2007), 29, accessed on June 3, 2015, http://www.minedu.govt.nz/~/media/MinEdu/Files/EducationSectors/InternationalEducation/PolicyStrategy/11950%20ie%20agenda%20final%20download%20100807.pdf.

22   Richard T. Arndt, *The First Resort of Kings: American Cultural Diplomacy in the Twentieth Century* (Washington, DC: Potomac Books, 2005), 388–89.

23   New Zealand, Ministry of Education, International Division, *The International Education Agenda: A Strategy for 2007–2012*, 4.

24   Quebec remains very active in diplomacy. See Richard Vengroff and Jason Rich, "Foreign Policy by Other Means: Paradiplomacy and the Canadian Provinces," in *Handbook of Canadian Foreign Policy*, ed. Patrick James, Nelson Michaud, and Marc J. O'Reilly (Lanham, MD: Lexington Books, 2006), 119.

25   There has been some notable recent work on parts of this subject area. Particular attention should be paid to Jennifer Wallner, *Learning to School: Federalism and Public Schooling in Canada* (Toronto: University of Toronto Press, 2014). Wallner provides an excellent and highly interesting analysis of the ways in which provincial ministries of education, the CMEC, and the federal government have created a structural network in contemporary Canadian education. Also, a doctoral dissertation by David Whelchel contains a useful discussion of Ryerson and the nineteenth-century roots of Canadian education diplomacy. See David Aaron Whelchel, "The Schoolmaster Is Abroad: The Diffusion of Educational Innovations in the Nineteenth Century British Empire" (PhD diss., Washington State University, 2011).

26   Phillips, Ron. "Council of Ministers of Education, Canada (CMEC) and the First Nation Education in Canada: International Implications." *International Journal for Cross-Disciplinary Subjects in Education* (IJCDSE) 4, no. 1 (2014): 1903-09.

27   For a better idea of what the view is like at the pinnacle of international corporate power in contemporary times and the inscrutability of the "machine," see Lewis Lapham, *The Agony of Mammon: The Imperial World Economy Explains Itself to the Membership in Davos, Switzerland* (New York: Verso, 1998), 45–46, 62.

28   Joel Spring's work brings several critical perspectives to this issue: Joel Spring, *Education and the Rise of the Global Economy* (Mahwah, NJ: Lawrence Erlbaum Associates, Inc., 1998), 173.

29   Ibid., 140–49.

30   The emphasis is on citizens as opposed to consumers. See Bernard Shapiro, "The Case for Public Education," *The University of Toronto Bulletin*, March 29, 1999, 16.

31   Ottawa was briefly involved in selling education through the Canadian Education Centres from the early 1990s until 2009. See Canada, Department of Foreign Affairs and International Trade, *Evaluation of the Canadian Education Centres Network (CECN)*, DFAIT, accessed June 8, 2015, http://www.collectionscanada.gc.ca/webarchives/20051229032850/http://www.dfait.gc.ca/department/auditreports/evaluation/evalCECN99-en.asp.

Index

CPSIA information can be obtained
at www.ICGtesting.com
Printed in the USA
LVOW10s0917100617

537659LV00012B/373/P

9 780995 340602